AMBER REVOLUTION
How the world learned to love orange wine

Brda dawn

AMBER
REVOLUTION

How the world learned to love orange wine

By **Simon J Woolf**

Photography by **Ryan Opaz**

WITHDRAWN

Interlink Books
An imprint of Interlink Publishing Group, Inc.
Northampton, Massachusetts

M C P
Morning Claret Productions
Amsterdam, Netherlands

First published in the Netherlands in 2018 by Morning Claret Productions
An imprint of The Morning Claret, Amsterdam, Netherlands
www.themorningclaret.com

First American edition published in 2018 by INTERLINK BOOKS
An imprint of Interlink Publishing Group, Inc.
46 Crosby Street, Northampton, Massachusetts 01060
www.interlinkbooks.com

Copyright © Simon J Woolf 2018
Original photography copyright © Ryan Opaz 2018
See list of additional photo credits on page 288
Cover, design, layout and artwork: Studio Eyal & Myrthe
Editor: Andrew Lindesay

Library of Congress Cataloguing-in-Publication Data available
ISBN 978-1-62371-966-1 *(hardback)*
Printed and bound in Latvia by PNB Print

10 9 8 7 6 5 4 3 2 1

Dedicated to Linda Woolf, Otto McCarthy-Woolf and Stanko Radikon
– I hope you'd have been proud

Orshimos, or ladles for getting wine out of a qvevri

Contents

Foreword by Doug Wregg

I assayed my first orange wine in 2006 (Dario Prinčič's Trebez 2002). I can still remember my initial shock at its profound, rich, almost burnished colour which seemed to change subtly in the light, and then encountering the wine's evolving aromas and textures which so challenged and reshaped my palate. It was a moment of real discovery, and a glimpse into the past and the future at the same time.

Orange (or amber) is most definitely an important colour in the wine spectrum. The colour denotes that grapes (which we normally associate with white wines) have been macerated with their skins – as if they were red wines. During the period of maceration, various components are naturally extracted, such as colour, tannin and other phenolic compounds.

The degree of colour depends on the grape variety, the nature of the vintage, the time of harvesting, and the winemaking – the length of maceration, the quality of extraction, whether the wines are made oxidatively or anaerobically and so forth. Skin contact wines may be golden-yellow, pinkish-grey, orange, amber or even ochre.

To make a meritorious skin-contact wine you need something worth extracting from the skins. Good farming, preferably organic or biodynamic, is a prerequisite, yielding excellent grape maturity but also balance within the grapes themselves. The extraction itself should be subtle and harmonious, the winemaker judging whether to use the grape stems, how many days to macerate, whether to rack the wine and expose it to oxygen, and so forth.

The tannic component is very important in orange wines – just as with red wines, it helps freshen the palate and balance the fruit. Also, colour, and last but not least, stability – all those phenolic compounds help preserve the wine from oxidation. There's a huge range of styles, ranging from wines where you'd barely know there'd been any skin contact, to those which coat the mouth with tannins and are practically a meal in themselves.

Simon's book is a celebration of these amazing wines, and the passionate and single-minded vignerons who craft them. This is certainly no dry academic thesis, rather it is a refreshingly jargon-free, thoroughly engaging narrative, written like a novel and a tale for our times of artisans following their hearts rather than genuflecting to received wisdom.

Dismissed initially by critics and even scorned by their peers, the amber pioneers stuck to their guns. The proof is always in the drinking. Their wines are now not only venerated by critics, sommeliers and wine drinkers, but have influenced and inspired scores of growers throughout the world.

Simon's book tells the compelling story of this renaissance of traditional winemaking methods and the people who helped to forge a 'new-old' style of wine, and links this movement to the historic winemaking culture of Georgia, where amber wines have been made using the whole grape — skins and all — for thousands of years.

The future for skin-contact wines looks very healthy. Whilst some commentators say that they are merely a fad, we are seeing more and more growers in every wine-producing country either experimenting with, or fully espousing, this style of winemaking. Meanwhile, the wines have undoubtedly convinced a generation of sommeliers and wine buyers. Orange has legitimately become the fourth colour on wine lists in many bars and restaurants.

If you are new to orange wines then *Amber Revolution* is an irresistible enticement to discover them. If, like me, you are already a convert, then it is an opportunity to become reacquainted with old friends and dig even more deeply into this fascinating subject. Most of all, this book is a rattling good read and really puts the wines into their proper context. So, pour yourself a glass of something amber and nourishing, and read on...

Doug Wregg *is sales and marketing director of the UK's largest importer of natural and orange wines (by some distance), Les Caves de Pyrene.*

Preface

Since the dawn of starched tablecloths and besuited sommeliers, restaurant wine lists have offered up their treasures in a time-honoured sequence: fizz to open, then still whites, perhaps followed apologetically by rosé, then more voluminously with reds, and finally sweets, including the occasional cameo role for port.

Those five sacred categories no longer stand alone – over the past decade, they've been increasingly augmented by a sixth: orange wine. The name isn't universally accepted – some prefer the more aristocratic and occasionally more accurate descriptor 'amber wine', others go for the full pedantry of 'skin-macerated white wines'. And there are those confused establishments who jumble orange together with rosé – a messy proposition, I can't help thinking.

Orange wine as a term is troublesome enough that immediate clarification is necessary. This book focuses only on wines made with white grapes treated as if they were red, fermented together with their skins (and sometimes stems, too) for a period of multiple days, weeks or months. The term 'orange wine' crops up in various corners of the globe in relation to other fermented beverages, but they are wilfully and summarily ignored here. Lovers of fruit wines truly made from oranges, or enthusiasts of the doubtless exceptional output from the Orange appellation in New South Wales, Australia may want to exercise their right to a refund before they angrily scuff the covers.

Conundrums aside, orange wine's time has well and truly come – bottles are proudly displayed on the shelves of countless independent wine merchants, in fashionable wine bars and top-flight restaurants as never before. The technique resists mass-production, requiring considerable patience and skill to execute properly, so these wines will never dominate supermarket shelves – but producers across the globe are now almost as likely to have an experimental 'orange' in their line-up as they are a traditional method sparkler or a late harvest dessert wine.

Yet for all the exponential growth of interest, a great deal of myth, superstition and plain old ignorance still surrounds the style. Its origins and rich heritage, in particular, have received very little love from the great and the good of the wine world.

Amber Revolution is an attempt to right that wrong and to distil a significant body of knowledge about this wonderful and unique beverage into one just about digestible volume. The greater part of the book delves into the histories of people, places and culture from orange wine's heartlands: Friuli-Venezia Giulia,[1] Slovenia and Georgia. The personal stories of winemakers in these regions are as rich and colourful as the wines they produce, and provide the all-important context for their output.

Just two decades ago it would have been impossible to write a major book about orange wine – it didn't even have a name. Now, the only problem is what to leave out. The explosion in availability, popularity and acceptance of the style unquestionably represents a revolution, whatever shade or hue it might be dubbed.

Simon J Woolf, *Amsterdam*

---

1   In truth, only Friuli Collio and Carso feature to any great degree in this book –
    but there is no easy way of referring to them collectively, without dragging in
    the whole of the Friuli-Venezia Giulia administrative zone.

INTRODUCTION

Grape skins in a qvevri, Alaverdi Monastery

1

A step into the void

I'm buried deep in the earth's crust,

clambering past densely packed fissures of elemental rock that drip with minerals and salty deposits. A sheer face of diagonally ribbed limestone rises up, stacked layer upon layer into the compressed fabric of millennia, of time itself. This is a primeval, ancient place, the path surely hewn by giants – or magicians wielding implements imbued with supernatural strength.

Just as the eyes adjust to the near total dark, shards of yellow light appear, illuminating a crevice, exposing a gaping void gouged out by an ancient spring. The inky blackness that lies behind it seems more impenetrable than the eye of a thunderstorm or the gravitational pull of a black hole. I take a cautious step back and bump into a conical oak vat.

And then a wine glass is pressed into my hand.

It contains a luminous amber liquid, seemingly tinged with an electric pink afterglow. The aromas hit first – they're as bright and vital as the surroundings are dark and mysterious. A tiny sip is enough to release the life force within. Intense yet refreshing sensations crowd into the mouth with such force and complexity that the brain can scarcely process them in any meaningful fashion.

It's truly a light-bulb moment, and I don't know it yet but it will revolutionise my life. But what is this strange yet compelling libation? Was it fashioned by the same otherworldly spirits that created the cavernous lair all around me?

Winemaking could be said to be a kind of alchemy, but wizardry it is not – this delicious elixir had a human hand behind it. The moment was October 2011, a crisp, sunny autumn day in the village of Prepotto near Trieste. The place was Sandi Skerk's winery, a cellar which *is* bored deep into the Carso region's unyielding limestone rock, although the manner of its creation doubtless involved nothing more occult than a jackhammer and a JCB.

Sandi Skerk and the Carso limestone in his cellar

That day was my first conscious experience of a venerable wine style, elegantly described in Italian as *vino bianco macerato* – literally, macerated white wine. That being a rather technical phrase, many wine lovers now prefer the more succinct term 'orange wine', referring to the deeper hues that maceration brings about, which can span anything from light orange to amber gold or russet brown.

My visit that day generated far more questions than answers. Why, as a self-confessed wine nut with a penchant for the exotic, had I never tasted a wine like this before? How exactly are they made? Who else makes them, and are they only to be found in northern Italy?

I returned home (London, at the time) with a mission. I would write an informative article on my then fledgling wine blog, aiming to convey the otherworldly experience of visiting Sandi's cellar along with those of two of his colleagues – and I'd explain what the wines were about, why they looked, tasted and smelled so different.

The modus operandi was surely simple – search online for a good primer, check my battered *Oxford Companion to Wine*, find the go-to book for the wines of Friuli and Carso – and perhaps a slim volume on *il vini bianchi macerati*, too?

I was in for a shock. There was very little information in English about Friuli's wines and even less about the more obscure Carso (technically part of the Friuli-Venezia Giulia region, but culturally quite separate to the rest of Friuli). The third edition of the *Oxford Companion to Wine*, published in 2006, provided no explanation of the revelations I'd experienced in the Carso. And when it came to resources for macerated white wines, the internet yielded a few cursory references but little more. There was categorically no book.

I pulled together an insubstantial piece about Skerk and his colleagues in the village of Prepotto, without any feeling of closure on the subject. My curiosity was piqued. Over the next two years, I devoured every scrap of information I could find online or off – every tasting note, opinion piece or blog post that seemed to have any connection to the Carso experience.

Slowly, the details came into focus. I learned that 'orange wine' is the most widely accepted description of the genre – at least, since 2004 when the term was first suggested by the UK wine importer David A. Harvey. Gratefully absorbing the output of Eric Asimov, Elaine Chukan Brown and Levi Dalton, I discovered the existence of a movement – a group of mainly Slovene and Italian families who had re-adopted the macerated white-wine style, after it had lain largely dormant for decades. The epicentre was not the Carso, but rather its similarly cross-border cousin Friuli Collio, and specifically the village of Oslavia.

Two winemakers from Oslavia cropped up again and again in the literature (such as it was). I was gripped by the gravitas of their names: Joško Gravner and Stanko Radikon. The orange wine trail lead inexorably to their cellars, yet who knew what their wines tasted like?

Gravner's story, it emerged, spread far beyond his country – to the Caucasus, and specifically to Georgia. A fascination with the republic's ancient tradition of making wine in large, buried amphorae (*qvevris*) compelled him to visit and subsequently adopt the technique for his own production.

I travelled to Georgia myself for the first time in 2012. It was still relatively underdeveloped in terms of wine tourism, but the utter uniqueness of the qvevri winemaking tradition was fast elevating producers to the status of natural wine shamans worldwide. The culture, the people and the wines were entrancing.

In May 2013, I contrived an opportunity to visit Gravner, off the back of another trip to the area. The occasion was not a success. Joško, like most Oslavians, has Slovene as a mother-tongue but is bi-lingual in Italian. My possibilities extended only to English, German and French. We could not communicate, and synergies stubbornly refused to flow.

Much has been written about Gravner, unofficially crowned as Italy's best white winemaker for more than a decade but then brutally discredited by many of those same fans after his stylistic rebirth in 1997. The naysayers appeared to hate orange wines with a venom I could not fathom. Their claim? That the results were unremittingly oxidised, volatile and faulty.

A gash in the limestone in Sandi Skerk's cellar

Luckily the wines spoke that day with a perfect clarity, unhindered by the shackles of language. They were – and are – some of the most elegant, complex and well-made wines to come out of Italy.

A year later, I made it to Stanko Radikon's door, where I discovered a warm-hearted man who appeared to be recovering well from the torture of a serious cancer. Together with his son and co-winemaker Saša, wife Susanna and daughters Savina and Ivana, we enjoyed a long lunch where more bottles than I can recall were opened, and many huge gaps in my understanding of the area's history and winemaking were plugged.

Just a few months later, while visiting producers in Slovenia's Vipava region (a little further east into the country from the border near Oslavia), I discovered the existence of a 19th-century book which confirmed that maceration of white grapes had always been the norm, at least in some parts of the country. It was becoming clear that there was a continuous narrative – a story to be told, showing how the Georgian traditions of macerated wines made in qvevri could be linked with Friuli Collio and its neighbouring Slovenian twin Goriška Brda.[2] Gravner provided the initial bridge between east and west, then Gravner and Radikon influenced just about everyone else after that.

At the same time it seemed that the ever-growing fashion for orange wines (including those of Gravner, Radikon, Skerk and many Georgian producers) might be peaking. Suddenly there were scantily researched articles popping up everywhere – some in the most unlikely places (*Vogue* magazine was one of the more incongruous). Fashionable wine bars from New York to London to Berlin and Paris were not just 'showing some skin', they were increasingly giving orange wines the honour of their own section on the wine list.

But still, no-one had gathered all the threads of orange wine's story together. Nowhere was it possible to read a complete history of the macerated white wine style – from its origins in the mists of time, to its more recent history around the Adriatic and its resurgence post-Gravner and Radikon. More and more adventurous drinkers were enjoying the wines (I've had the great pleasure of meeting many of them at tastings over the years), but very few realise quite how far back the history goes, or how difficult it was for these wines to gain acceptance when they first appeared commercially in the late 1990s.

My fate was sealed. There had to be a book, and if no-one else was writing it, I would take on the job. Prevarication and a well-paid IT job were the only obstacles. After successfully showing both the door, all I had to do was to persuade publishers that the world needed a book about orange wine.

---

2 Both Collio and Brda mean 'hills' in their respective languages – hence the names Friuli Collio and Goriška Brda are just two ways of saying more or less the same thing.

None were persuadable — at least not when the author was an upstart wine blogger with little experience of researching and writing a book.

Luckily, the ever-growing global network of orange wine lovers, producers and pundits proved to be more visionary, and this book was successfully crowd-funded on the Kickstarter platform during autumn 2017.[3]

Sandi Skerk pours a glass of his pét-nat, at the winery

---

3 The full list of the supporters can be found at the back of the book.

Sandi Skerk's dramatic cellar carved out of Carso limestone

2

The fight to reclaim identity

What links the republic of Georgia

W hat links the republic of Georgia with Friuli-Venezia Giulia and western Slovenia? Not much, on the face of it – there are no cultural or linguistic overlaps, no shared borders, seas or mountain ranges. But dig a little deeper and the links are there.

Although Georgia's struggles with its powerful Russian neighbour might appear at first glance to have little to do with the strife suffered by Slovenes, Italians and their ex-Austro-Hungarian neighbours after the two world wars, there are parallels. Both regions saw their ancient winemaking cultures almost lost and erased from history, as they were obscured by political upheaval and modernity.

Georgians lived with a paradox during the Soviet era; their distinct language and customs were loosely tolerated but at the same time subject to Russian dominance. Winemaking in particular was homogenised and restructured to suit the needs of a thirsty empire – quantity, not quality, was the watchword.

By comparison, Slovene families who ended up on the Italian side of the newly drawn border after the second world war endured more severe cultural repression, as their ethnicity and language were persecuted under Mussolini. Their neighbours on the Slovenian side of the fence fared little better. The creation of Tito's communist Yugoslavia and the brutal civil war that lead to its break-up after 1991 successfully throttled Slovenia's ability to compete as a serious winemaking nation – a setback of many decades from which it is only just beginning to emerge.

20th-century populations of both these regions, the Friulians, Triestines, Slovenes and Istrians on the one hand, and Georgians on the other had the bad luck to live in geopolitically volatile parts of the world, with their borders continually redrawn, and their governments similarly in flux throughout the post-second world war period. The extent to which their identities and livelihoods were damaged during this time and the effort required to repair the resulting physical and emotional scars are hard to imagine.

History has also obscured their stories, sometimes almost to oblivion. Georgia is now acknowledged by many as one of the most important wine nations in antiquity. Since the work of Patrick McGovern and his team uncovered archaeological evidence dating wine production and consumption back to 6,000–5,800 BC, Georgia can boast of the longest and most continuous tradition of winemaking in the world. Yet as recently as 2000, a much-praised book entitled *A Short History of Wine* had barely a single mention of the republic, and nothing about its ancient but living tradition of making wine in buried clay pots. Rod Phillips's work is excellent, and was unequalled at the time of publication, but clearly the extent to which the Soviet Union had obscured Georgia's history, and the difficulties of travelling there to undergo research created a blind spot. Phillips mentions evidence of wine consumption in Iran (then the oldest on record), and puts forward various hypotheses regarding winemaking in Mesopotamia and the Middle East. But on the Caucasus and Georgia there is merely a short sentence, recognising that this part of the world might yet have secrets to be revealed.

Locked away behind Yugoslavia's communist gates, Slovenia suffered a similar fate, largely ignored by the western wine world until the 1990s. Its modern history has barely been examined outside the country. Where there are whole shelves in libraries dedicated to first world war history focused on the battles at Passchendaele, the Somme and the Marne, the protracted bloodbath that were the battles of the Isonzo is still little known.

In the case of Slovenia and neighbouring Friuli, the relative lack of major urban centres probably didn't help. Goriška Brda, the Isonzo and Collio are all farming districts that languished in poverty for much of the 20th century. The world's spotlight has skipped over these peasant lands for decades, ignoring the jewels that lie within.

Alongside the tribulations of war, ever-changing borders and fragile politics, the splintered nations around the Adriatic lost something else – their traditional style of macerated white wine disappeared in the post-war decades, as modern winemaking technology gained ground. Decades later, two visionary wine-makers (Joško Gravner and Stanko Radikon) from a small village in the Italian Collio would become the catalysts who put macerated white wines back on the table (both literally and figuratively). They would be regarded by their peers, customers and critics as madmen and heretics. Their struggle, just like that of their ancestors, was ultimately an attempt to assert a lost identity.

Home-cured ham at Mlečnik

Cultural identity can take many forms. It can be about art, cuisine, ethnicity, language or frequently a mixture of all these. In parts of the world where farming is the predominant industry, it is also determined by what produce comes from the land. What is Friuli without its melt-in-the-mouth San Daniele ham, its hard and tangy Montasio cheese or its slightly tannic, sweet Ramandolo wines? What is Goriška Brda without its intense *pršut* (prosciutto), some freshly picked cherries in the summer or a glass of rebula?

Stanko Radikon at home, 2011

In terms of wine, these identities were distorted for much of the 20th century, as the march of industry and globalisation enforced decisions about what was and was not valid as a means of production. Both Friuli Collio and Slovenian Brda mutated into centres for modern winemaking, but at the cost of erasing parts of their region's very DNA. Attempting to reverse that process to reclaim authenticity and heritage has been almost as difficult as travelling back in time.

Georgian winemakers have been through a very similar process, watching their tradition nearly die out, but saving it at the eleventh hour. More than perhaps any other modern nation, the country has retained a deep connection between its folk traditions and its wine and food – they are well-nigh impossible to untangle. Anyone who has had the luck to visit the country, or participate in a *supra* (a traditional feast, with much singing, toasting and imbibing) will have been touched by the warmth and sociability of its citizens. It's a clear demonstration that wine can be more than a mere liquid and be part of a profound sociological continuum rich in meaning, heritage and identity.

Qvevris are everywhere in Georgia

The struggle of winemakers who wanted to rediscover this true identity has been a battle with modernity, a realisation that the best wines don't always come from a high-tech cellar gleaming with the latest machinery, but often from more humble properties where the priorities are clearly understood: perfect fruit, maximum respect for the land and a healthy nod to the traditions and culture of the past.

In the personal histories which follow, deeply hued, macerated wines provide the accidental linkage between these two distinct cultures, the ex-Austro-Hungarian Adriatic and the Caucasus.

Musicians at Barbarestan restaurant, Tbilisi, Georgia

Family and friends toast at Brothers winery, Bolnisi

A woman prays at the 6th-century Jvari monastery near Mtskheta, Georgia

Orange, amber, macerated or skin-contact wines?

Nomenclature is a tricky beast. Sometimes the names that fall into common usage aren't the most logical or the most useful – but if they are generally accepted, that's probably more important.

In this book, I use the term 'orange wine' by default. "But these wines are not always orange", the pedants cry. And they're absolutely correct (as pedants often are, annoyingly), yet white wines are not always white, and red wines are never really red. It's all a matter of common parlance and of agreeing the simplest method of communication.

Statistically speaking, orange wine has won the battle. It's the most widely used term, appearing on the labels of countless bottles and used by many restaurants to denominate the skin-macerated sections of their wine lists.

A sizeable contingent of winemakers don't like the term, either because, they protest, their wines are not orange in colour (see above) or one suspects because the associations with the natural wine movement are unwanted. Joško Gravner prefers the term 'amber wine', which is also now commonly used in Georgia.

Others have suggested it's better to talk about 'skin-fermented white wines' or 'skin-contact white wines'. These phrases are accurate, but don't fit very well into our modern paradigm for grouping wine styles. They adopt a technical vernacular, rather than the simple colour grouping that most wine drinkers are used to encountering.

Lecturer and winemaker Tony Milanowski offers this very clear piece of thinking, which provides the perfect justification for a four-colour system: "We talk about red and white grapes. We talk about wines from the juice and wines from the skin. That gives us four combinations, so why not four wines?"

Here's how that breaks down:

White wine
Juice from white grapes
(without skins)

Orange wine
Juice and skins
from white grapes

Rosé wine
Juice from red grapes
(almost without skins)

Red wine
Juice and skins
from red grapes

FRIULI AND SLOVENIA

Brda vineyard

June 1987

All Joško Gravner wanted to do on his return from California was to get home to Oslavia and check that his beloved vineyards hadn't succumbed to disease. Early summer was a critical period, so his 10-day absence was far from ideal. Instead, he was stranded at Venice Marco Polo Airport with no car, frustrated and angry.

He'd phoned his wife Marija to let her know she could come and pick him up as arranged, but the line just rang and rang cryptically with no answer. Gravner had no way of knowing that a heavy thunderstorm had severed the telephone cables, and with it Oslavia's connection to the world. His call had vanished into the ether.

Eventually, he managed to get through to his sister in Trieste, who in turn got a message to Marija. Hours later, she arrived at the terminal to find her downcast husband. "So, what did you learn in California?" she asked. "I learnt what not to do," Joško replied.

It had seemed like a great idea. Gravner's fellow winemakers in nearby Alto Adige invited him to join the trip, with a ready-made itinerary. California at that time looked like the ideal model for building a modern wine industry. Ever since its triumphs in the 1976 Judgement of Paris blind tasting,[4] The Golden State's star had been in the ascendant. Viewed enviously from the rural backwaters of northern Italy, it appeared to have perfect infrastructure and a peerless sales engine.

Close-up, the reality was rather different. California's top cuvées were utterly unable to touch his soul – there was too much of everything. Too much alcohol, too much oak and too much irrigation in the vineyards. After tasting a reported 1,000 wines over the course of the trip, he just felt fatigued and sick. Worse still, the 35-year-old winemaker saw his own trajectory reflected

---

4 See page 175, note 66 for more about this legendary tasting.

back at him, as if in a mirror. Just as California's high-tech, gleaming, no-expense-spared wineries were using the latest techniques to primp and polish their wines, so Gravner had abandoned his father's old-fashioned but honest production methods when he took control of the family winery in 1973.

With youthful fervour and ambition, he'd mercilessly sold off the huge old *botti*[5] and replaced them with modern stainless steel tanks and every piece of modern technology he could afford. Finding that steel alone wasn't enough to create complex, fine wines, he'd also invested in new French oak *barriques* – a winemaking fashion that swept Italy in the 1980s at the same time as shoulder pads and poodle-permed hairdos, and which would later seem just as outdated.

Nevertheless, Gravner's output was hot. His wines were in such demand that they were constantly sold out. But instead of being content with this extraordinary success, Gravner felt as though he had reached an impasse. California had shown him a vision of his future, and it was not the one he wanted. How could he best regain his authenticity as a winemaker?

It would take another decade to arrive at the right answer, but its implications would send shock waves through the Italian wine industry and far beyond. And it would finally reassert the identity of a village which had quite literally lost everything just a few short decades ago.

---

5 Large, old barrels with a capacity of 1,000 litres or considerably more, usually made of Slavonian or Austrian oak.

3

Destruction
and
persecution

The nondescript hamlet of Gonjaĉe lies

just a few kilometres across the Italo-Slovene border from Oslavia, but ascend the green hill just outside the village and a spectacular panorama unfolds. The rolling vineyards of Goriška Brda and its Italian namesake Friuli Collio undulate across the landscape for what seems like infinity. On a clear day the Julian and Carnic Alps are visible, and with luck you can even glimpse the Dolomites. This particular peak is dominated by a look-out tower, a brutalist if utilitarian concrete structure that elevates its visitors 23 metres above the trees. Gazing out over the 360-degree vista, it's easy to imagine that this peaceful, bucolic landscape has barely woken from its slumber in 1,000 years. The transition between Italy and Slovenia is seamless – invisible, even. There are no border patrols, no barbed wire, and no armed guards, only handsome amphitheatres of vines, interweaved in a patchwork of hilltop villages, woodland and mountains.

The history buried in these *colli* is rather different. The tower forms part of a memorial, commemorating 315 sons of Goriška Brda who lost their lives fighting in the second world war. But step back another 25 years to the first world war, and the body count multiplies horrifically. The region was brutally torn apart between 1915 and 1917 as a set of bitter, bloody and ultimately futile battles between the Austro-Hungarian and Italian armies transformed the area into a wasteland.

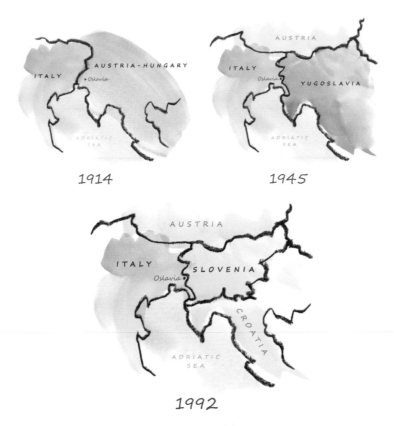

1914   1945

1992

Shifting borders around the Adriatic during the 20ᵗʰ century

Oslavia destroyed, 1916

The twelve battles of the Isonzo, so called as they raged along the length of the Isonzo river that descends from Alpine Slovenia into Friuli, claimed or wounded an estimated 1.75 million soldiers over the course of 29 months. Although Austro-German forces gained and occupied Friuli and the Veneto for about a year, by the end of 1918, Italy managed to win back its north-easterly extremities plus a substantial slice of the old Austro-Hungarian empire. This included Trieste and the surrounding Carso, Istria and what are now the Slovenian Goriška Brda and Vipava valley regions.[6]

The scale of the destruction exceeded even the more famous battles of the Somme or Passchendaele, yet history has largely forgotten this brutal and unnecessary slaughter. Oslavia was situated at the epicentre of the fighting, and as author and contributor to the Veronelli wine guide Marco Magnoli relates: "The first six battles annihilated an entire hill, and with it the personal and social identity of those who lived on it".[7] After being bombarded with half a million rounds of ammunition and 35,000 artillery shells during the battle for Gorizia (1916), Oslavje (to give it its Slovene name) was so badly destroyed that, after the war, it had to be rebuilt in a different location – the very contours of the land were permanently altered, leaving only "a shapeless hill, yellow with sulphur and pulverized stones".[8]

Only a single house still stands in the original location, having miraculously survived both world wars. The address is Lenzuolo Bianco 9, and the family that has owned it since 1901 are called Gravner.[9] Lenzuolo Bianco or 'white bedsheet' is itself a *nom-de-guerre* dating from the first world war, referring to a sole remaining whitewashed wall which soldiers used as a shooting target from across the valley. The house itself was used as a military hospital during the war.

---

6 John R. Schindler, *Isonzo: The Forgotten Sacrifice of The Great War* (Westport, CT: Praeger, 2001).

7 Brozzoni, Gigi, et al. *Ribolla Gialla Oslavia The Book* (Gorizia: Transmedia, 2011).

8 Ibid, p. 51.

9 Gravner is a Slovene name and would originally have been pronounced 'Grauner' (to rhyme with 'browner'). However, the family confirms that they pronounce the v as it is written.

The battle-scarred, famine-weakened families of Oslavia and its environs found it difficult to relate to the Italian government's propagandising about a massive victory in 1918. Not only was the disastrous human and economic cost impossible to hide, but into the bargain almost all the area's residents were Slovenes who had just involuntarily become Italian. Their troubles were only just beginning.

327,000 Slovenes found themselves on the Italian side of the new border after the first world war, including a substantial number of winegrowers in Friuli Collio and the Adriatic-hugging spit that is Carso – even if their vineyards sometimes remained inconveniently on the other side of the fence. A sustained and some-times bloody game of back and forth ensued with the same borders during the second world war and into the early 1950s, with Yugoslavia eventually gaining a slice of what had previously been Venezia-Giulia (the Italian coastal region around Trieste). Again, the borders paid little respect to those living in their proximity.

There is no shortage of anecdotes about the seemingly arbitrary nature of the shifting borders. A farmer's stable had an entrance for his cows in Italy, but the exit was in Slovenia. Family houses and other buildings found themselves split into two. Sometimes the stories take on a darker hue. Roberto Prinčič, currently president of the local winemakers association (Consorzio Collio[10]), tells the tale of the unfortunate Mirko who was living near San Floriano del Collio – a village perched even higher into the hills than Oslavia, and even closer to the Italian-Yugoslav border after 1945.

Mirko's house only had an outside toilet, as was the norm in the 1940s. His house was technically still in Italy, but the toilet ended up in Yugoslavia. Luckily Mirko befriended the border guard stationed in his street, and the two men achieved a level of understanding which allowed Mirko to relieve himself at leisure. Then one dark evening, Mirko stepped out to answer a late-night call of nature, only to find that his friend had gone off duty. An unfamiliar soldier pointed a gun at him and ordered him to stop. Mirko attempted to explain the situation but was arrested and ended up in jail for a few days.

---

10 A *consorzio* is an association of producers. The *consorzio collio* manages the
    interests of its member winemakers in the Friuli Collio DOC area.

The Sacrario militare di Oslavia commemorating 57,000 dead Italian soldiers after the first world war

Slovenian border, modern era

First world war shells at Francesco Miklus winery

Most of Oslavia's now famous winemaking families – Gravner, Radikon, Prinčič and Primosic, to name a few – have Slovene origins. Life was hardly comfortable for ethnic Slovenes in Italy after 1918. After the rise of fascism and Mussolini's accession to power, all Slav languages were banned from schools and general usage, to the extent that church was the only possible place for Slovenes to converse in their own tongue. Slovene and Croat families were widely persecuted and 'encouraged' to leave the country for good.

Mussolini's totalitarian state went further in its attempts to erase any traces of non-Italian culture. The Italianisation programme commenced in 1922, essentially as a way to force assimilation and integration of ethnic minorities. From 1926, Slavs living within Italy's new borders were forced to change their first and second names to appropriately Italian sounding alternatives. Cosič became Cosma, Jožef became Giuseppe and Stanislav became Stanislao.

Lojze Bratuž

It's for this reason that Luigi Bertossi isn't a name that features often in the history books but this was the alias forced on Lojze Bratuž, a choirmaster and composer, and an advocate for Slovenian culture who lived and worked in Gorizia between the wars. His main activities were conducting the few local choirs sanctioned by the authorities, and arranging traditional Slovenian songs for them to sing. In 1936, as a result of his work, he was brutally beaten up and force-fed castor oil and petrol by fascists. He died from poisoning two months later, aged 35. In general, Slav intellectuals and educators were barely tolerated during Mussolini's reign and as a result many emigrated between the wars rather than stay and undergo a similar fate to the hapless Bratuž.

Shutters outside the winery at Mlečnik

While the attempt at cultural genocide that was Italianisation was theoretically abandoned after Mussolini's overthrow in 1945, in practice it continued long after that year in subtle and insidious ways. As Joško Gravner's daughter Mateja confirms, up until the early 1970s government officers registering a new-born baby wouldn't accept Slav or other so-called foreign first names. So, Joško (born 1952) became Francesco on paper, just as his father Jožef was forced to become Giuseppe for the sake of officialdom. To this day the family's business is officially owned by the somewhat fictitious Francesco Gravner, and a new trading subsidiary called Francesco Joško Gravner was only added in 2016 as a slight redress to history.

Energy (of the human, physical kind), resources and funds to rebuild home-steads or replant vineyards were in very short supply between the wars, thus the Italian Collio (which now included Oslavia) languished in obscurity as many of its residents deserted to more prosperous parts of Italy. Along with the whole of Friuli-Venezia Giulia, it would remain a backwater until it became an autonomous state in 1963 – the "Mezzogiorno of the north", as it was described by the wine historian Walter Filiputti.[11]

---

11 Mezzogiorno refers to southern Italy and its sunny climate but is also used as a rather pejorative term to describe the supposed laziness or backwardness of the South. Filiputti coined this phrase in his book *I grandi vini del Veneto, Friuli, Venezia Giulia* (2000) to describe Friuli in the 19th century and up until the end of the second world war.

Damijan Podversic's vineyards in Collio

Mount Sabatino, the scene of many of the Isonzo battles during the first world war

Goriška Brda's population had two decades to adjust to their new Italian status before the area was annexed by the Nazis in 1941, subsequently becoming part of Yugoslavia in 1945 after the collapse of the Third Reich. It would be obscured from view for even longer than Friuli, as the Federal People's Republic of Yugoslavia inaugurated itself as a Soviet-friendly communist state in 1946, effectively placing itself behind the Iron Curtain. Under Josip Broz Tito's 34-year rule, farmers had to deliver the majority of their grape harvest to one of the state cooperatives, where it would be transformed into wine of mediocre quality at best.

At least Yugoslavia's winemakers didn't have to contend with the persecution suffered by their countrymen over the border, but the arbitrary division between nation states brought its own unique challenges. Winemaker Janko Štekar lives just on the Slovenian side of today's border, in the tiny village of Kojsko. He remembers the checkpoints between Italy and Yugoslavia up until the 1990s. By luck, all of the Štekar family's property ended up on the Yugoslavian side of the border, but a friend was less fortunate. He had to cross into Italy just to carry out routine work in the vineyard, but the nearest checkpoint was only manned from ten o'clock in the morning. During summer and harvest time this is far, far too late to begin the working day – it's typical for vineyard workers and grape pickers to start at 6 AM or even earlier. This was impossible without a two-hour detour to the closest checkpoint with 24-hour access.

Many other estates found themselves with similar logistical issues to solve. Movia, a long-established estate in Goriška Brda run by the formidable Aleš Kristančič, has vineyards split equally across both sides of the border, requiring some bureaucratic sleight-of-hand to be bottled as Slovenian wine.[12] Uroš Klabjan must cross national borders twice if he takes his truck from the winery, in the Slovenian Karst, winding up the hill to some of his higher altitude vineyards – nowadays an unhindered 10 to 15-minute drive.

The concept of national or cultural identity was at best blurred, and at worst erased for the residents of these shifting territories. Between 1914 and 1991,

---

12 Slovenia allows grapes harvested in Italy to be bottled as Slovenian quality wine, however the reverse (Slovenian grapes being bottled as Italian quality wine) is prohibited. A clear piece of symbolism which shows who is top dog.

ethnic Slovenes living in Goriška Brda or neighbouring Vipava would go from being Austro-Hungarians, to Italians, to Yugoslavs, and finally in 1991 to Slovenians when the country declared its independence. Štekar paints a picture of how bizarre it was to grow up during these turbulent times: "I was born Yugoslav, my grandfather Italian and my children Slovenian – even though we all grew up in the same house!"

Thankfully for everyone who had to work within and around such bureaucratic madness, the situation became considerably more relaxed once Slovenia joined the European Union in 2004 and then the Schengen Agreement in 2007 – at which point sentries and checkpoints vanished almost for good.[13] Today, driving around the peaceful country roads of Goriška Brda and the Collio, it's possible to cross back and forth between the two countries in blissful ignorance of the political and personal strife that was once a part of daily life.

Other maceration techniques

It's simplistic to say that most white wines are made without any maceration. Here are two techniques which involve some skin contact, but do not result in an orange wine:

Pre-fermentation cold-soak

Some winemakers like to macerate their white grapes for one night, or up to 24 hours, at a low enough temperature that fermentation does not start (typically 10–15°C). Sulphur dioxide may also be used to prevent any native yeasts on the grape skins from getting to work. The aim is to extract aromatic compounds from the skins, without the extraction of phenolics (tannic compounds) or excess colour.

Macération pelliculaire

This French term refers also to a pre-fermentation maceration, but one which is normally at a higher temperature than a cold-soak (typically around 18°C). This practice was very popular for Bordeaux white winemaking in the 1980s and 90s. The maceration time is usually four to eight hours.

---

13 Sporadic border checks on cars entering Italy from Slovenia apparently reappeared briefly in some locations during 2016–17, owing to large numbers of immigrants entering the EU via south-eastern Europe.

4

Friuli's first winemaking revolution

U p until the 1960s, the profession of winemaker was nothing to boast about in Friuli – quite the opposite, as demonstrated by the Friulian riposte *"Tas ca tu ses un contadin!"* (Shut up, you're just a farmer).[14] Winemakers were seen as little more than peasants, working the land much like anybody else. But it all started to change in 1963, when Friuli-Venezia Giulia gained special status as one of Italy's five self-governing autonomous regions.[15]

The newly elected regional government wasted no time introducing incentives and statutes to stimulate the region's agriculture and specifically its viticulture. Statute number 29, poetically sub-titled 'A vineyard called Friuli', set forth an ambitious plan to revitalise and upgrade Friuli's wine production. Grants and training were made available for wineries, and financial incentives were offered to those producers who could meet the strict quality requirements defined by the new *Denominazione di Origine Controllata e Garantita* regulations, which constitute Italy's official wine classification system, coincidentally also launched in 1963.

---

14 Friulian (or Friulano in Italian) is an official language spoken in some parts of Friuli-Venezia Giulia, mainly the provinces of Udine and Pordenone and half of the province of Gorizia. It is not spoken in Oslavia.

15 The others are currently Sardinia, Sicily, Trentino-Alto Adige and Val d'Aosta.

The timing was perfect. Italy enjoyed a small economic boom during the 1960s, and by the end of the decade the demand for quality wine was higher than ever before.[16] Many of Friuli's future big names set up shop during this period, including Mario Schiopetto, Livio Felluga, Collavini, Volpe Pasini and Dorigo. Their business model was completely different to what had gone before; the aim was to bottle high-quality wine and sell it all over Italy, and even beyond. Before the 1960s, most of Friuli's wine output was sold in bulk and consumed locally, and even talking about a business model would probably have produced nothing more than quizzical stares.

As Friuli's war wounds healed, and its bloody past finally receded, a new non-violent revolution began to sweep the region. Winemaking science had evolved quickly in post-war Germany, and first crossed the Italian border into the largely German-speaking Alto Adige (Südtirol) region. Courtesy of an ex-lorry driver named Mario Schiopetto, it soon found its way to Friuli Collio.

A 1970 wine from Primosic. The wording "Ribolla Oslavia" was later forbidden as the Collio DOC established itself

Schiopetto was young, savvy and well-travelled due to his previous profession. He'd grown up in the world of hospitality, as his parents ran the fireman's hostelry, which he took over in 1963 at the age of 32. He started making wine in Capriva del Friuli, using vineyards rented from a nearby church. He drew heavily on the expertise of oenologist Luigi Soini, who had gained experience in the new German winemaking methods in Alto Adige. Soini was winemaker at the Collio estate Angoris from 1969, and later director of the Cantina di Cormons.

---

16 See Paul Ginsborg, *A History of Contemporary Italy: Society and Politics, 1943–1988* (London: Penguin, 1990).

He was well versed in all the latest technology, and, as the Friulian wine expert Walter Filiputti put it, "talked a whole new language of controlled fermentations and sterile bottling".[17] Schiopetto had also befriended Professor Helmut Müller-Späth, head of research at the German company Seitz, a market leader in fermentation technology and machinery.

This technical powerhouse allowed Schiopetto to create a style of white wine that turned Friulian winemaking on its head. Filiputti remarked that, "Tasting these wines was like experiencing a new world".[18] Schiopetto's clean, crystal-clear offerings had upfront fruity aromas and a fresh, lively character. They were radically different to most white wines of the day, which tended to be much deeper coloured, and rather flat and tired in comparison. They were, in fact, the first modern-style biancos to be made in Italy, earning Schiopetto a permanent place in the nation's winemaking history books.

How had he achieved this miracle? Certainly, all his neighbours and colleagues wanted to know, especially as he was asking and getting significantly higher prices for his wines than many more established hands. While there was mild outrage about the upstart Schiopetto in public, in private winemakers were frantically acquiring his bottles, tasting and analysing them to ascertain his secrets.

Avoiding oxidation

Oxidation is the enemy of freshness, and most modern white wines depend on a dose of SO_2 for protection. White wines are more fragile and susceptible to spoilage mainly because they lack the strengthening phenolic compounds from the grape skins. Skins and stems are typically discarded immediately when the fresh grapes are pressed, unlike red wine where they are retained as a key part of the ferment.

Schiopetto's achievement was no party trick, but rather just the appliance of the latest winemaking know-how, which had not previously reached the Collio. Temperature-controlled stainless steel tanks were key for fermentation, replacing cement tanks or the traditional large Slavonian oak barrels (*botti*). They allowed much cooler and more controlled fermentations to proceed at

---

17 Walter Filiputti, *Il Friuli Venezia Giulia e i suoi Grandi Vini* (Udine: Arti Grafiche Friulane, 1997), p. 70.

18 Ibid.

the winemaker's behest, instead of relying on ambient temperatures or stone cellars to stop a raging ferment from overheating.[19] Pneumatic presses, invented by German company Willmes in 1951, allowed the grapes to be processed more gently than the Vaslin presses that had preceded them, and with far less risk of premature fermentation or oxidation when compared to old basket presses.

A wide range of manufactured winemaking products introduced onto the market during this period were also significant: They included laboratory yeast strains, guaranteed to ferment wine reliably to dryness without the unpredictability of naturally occurring wild yeasts, and Campden tablets, which provide an easy way to dose grapes, barrels and ferments with the antioxidant, antibacterial sulphur dioxide (SO_2). Every aspect of a wine's production from vineyard to the final bottling could now be precisely controlled and regulated.

Ramato –
a copper-coloured pinot grigio

Friuli's pinot grigio has long been popular all over the Veneto, but in the past it was often far from water-white in colour. Pinot grigio is a clonal mutation of pinot noir and has pink skins. Leave those skins in contact with the fermenting must for even a few hours, and the wine takes on a distinctively pink or even copper hue.

The popular Venetian name for these pinot grigio wines was *ramato*, from *rame*, Italian for copper. Pinot grigio ramato was typically made with a short skin maceration from eight to 36 hours. It may even have evolved as an accident, as separating the skins from the juice in a basket press was time-consuming, meaning that some colour pickup was almost inevitable.

The *ramato* style of pinot grigio persisted long after skin contact was abandoned after the 1960s for other white wines, but has declined sharply in popularity since the 1990s. However, the term is starting to crop up in other parts of the world, but more as a kind of homage to its origins. Wines such as Ramato (macerated 10 to 12 days) by the Long Island producer Channing Daughters reference this old tradition, but are stylistically different.

---

19 Fermentations can easily reach 30°C or even higher in warm conditions. When they do, many of the more subtle aromatics of the grape variety may be lost.

Oak fermenters at La Castellada

Klemen and Valter Mlečnik with an old basket press from 1890 which is still in use

Schiopetto's innovations took a few years to gain acceptance, but by the early 1970s two other major Collio wineries had adopted his ideas. In nearby Ruttars, Silvio Jermann had newly taken over the reins from his father, and would start building his huge empire (which today extends to some 160 hectares of vineyard). Marco Felluga, working at his family's new winery in Brazzano, was also a convert to the new style. Others quickly followed suit. Collectively, they offered what seemed like the holy grail to Italian consumers. Their clean, fresh, fruity white wines represented a modern style that simply didn't exist in Italy before.

These methods represented a sea-change from the way that white wine had previously been made, not just in the Collio but across the whole of Italy. Most winemakers in poor rural areas such as Friuli relied on ancient equipment that had been in their family cellars for decades, if not centuries – old basket (screw) presses and large oak or chestnut *botti* were often in service for several generations. Hygiene was often regarded as a luxury option. Pressing grapes with a basket press was a slow and labour-intensive process taking hours rather than minutes. It exposed the grapes to two risks – firstly, oxidation, and secondly the chance that fermentation might begin spontaneously before the winemaker intended.

Pre-war winemakers did not have easy access to scientific research on how to avoid oxidation or maximise youthful aromatics. Without the predictability of cultivated yeasts and an easy method of dosing SO_2 to preserve freshness, white wines would sometimes end up off-dry[20] or partially oxidised by the time they found their way to their thirsty public. That said, winemakers in Friuli and Slovenia had long held a secret weapon to solve the oxidation problem, a venerable method handed down from generation to generation – long skin maceration. Allowing the white grapes to macerate/ferment with their skins for an extended period of a week or more not only extracts more flavour and aroma, but also provides tannins and structure in the wine, making it considerably more robust. Winemaker Stanislao 'Stanko' Radikon recalled that his grandfather macerated his ribolla gialla grapes quite simply as it was the only way to ensure that the family's wine would last the whole year without spoiling.

---

20 If a wine is fermented with the wild yeasts found naturally on its skins or in the atmosphere, it may or may not ferment all the grape sugars completely to dryness.

The technique of macerating white wines for days or even weeks was common all around the Adriatic and is documented in a number of books from the nineteenth century. *Vinoreja za Slovence* (Winemaking for Slovenians) was written in 1844 by the celebrated Slovene writer, priest and farmer Matija Vertovec, in a now archaic Slovene dialect. Vertovec was based in Vipava, a small Slovenian village about 40km east of Oslavia and was well travelled and highly educated. His sermons attracted huge crowds as he was also a formidable orator. His pragmatic winemaking manual was written in a simple but some-times surprisingly poetic manner, in order to be easily understood by the largely uneducated farmers in the area. It's extremely well researched, and partly based on Vertovec's own experiments. He begins, however, with a caution:

> Whatever good God provides, man in his presumptuousness and insolent ingratitude ruins. Wine is God's special gift that according to the Bible makes the heart rejoice; man should therefore drink it with restraint and when he needs spiritual and physical strength. That way, like oil in a lamp, the flame of life will light up in him and he will lead a long and healthy life.[21]

Amongst a raft of technical detail and discussion, he notes that in Vipava grapes are typically left with their skins "from 24 hours to 30 days", and that "it improves the flavour and durability of the wine, and ensures it will ferment to dryness". He even refers to the skin fermentation technique as "the old Vipava method", implying that the technique was already well established more than 150 years ago.

Just over a century later, this old method of making white wine fell quickly out of fashion in the 1960s and 1970s, as Mario Schiopetto's newer methods of making fresh white wine spread across the Collio and beyond. The old macerated style began to be regarded as an example of rustic memorabilia – such wines were OK to serve on the farmer's table, but not worthy of being bottled and sold to the grander households of Venice or beyond.

---

21 Matija Vertovec, *Vinoreja za Slovence* (Vipava, 1844).

The only known photo of the Slovenian priest and scholar Matija Vertovec

Commercial wine production was about to become Friuli's lifeline. It had just about managed to survive the two world wars, suffering substantial population drain, famines and a general move away from the land and into the cities, but was still crippled by poverty and lack of infrastructure. On 6 May 1976 disaster struck again, when a 6.5-magnitude earthquake killed almost 1,000 people and destroyed a number of villages across Friuli and Brda in just one minute. In total, 77 villages were affected and 157,000 people became homeless, but the region's vineyards sustained almost no damage. 1976's harvest became a beacon of hope, and suddenly vines and their produce assumed symbolic status as Friuli's bright shining light of opportunity.

Orange wine in the Renaissance?

Isabelle Legeron MW suggests in her 2014 book *Natural Wine: An introduction to organic and biodynamic wines made naturally*, that the reason wine often appears to be more orange than translucent in Renaissance paintings is because people were probably drinking orange wine. Tempting though this analysis might be, Dutch historian and wine expert Mariëlla Beukers asserts that it is almost certainly wrong.

"It's much more likely that these paintings show the nobility drinking sweet wines, which had huge status at the time," explains Beukers. There are other explanations for the darker colour: almost all wine was stored in barrels, not in bottles. Also, the lack of scientific knowledge about fermentation meant white wines were much more liable to oxidise quickly, taking on a darker hue.

Orange wine in 19th-century Austro-Hungary

The priest and writer Matija Vertovec's *Vinoreja za Slovence* (published in Vipava in 1844) notes that it was common in Vipava and some other parts of Slovenia to ferment with the skins, however he was not a wholehearted fan of the process, even though he pointed out its very practical basis of making the wine more stable. He quotes the director of the Klosterneuburg wine school August Wilhelm von Babo at length, and sings the praises of what he terms the northern or German method of making wine, where white grapes are pressed and then fermented without their skins in oak barrels.

He sums up the pros and cons, describing the German style as "more appetising and palatable" but also cautioning that it lacks noble aromas, has less alcohol and even is not as healthy or suitable for the weak or infirm due to its lack of tannins.

Following his own experiments in the 1820s, Vertovec concludes that a maceration time of around four to seven days is probably optimal, even though he mentions that some winemakers in Vipava macerate for up to a month.

Vertovec describes northern and southern fermentation processes in some detail. In the colder northern countries, he says, the grapes are usually pressed, and the juice is stored in enclosed wooden barrels where it ferments, sometimes rather slowly. He also notes that people in the colder, northern countries have to eat and drink more to be satisfied; there is more than an implication here that he regards northern dwellers as slightly uncivilised, and with a tendency to drunkenness.

In the warmer southern regions, the custom was to macerate the grapes in open-topped vats, allowing a more vigorous and faster fermentation to occur. He goes into some detail about how winemakers can control the temperature of their ferments, by keeping cellar doors open or closed, and by pouring water over the covered vats if emergency cooling is required.

He also mentions, somewhat confusingly, that in the Collio (which was almost all Austro-Hungarian at the time) the northern method was more popular. This is slightly at odds with the large amount of anecdotal evidence from the region's modern-day winemakers, who claim that their forefathers used to skin ferment their white grapes.

Vertovec is often rather vague about whether he is writing about white or red wine – possibly because not everyone separated their grapes in this way. A slightly clearer picture emerges from the exhaustive survey *Die Weinproduction in Oesterreich* by Arthur Freiherr von Hohenbruck, published in Vienna in 1873. Von Hohenbruck confirms that the very particular white wines from the Vipava valley were strong and tannic, and made with around five to six days of skin contact. However, for other Austro-Hungarian regions such as Dalmatia, he notes that it was unusual for red and white grapes to be separated. In Styria (it's not entirely clear whether he refers to the modern-day Austrian or Slovenian part), he mentions that riesling and muscat were commonly skin fermented.

Both these books make it very clear that the more traditional, rustic winemaking tradition of southern Europe (which logically included most of Austro-Hungary and Italy) was to make what we now know as orange wine, whereas the northern method, popular in Germany and northern France aimed for a lighter, more elegant style by pressing white grapes and removing the skins immediately.

Franz Ritter von Heintl wrote in *Der Weinbau des Österreichischen Kaiserthums*, published in 1821, also in Vienna, that it was common in some parts of Austro-Hungary to make white wines as if they are reds, fermenting them in open-top vats. There are many other brief references to this style of production in German and Austrian texts throughout the 19th century.

Further back in winemaking history, it becomes increasingly difficult to separate white and red winemaking, as all varieties were commonly grown, harvested and vinified together. The exceptions are those parts of the world where a culture of more expensive fine wine goes back many centuries, such as Bordeaux, Burgundy and the Mosel.

The historian Rod Phillips notes in his book *A Short History of Wine* that neither ancient Greeks or Romans made a clear distinction between red and white wines, probably, he surmises, because everything was fermented with its skins. He does however note that the Romans prized sweet white wines, which would have been made in a maderised (deliberately oxidised) style.

5

Friuli's second winemaking revolution

Jožef Gravner built up a peerless reputation

as a winemaker, even though prior to 1968 he had never considered bottling any of his production. His wines were typically sold to local restaurants and bars in *damigiane* (demi-johns[22]), after maturing in the cellar's *botti*. In the words of his son Joško, "he made a little, but it was good". To underline the importance of quality over quantity, he would joke that the best manure came from rabbits. Key to his success was meticulous hygiene in the cellar – a much overlooked factor in an era before wine science was properly understood.

Gravner senior lived in an age when integrity was sufficient as a sales tool. "If you produce high quality, it will sell", was his philosophy. Joško took his words to heart, but felt that he could extend quality to quantity as well. He took over production from his father at Lenzuolo Bianco 9 in 1973, and looked initially to Mario Schiopetto for inspiration. "Schiopetto was smart", he recalls with a note of caution, "but he was a bit of a 'money' sort of person".

By the 1980s, Friuli discovered it had a whole new identity on the national stage, widely acclaimed across Italy as the go-to region for pure, aromatic white wines.

---

22 Glass containers of 20 to 60 litres with a wide body and a narrow neck.

And if Friuli was the source of this sacrament then Joško Gravner would soon be ordained as its high priest, as he rapidly perfected the emerging style of fresh, cold-fermented wines from international varieties such as chardonnay, sauvignon blanc and pinot grigio – all plentiful in the region since the Napoleonic era.

From left: Giorgio Bensa, Edi Kante, Joško Gravner, Stanko Radikon, Nicolo Bensa, 1992

A thoughtful, intellectual and sometimes brooding character, Gravner was also ambitious and keen to push boundaries. He pioneered modern viticulture techniques such as green harvesting, removing a proportion of unripe bunches from the vine in the summer to encourage it to produce a smaller but higher quality yield. Green harvesting is standard practice in quality wine regions these days, but for the older residents of Oslavia who had survived the brutal famines between the wars, the sight of nature's bounty being discarded and left on the ground was beyond heretical. Many of them stonewalled Gravner for years after he first tried the technique in 1982.

A group of similarly innovative, enthusiastic winemakers, mostly of Slovenian extraction, coalesced around Gravner between 1985 and 1999, meeting to taste and talk shop. Stanislao 'Stanko' Radikon, Edi Kante, Valter Mlečnik, Nicolo and Giorgio 'Jordi' Bensa (whose estate is La Castellada), Angiolino Maule (La Biancara) and Alessandro Sgaravatti (Castello di Lispida) were core members. Staged but evocative photos from the late 1980s and early 1990s document this powerhouse of winemaking talent. Gravner wrote about his colleagues with great fondness in the first of the two G monographs:

> Niko, Walter, Angiolino, Stanko, Edi, Jordi, Alessandro are friends and fellow winemakers. Serious people, producers who are not lured into compromises by the promise of quick returns. Contadini[23] who know what needs to be done to make better wines and follow these precepts day in day out, in the cellar and the vineyard.
>
> We get together often, to compare ideas and wines. Each of us has a difficult path ahead, years of hard work, mistakes to make and to be paid for. We will learn from them.
>
> One day perhaps they will help us to make a better wine than any we have ever made before.[24]

It's more than a little ironic that shortly after this book was published in 1997, he would shut all these friends out of his life and continue his work alone.

---

23 Farmers.

24 G, published by the Gravner estate 1997, and presented to friends and visitors to the winery.

From left: Alessandro Sgaravatti, Giorgio Bensa, Angiolino Maule, Stanko Radikon, Joško Gravner, Edi Kante, Valter Mlečnik, Nicolo Bensa, mid-1990s

Although the relationships were no doubt a complex hybrid of mentor, collaborator and pupil, it's very clear from Gravner's inevitable placement at the centre of the photos that he was the dominant force. Edi Kante recalls clearly, "He was the master and we were the scholars". Gravner wasn't content just to produce fresh, young white wines fermented in steel tanks. Inspiration for something more grandiose came first from France and the fine wines of Burgundy. In the mid-1980s he began to age wines in new French oak *barriques* in order to achieve a richer and more intense result. The accolades and prizes flooded in, but Gravner wasn't satisfied.

The cellar full of modern technology and expensive French *barriques* had resulted in a loss of identity in the wines – a huge irony, given that this modern, slick approach to winemaking had helped to define post-war Friuli. After the wake-up call in California, it was clear he had to look elsewhere for inspiration. The seed had already been planted by a chance conversation with friends Luigi 'Gino' Veronelli (Italy's most celebrated wine critic, who revolutionised writing about wine with his poetic language) and Professor Attilio Scienza (professor of vine biology and genetics at the university of Milan), who suggested that Gravner should study the traditions of ancient Mesopotamia, the generally accepted birthplace of wine. Gravner's subsequent research lead him slightly further north-west, right to the foot of the Caucasus mountains.

Now widely held as the cradle of wine production, Georgia has documented evidence of wine consumption going back 8,000 years, in the form of grape seed deposits at the bottom of a qvevri (Georgian amphora) fragment.[25] Unfortunately, in the late 1980s it was nigh on impossible to visit Georgia, which remained hidden behind the Iron Curtain as part of the USSR until 1991. A violent military coup lead to almost a further decade of terrorist activity, the 1993 civil war, and general political instability. Still, Gravner was fascinated by the description of an ancient tradition, and the idea of fermenting wines in buried amphorae with close to zero intervention from the winemaker.

His first experiments would not be with an amphora, but rather fermenting white grapes with their skins. After a successful trial with a small batch in 1994, Gravner could see that simplicity and a return to the roots of winemaking held the key. He would abandon the technology and the interventions that had come to define post-war winemaking, returning instead to the simple way his father – or even his grandfather – had made wine. In summer 1996, two brutal hailstorms destroyed around 95% of his beloved ribolla gialla crop, the estate's most important indigenous white grape variety. There was a bizarre symbolism to this act of God, a destruction that would ultimately lead to rebirth. Scraping together a minuscule harvest from vines hidden behind walls that had survived

---

25 Patrick McGovern et al, 'Early Neolithic wine of Georgia in the South Caucasus', published in November 2017 on the website of the Proceedings of the National Academy of Sciences of the United States of America at doi.org/10.1073/pnas.1714728114.

"L'arrivo delle Anfore" - Joško Gravner takes delivery of qvevris in 2006

the hail, he played around with the parameters – with or without laboratory yeast additions, with or without long skin maceration. The results were not sold commercially, but Gravner could see the way forward.

In 1997, a friend working in Georgia for the World Wildlife Foundation managed to sneak out a small 230-litre qvevri which he presented to Gravner. This sharp-bottomed terracotta vessel is traditionally submerged up to its neck in the ground, with only its small opening protruding. Gravner used it to ferment an experimental batch of wine that autumn, working in the small cellar of his grandfather's house in Hum.[26] After so many years of research, and the unfulfilled desire to visit the country, it was an emotional moment. "My heart trembled watching the wine ferment in the terracotta," he recalled. The results delighted him so much that he decided there and then that he would never analyse or try to influence his wines in any way again while they were fermenting.

From that year, he began using only large Slavonian oak vessels for fermentation and ageing, quietly selling off the fancy temperature-controlled tanks and

---

26 Hum is a rather spread-out village just over the Slovenian side of the border, about two kilometres from Joško Gravner's home and current cellar.

French *barriques* to other wineries in the area. All of the white grapes remained with their skins for 12 days during the fermentation, and were bottled without filtration or other processing. The results were dark, amber coloured and slightly hazy due to the lack of filtration, with heady aromas of spices, dried herbs and honeyed autumn fruits.

Not only were these wines quite unlike anything produced in Collio at the time, they were quite possibly unlike anything that had previously been bottled in Italy. Despite the practice of skin maceration during fermentation being as old as the Collio hills, it had never been thought of as a fine wine that anyone would bottle or sell. Gravner's first challenge was to get the wines accepted by the Consorzio Collio. It took two attempts in 1998, and the intervention of the influential Luigi Veronelli, but the 1997 wines were eventually approved. A year later, Gravner felt confident enough to print his DOC Collio labels in advance of the regulatory tasting. It proved to be a bad decision. The *consorzio* had no more patience for these proudly amber wines and the 1998 Breg and Ribolla Gialla were downgraded to IGT Venezia Giulia status instead, necessitating a reprint of the now useless labels. Gravner's patience with the *consorzio* was also at an end. He left the membership organisation shortly after and has never rejoined.

Whatever appeared on the label, a much bigger test came in 2000 – the first of Gravner's new style wines, the 1997s, were ready to release. Just after the year's allocations had been dispatched across Italy, *Gambero Rosso* published the preview supplement for their prestigious awards with a staggering headline: "Joško has gone mad! Come back Joško, we miss you!" It continued to detail the stars of Friuli – Schiopetto, Jermann, Felluga – but one star was in freefall: Gravner. Joško was in tears as he read it – not just because of the injustice and prejudice against his back-to-the-roots style, but also because he understood the implications. *Gambero Rosso*'s influence on the Italian wine-buying public and professionals was enormous, so much so that orders of the Gravner 1997s were returned to the winery, or in some cases the deliveries were not even accepted at their destinations. Some 80% of that year's wine was sent back, mostly without ever having been tasted. It was a bitter pill to swallow, especially when Gravner knew for sure that he was finally on the right track.

The end of the 1990s had claimed another casualty. Gravner broke with his previously tight-knit group of colleagues. By 1998, he no longer wanted the burden of collaborating, concerned that he might be thrown off his path with distracting or conflicting ideas. "If you want to climb Everest, you can't do it in a bus," is his justification for the split. As Angiolino Maule put it, "Joško broke the umbilical cord with his 'children' in 1998 – I was one of his 'sons'." Joško's daughter Mateja offers a more diplomatic analysis of the group's break-up: "There was always a bit of competition between everyone. Imagine that one importer was selling Radikon's wines, or ours – they'd be unlikely to take two producers from the same village, making the same style of wine. I think this competition in the end made it difficult for everyone to keep working together."

Stanko Radikon in the vineyards, 2011

Still, even if some colleagues regretted Gravner's withdrawal or even resented his success, the group had created something extraordinary. Now there was a core of educated, passionate winemakers spread around northern Italy and western Slovenia, all pushing the boundaries and all absolutely sure that the modernist wine revolution spearheaded by Schiopetto was not the only way forward.

Many would go on to become iconic in their own right. Edi Kante decided that macerated white wines were not ultimately his style, but his precise, expressive white wines from the stony Carso region are now as legendary as his extraordinary cellar, tunnelled three stories down into the Karst plateau and decorated with his exuberant, abstract paintings. Valter Mlečnik's Ana has become one of the greatest expressions of the Vipava valley's terroir. Angiolino Maule has redefined ideas of what garganega, Soave's major white-grape variety, can express. And then there was Stanko.

Stanislao 'Stanko' Radikon's family home and winery is about 400 metres up the hill from Gravner's front door. Early in his professional life, Radikon worked as a car mechanic. Gravner, who is two years his senior, advised him to return to working in the vineyards. Radikon did just that and officially took over the family property in 1979.

The two iconoclasts worked together closely for almost two decades, before Gravner's parting of the ways in the late 1990s. A kind and humble man, Radikon's philosophical side was gentler and less austere than his colleague. His wry stare seemed to be carefully sizing you up, but he could break out into a smile or a chuckle at any moment. Only two generations previously, Radikon's grandfather had cannily bought up land laid bare after the second world war and planted it with vines. Perhaps it was this relative proximity to destruction that helped shape Radikon's powerful drive for sustainability and care for the environment. Reminders of the horrors of war lie all around the family's property, from unexploded bombs to primitive gunpowder cartridges dating from the first world war. The family's Slatnik vineyard faces Mount Sabotino, one of the key battlegrounds over which the bitter Isonzo battles took place. Radikon's son Saša remembers that, even as recently as the 1990s, the entire top half of the mountain remained bare. More than two decades later, nature has finally managed to regenerate itself and green the peak once more.

Open-top fermenters at Radikon

Farming organically is close to being a default choice for top wine growers in the 21st century, but in the 1980s when Radikon was starting out it was as radical as the sound of the family name. Like Gravner, Radikon enjoyed considerable commercial success with wines made in a modern style throughout the 1980s and early 1990s, but it wasn't enough to satisfy his restless energy. The light bulb moment came in 1995, with the realisation that his Ribolla Gialla was missing the special aromas and flavours that were so entrancing when the grapes were eaten directly in the vineyard. Radikon took a spare 225-litre oak barrel and fermented some of his ribolla gialla grapes for a week with their skins, just as his grandfather had done fifty years previously.

When the wine had finished fermenting, its contents were revelatory. "The really big change was when I tasted the wine," Radikon said. "It was something completely new, totally different and exciting. It made me crazy, just tasting it." Was it a coincidence that both he and Gravner rediscovered this ancient method practically within the same 12-month period? Both men have referred rather cryptically to their ability to communicate without speaking, however it is likely that they discussed the idea of extended maceration at some point during the 1990s. Joško Gravner adds, "It's not important whether Stanko or I were the first – we were both returning to it 500 years after wine was first made in this way in Oslavia."

Never one to do things by halves, Radikon decided to switch the estate's entire production of white wines to the skin fermented method, a decision he'd later justify by saying, "There are two times when you can make a big change – when things are going really, really well, or when they're going really, really badly. Luckily for us, things were going well!" Experimentation continued for the next few years, to find the perfect amount of skin contact. Radikon tried macerations with the skins for up to six months, but eventually settled on two to three months as the optimum period. His now famous Oslavje, Ribolla Gialla and Jakot[27] wines crystallised into their autumnal, russet coloured personas, defiantly cloudy, brilliantly alive and expressive.

Just like Gravner, Radikon was met with what was best described as puzzlement, if not outright hostility when his new wines were released. He soldiered on, happy that the right customers would eventually come to the wines – which indeed they did, even if they were often quite different customers than before. His 1997 was the first orange vintage put up for sale – like Gravner, he had to write off the 1996 due to hail damage. The 1995 experimental Ribolla was bottled but never sold. Tasting it in 2016, Radikon's face clearly showed mixed feelings – the wine's character remains cast as a slightly geeky teenager, not quite sure of itself and not yet fully comfortable in its new garb.

Innovation remained a constant theme during Radikon's 36 vintages. With a streak of the mad inventor about him, he designed an automated machine which would

---

27 Jakot is Radikon's slightly rebellious name for his wine made from 100% friulano. Friulano (aka sauvignonasse or sauvignon vert) had always been known in Friuli as tocai friulano, but from 2008 this name was banned by the EU in response to a complaint from Hungary that it might be confused with its Tokaj appellation wines. Radikon's cheeky solution was to spell Tokaj backwards. As a fantasy name for friulano, it has also been adopted by Dario Prinčič, Franco Terpin, Aleks Klinec and many others.

assist in the labour-intensive task of punching down the skins during fermentation. Looking for all the world like a primitive robotic arm on a plinth, it is still in use today. One consequence of the extended skin contact was that it was possible to reduce the amount of sulphur dioxide required to stabilise the wine. The polyphenols from the skins gave it more than enough strength to preserve it. By 2002, Radikon had enough confidence to stop adding any sulphur at all, pre-empting a fashion for zero-added sulphur wines which only picked up speed a decade later.

In 2002, Radikon and Edi Kante prototyped alternative bottle and cork sizes, out of frustration that the traditional 75cl bottle was too much for one person, but not enough to last a whole meal with a couple. Radikon's premium wines are now bottled in 500cl and 1 litre bottles, with specially made corks which imitate the glass/cork proportions and ratios of traditional magnum bottles (150cl).[28] Edi Kante likes to joke that the one litre bottle is "perfect for two people. If only one of them is drinking!"

This focus on hedonistic enjoyment of the wines was typical of Radikon, a man who lived life without pretension. Despite the fact that Radikon has become a cult producer worldwide, the family's house is modest and tastings were still conducted at the kitchen table until 2017. The winery is simplicity itself, an old cellar with rows of Slavonian oak fermenters and large *botti* where the previous vintages age. Saša likes to draw attention to one section of the cellar wall which is open to the bare rock, seeping with mineral salts and moisture – "that's our temperature control system", he remarks wryly.

Radikon spent the last few years of his life battling with a brutal cancer. Just a few weeks before his death, he was still active, as willing as ever to sit at the kitchen table, tasting wine, opening bottles from his back catalogue and offering discourse on everything from politics to winemaking. Asked if he was satisfied with his achievements, he replied "kind of", a typically low-key response from

---

28 It's generally accepted that wine ages more slowly and satisfactorily in larger format bottles such as magnums. This has been partly attributed to the ratio between the neck and cork of the bottle and its main body, which is larger for a magnum than for a conventional 75cl bottle. The larger ratio means that proportionally less of the wine is in contact with either the glass or the cork itself.

Stanko Radikon noses his wine, 2011

Cardboard covers the qvevris at Gravner during fermentation

this modest, intelligent and resolute man. His wife Suzana had an air of grim determination about the way ahead: "He's fighting this battle, and he has to win!" But it wasn't to be, and just days before the harvest, Stanko passed away on 11 September 2016 aged only 62. Saša announced the news to the world in a typically 21st-century manner, with a poignant Facebook post: "Tonight I missed a friend and collaborator. But most of all, I missed dad. Ciao Stanko."

Saša Radikon is cut from the same cloth as his mother – both solidly built, they have an initially gruff manner which recedes quite quickly to show their kindness and humanity. As Saša explains, there was never any discussion about him taking over in the winery – he and his dad simply worked together in a natural partnership. Saša unveiled his own innovations with the 'S' line wines more than a decade ago – the Slatnik blend and a Pinot Grigio, made in a slightly lighter style with less maceration and released relatively young. Although it has been a painful process getting accustomed to life without Stanko, Saša takes comfort from a cellar still full of wine which the two made together. Many more years of Stanko's incredible legacy are still to be bottled, sold and enjoyed by a fan base which now spans every continent.

Stanko and Saša Radikon, September 2014

Joško Gravner punches down a qvevri with fermenting ribolla gialla grapes, ensuring the skins are kept submerged and moist

How are orange wines produced?

Orange wines are always made from white grape varieties, with the proviso that pink-skinned varieties such as pinot grigio are usually included in the definition of white. Instead of pressing to separate the juice from the skins before fermentation (as is the case in standard white wine production), skins and sometimes stems are left in the fermentation vessel for days, weeks or even months.

Saša Radikon's view is that a true orange wine must ferment spontaneously (with wild yeasts rather than an inoculation of selected or laboratory yeasts),* and without any temperature control. If the fermentation is controlled and held at a low temperature (for example, 12–14°C), as is common in modern mainstream winemaking, the character from the skins will be muted or even lost. The same is true if the grape's native yeasts are not used.

Fermentation often takes place in an open-topped vessel (for example, the now classic conical oak fermenters favoured by many producers in the Collio and Slovenia), facilitating the frequent punchdowns that are preferred by producers such as Radikon and Gravner. After fermentation, vessels are usually topped up and sealed, to prevent oxidation. The carbon dioxide produced by fermentation protects the wine from oxidising up until this point.

Many orange wines only remain with their skins during fermentation (typically between one to two weeks) before being pressed and racked. The wine is then often aged for many months or even years in the vessels of the producer's choice. These could include barrels made from oak or other woods, stainless steel tanks, or amphorae.

In some cases, the winemaker decides that the skins have more to give, and the wine will stay with its skins for further weeks or even months. Where an orange wine is made in an amphora or qvevri in the traditional Georgian style, the skins, stems and pips (collectively 'the mother' in Georgian parlance) will typically stay in the vessel even longer, perhaps for three to nine months, with no interventions at all by the winemaker.

Orange wines can also be sparkling – several producers ferment their grapes with the skins for weeks or even months, then bottle them with a little extra grape juice to stimulate a second fermentation in the bottle. This produces a gently sparkling, or 'frizzante' wine as the Italians call it. The style is particularly popular in Emilia-Romagna.

---

* The *pied-de-cuve* method is a popular way of kick-starting a wild-yeast fermentation, by first enticing a small quantity of grapes to ferment with their own yeasts, and then using this live ferment to stimulate larger vats. Since no laboratory yeasts are added at any stage, this is still considered technically as a spontaneous or wild ferment.

Radikon – Ribolla Gialla

Saša Radikon de-stems all his grapes before they go into a large conical, open-top fermenter made of Slavonian oak. Fermentation starts naturally, and Radikon punches down the cap (the solid mass of skins which rises to the surface) roughly four times a day. During this period, the fermenter remains open, allowing the carbon dioxide produced by the fermentation to escape. Due to the presence of carbon dioxide, oxidation is not a problem.

Once fermentation is complete, the fermenter is sealed and made air-tight. It will also be topped up, so that there is no room for oxygen in the vat.

The wine will stay with its skins for a further three months, before it is eventually racked into large oak *botti*. Here, it stays for around four years before bottling. Radikon do not add any sulphites to the wine at any stage, neither do they filter or fine the wine.

The bottles are then further aged for at least a further two years before being released onto the market.

Gravner – Ribolla Gialla

Unlike Radikon, Joško Gravner prefers to include the stems in his ferments. His grapes are given a very light dusting of sulphur as they enter the winery (although even this is only done with the first few batches, just to ensure that fermentations begin as cleanly as possible).

Fermentation happens 100% in Georgian qvevris buried in the cellar. Grapes are delivered via gravity into the qvevris, and fermentation begins naturally. Punchdowns are administered according to a strict schedule, every three hours between about 5 AM and 11 PM. It's an exhausting process, which can take well over an hour to complete. During fermentation, the qvevris are covered with pieces of cardboard just to keep the flies out. After fermentation, they are tightly sealed to prevent the ingress of oxygen.

Ribolla Gialla stays with its skins and stems in the qvevri for around six months. After this time, it is racked off the skins and transferred to another qvevri for a further five months.

After the first year, the wine is racked into very large Slavonian oak *botti* (with capacities of 2,000 to 5,000 litres) where long ageing continues for a further six years. Finally, the wine is bottled, without filtering or fining, and then released a few months later.

Gravner prefers to use a small amount of sulphite when racking the wine, although the total levels in the finished wines are still very minimal.

6

The Slovenian
new wave

History tends to shine its light most brightly

on the two visionaries of Oslavia, but to some extent they were lucky to be in the right place at the right time. Many of Joško Gravner and Stanko Radikon's good friends based just a kilometre or two away from Oslavia did not share the advantage of being based in a relatively wealthy western European nation.

Until Slovenia became independent in 1991, its winemakers were largely bound by the limitations of the system that ran under communism. Grapes had to be delivered to the state-owned cellars, where they would be vinified and bottled under a state-owned label. Slovenia took a more relaxed attitude to individual production than elsewhere in the Soviet bloc, allowing some growers to make small quantities for private sales, but it is not a coincidence that so many of today's best-known Slovenian wineries date their commercial history back to 1991 and no earlier. Even after independence, Slovenians have had to fight for a place at the table, with a weaker economy and therefore lesser status than their richer Italian or Austrian neighbours.

No-one feels this more keenly than Aleš Kristančič, proprietor, winemaker, mover and shaker at the Movia estate in Goriška Brda. The estate dates back to 1700, but came into the family in 1820. Its vineyards have been neatly divided in two by the Italo-Slovene border since 1947, although all of the harvest can be legally bottled as Slovenian wine. Kristančič is a restless soul, weather-beaten and bald-headed, with the look of a true fighter but also the raw excitement of a child. His mini-empire (winery, restaurant, tasting rooms and a magnum cellar which resembles a nightclub) now dominates the small village of Ceglo, and also includes a wine bar and shop in Ljubljana.

Kristančič is a born showman and storyteller, yet oddly without any arrogance – even if on occasion he requires some *amour-propre* to fuel the fire. He can be close to impossible to pin down, because no sooner than he follows one thread, than "tzak!" (as he likes to say for emphasis on just about everything) and he's off on a new tangent. He's bitter about the communist years, and also about Slovenia's unfair treatment as an underdog in the EU. "Imagine you have a culture, a tradition, mature vines, you are doing everything right – but you're still treated like a beast", he says of the Yugoslav era. His formative experience came as a young boy at school. He and his classmates were asked by their teacher to write down the professions of their parents. Aleš wrote "farmer" for his dad, only to find himself hauled up in front of the class. "You made a mistake Kristančič – your father is an *unorganised* farmer". The distinction referred to the fact that Kristančič senior was not a member of the local cooperative – in Yugoslavia's communist climate, a very unusual choice that placed him on the fringes of society. He might as well have been accused of being an axe murderer.

Kristančič clearly still smarts at the memory of this humiliation, but has gone on to have the last laugh, becoming one of the best known and most loved wine-makers in Slovenia. Pinning him down on dates is a leviathan task, but it is clear that Kristančič started to move away from more overtly modern winemaking methods in 1988. By the early 2000s he had evolved a pure, low-intervention style of production which reached its extreme in his Lunar wines. Made from rebula[29] and chardonnay left with their skins for up to nine months, the Lunar range is harvested, racked and bottled by the phases of the moon, and made without added sulphites or additions of any other kind.

---

29 Ribolla gialla is known as rebula in Slovene.

Aleš Kristančič (Movia) in the cellar

Valter Mlečnik's cellar book

When winemaker Valter Mlečnik talks about his past friendship with Joško Gravner, it's clearly an emotional topic. Mlečnik has a gentle, spiritual air about him (and given his considerable height, he's probably breathing more rarefied air than the rest of us!) but is not given to unnecessary displays of sentiment. "Joško was like a second father to me," he recalls fondly. At their first meeting in 1983, Gravner had lots of advice for Mlečnik, whose output he dubbed "a good table wine". Despite this damning with faint praise, the pair became close friends, and Mlečnik would become the only member of Gravner's inner circle based in Slovenia.

His relative poverty compared to the Italians turned out to be a blessing in disguise. Mlečnik couldn't follow fashions and snap up the latest technology or invest in new French-oak barrels as readily as his Italian colleagues. He bought second-use barrels from Radikon and Gravner, pre-empting future trends when less overt oak influence became desirable. He also stood by and watched as Radikon, Gravner and others invested in expensive temperature control systems and sterile bottling lines, only to junk them a few years later when they discovered that it was all totally unnecessary. "Joško was always one step ahead, though," Valter confirms, "and he also gave us all our faith back in ribolla gialla." Gravner did more than just advise on production methods. He also engineered an introduction with Joško Sirk, another Slovenian who ran one of the Collio's top restaurants, so that Valter Mlečnik was able to start selling his wines on the more lucrative Italian market.[30]

After years of being in constant contact, Gravner suddenly cut Mlečnik and everyone else off. Mlečnik remembers the moment well: June 1999 was the month when NATO bombed Serbia to try to dampen down the horrific Kosovo war. It was an uneasy time to be anywhere in the former Yugoslavia. There were no more phone calls, no more get-togethers to taste and discuss with the group, no more visits. The two would not meet again until they showed up at a memorial event for Stanko Radikon, on 20 December 2016. "Joško said hello, as if it had just been last week!", Valter recalls.

---

30   La Subida currently has one Michelin star. Joško Sirk is still at the helm, but his son Mitja has now taken over as head sommelier.

Valter Mlečnik

The Vipava valley in the Kranjska Gora sub-region

Still, by the late 1990s Valter was well on the path to the stripped-down style of winemaking that he's now perfected, together with his son Klemen who is now an integral part of the operation. Using a cellar where little has changed for centuries, the pair follow a tradition that is well documented in Vertovec's 1844 manual – even down to some of the pruning recommendations. The one concession to technology, a pneumatic press bought in 1996, was finally sold off in 2016 in favour of an old basket press from 1890 – now used for the entire production. The Mlečniks took a similarly reductive ethic to their production methods as Gravner, albeit with quite different parameters.

The stunningly beautiful Vipava valley, with its backdrop of the distant Julian Alps, is home not only to the Mlečniks but to many other producers who have since built great reputations for their macerated wines. Virtually all cite Gravner as an influence, as the one who gave them the confidence to go back to their roots. One such winemaker was Ivan Batič, who started out selling his wines from door to door in the small village of Šempas in the 1970s. He also counted Radikon, Gravner and Edi Kante as friends. A serious heart attack in 1989 made him pause for thought. Recovering on a diet of locally grown cherries and water, he began searching for a more sustainable, chemical-free way of working in the vineyards, and a quest for more authenticity in the finished product. This entailed replanting vineyards with the region's native varieties (zelen and pinela) in lieu of chardonnay or sauvignon blanc. He also returned to the old tradition of macerating white grapes. As his son Miha confirms, "Everyone in the village was still using extended skin contact in their white wines until the 1980s, but then pneumatic presses became available around 1985 or 1986 and that was the death of it." Now, the estate is at the forefront of natural winemaking in the area, and is part of a growing trend to switch to biodynamic viticulture.

As Primož Lavrenčič leaps athletically up onto a gantry at his new winery, with a dramatic wall of exposed rocksalt behind it, his passion for mountaineering is clear to see. Lavrenčič is based at the opposite end of the valley to Mlečnik, towards the south-east. He's also part of the biodynamic movement, recognising the absolute importance of healthy soils. "I'm the worst cellar-master", he jokes, "but the soil here is making good wine." Lavrenčič has a way of taking quite deep intellectual concepts and applying them in an easy, unpretentious way to his work. He's no slouch when it comes to the history of his region's winemaking, citing not just Vertovec's seminal work but also an even older book, *Die Ehre deß Herzogthums Crain* (*The Glory of the Duchy of Carniola*) by Johann Weikhard von Valvasor, which was published in 1689 in Nuremburg and mentions the special qualities of the Kranski sub-region for growing vines. Lavrenčič was given some ribolla gialla vines by Joško Gravner in 2003, while he was still working for his family's Sutor winery. He left the family business in 2008 (still run by his brother Mitja), wanting to explore more stripped down, less mainstream winemaking, which includes maceration for all of his white grapes, in the age-old tradition described by Vertovec.

The stories of younger winemakers being mentored and influenced by Gravner are legion, but not everyone needed his blessing to return to the old ways. Branko Čotar has been making macerated white wine in the stony Slovenian Karst region since 1974, and still has extraordinarily deep-hued bottles from the 1980s in his cellar to prove it. His son Vasja is now in the driving seat, but Čotar, with his Einstein-like shock of hair and a wild, rather mischievous twinkle in his eyes, still regularly presides over the tasting room. He originally just made wine for the family's restaurant – a teran (the region's lean, high-acid red grape) and the house white wine, which was always macerated. The first bottled

Primož Lavrenčič in the cellar and the vineyard

vintage was 1988, but it wasn't until 1997 that the family decided to close their restaurant and concentrate on wine – an option that simply wasn't feasible while Slovenia was still part of communist Yugoslavia. Čotar is one of very few winemakers who never switched from the traditional macerated style (Joško Renčel is another), and had it not been for his estate's relative obscurity during the communist years, this book might be telling a different story today.

If Slovenians occasionally cast a jealous look at the over-performing Collio, and its rise to fame and fortune within the wine world, so too have the Carso's inhabitants. This thin strip of inhospitable, stony land which runs southwards down the coastline towards Trieste is the Italian continuation of the Slovenian Karst. It's a tough place to farm or grow grapes, as instead of topsoil there is mostly just hard, unyielding limestone. Then there's the vicious Bora wind which can easily rip vines (or any other sort of plant) to shreds if they're not well trellised. For a long while after its Collio cousin shook off the stigma of being a poor farming region, Carso remained a rural backwater with little wealth and increasing population drain to Trieste. Generalisations may not always hold true, but there's also a certain ingrained Carso character – quiet intensity, stoicism, few words but no lack of actions.

Brežanka

Historically, vitovska was probably always macerated as part of a white blend called brežanka, together with malvasia and glera (prosecco). It's celebrated in a short poem 'Peter Mali' by the Slovene poet Valentin Vodnik (1758–1819), written in 1814. "Long live brežanka", says the protoganist as he eagerly sits down to dinner one evening, "I hope we will always have it!"

Paolo Vodopivec certainly fits this mould. Even though his wines have achieved a cult status on a similar level to Gravner and Radikon, Vodopivec is no fan of the limelight. He doesn't like receiving journalists, and strongly prefers not to appear in photographs.[31] "Wine shouldn't be about ego", he explains, "it should be about expressing what's in the vineyard." Vodopivec's extraordinary elemental cellar is a reflection of his character – uncompromising, austere but with an aesthetic

---

31 We have respected his views in this book, however he did agree to be in the picture with his qvevris – you see just him from the back.

Paolo Vodopivec's qvevri and barrel cellar

that would make a Scandinavian interior decorator proud. Together with his brother Valter (who is no longer involved in the business), the two decided in 1997 to focus purely on Carso's indigenous vitovska variety – and also to vinify it with its skins, as Paolo remembers was always done in his youth. He visited Gravner in 1998, but these two intense, almost reclusive characters failed to establish a close bond. Vodopivec was impressed by Gravner's achievements, but knew that his vision was different.

Unbeknownst to Gravner, Vodopivec undertook his own experiments with terracotta in 2000. He vinified some wine in a small Spanish *tinaja* (amphora), but was unhappy with the results. "I threw both the wine and the amphora away," he deadpans. He visited Georgia alone in 2004, resolving that he would explore the whole country and find out as much as possible about its winemaking traditions. Vodopivec is resolute and robust, but had perhaps underestimated the dangers of travelling through Georgia at that time. Wanting to ship a batch of qvevri back to Italy, he fell foul of the local mafia and had to negotiate a mutually beneficial agreement before both he and his qvevri were released.

It's fortunate that it all worked out because Vodopivec's wines are some of the most elegant ever made with extended skin maceration – and it is *very* extended. Although his initial experiments looked to tradition, with around eight days of maceration, that has steadily increased to up to a year in the qvevri for the 'grand cru' wine Solo. Vodopivec hates his wines being categorised as orange wines or even natural wines, partly one suspects because the non-conformist in him resists any kind of pigeon-holing, but also because he doesn't like the association with the more rustic or clumsy wines which cohabit the genre.

Contrary to popular legend, perhaps it was neither Gravner nor Vodopivec who were the true pioneers of amphora winemaking in the modern age. Božidar Zorjan and his wife Marija have been farming in Slovenia's north-easterly Štajerska region (the Slovene name for Styria) since 1980. They were early converts to organic farming, and then to biodynamics in the 1990s. Zorjan has a deeply spiritual bent, and feels a duty to continue making natural wines in the grand tradition of the long disused but symbolic monastery Žiče Charterhouse, which is close to his vineyards in Pohorje.

He began using amphorae to make some of his wines (all the white grapes stay with their skins for weeks or months) in 1995, starting out with small Croatian vessels, and moving later to Georgian qvevri when his supplier in Croatia died. The qvevri are buried outside, lying under the stars in order to harness energies, which for Zorjan are vital:

> Cosmic forces turn grapes through the winter into wine and thus give us a unique live wine, where the man with his ego is just a mere observer. Ever since I was a child I dreamed about making wine without a cellar or a press. Now, I always dream beautiful dreams, which are brought to me by tasting the spirit of my wine.

Zorjan and Gravner have never met. Just as Gravner and Radikon began separately but simultaneously searching for a way back to a more authentic and honest way to work in their wineries in the late 1990s, perhaps there has been a kind of shared consciousness in these quiet country regions spread around former war zones and hard-fought political borders. The deep thinkers, iconoclasts and visionaries were all searching for an identity that had been destroyed during the modern industrial age. They found it either by searching their own heritage, or with a little help from a yet more ancient culture that had somehow retained its integrity, despite the ravages of war and ethnic oppression. Namely, Georgia.

Aleks Klinec tops up a barrel in his cellar

Franco Sosol (Il Carpino) in the cellar

Damijan Podversic ploughing the grass between the rows

Miha Batič

Andrej Cep (Gordia)

Matej Skerlj inspects some high-trained Vitovska

Dario Prinčič

Stanko Radikon in the cellar, 2005

Popular grape varieties for orange wine

In theory, any grape variety can be skin fermented to produce an orange wine, however some varieties seem to respond better than others. Good acidity is important, especially when grapes are macerated for many weeks or months to create more full-bodied, structured wines. Here are a dozen of the most successful:

FRENCH / INTERNATIONAL VARIETIES

Chardonnay

A fairly neutral variety, but with potentially superior finesse and terroir expression, chardonnay can give a seriously structured, complex wine when macerated for long periods.

Best examples: Vipava (Slovenia), Southern Styria (Austria)

Gewürztraminer (and other traminers)

Aromatic varieties such as the floral gewürztraminer work extremely well with prolonged skin contact. Gewürz's character is so dominant and recognisable that even a maceration of many months will not subdue it – indeed it often turbocharges the experience! The thick skins provide ample tannins, which act as the perfect foil to the sometimes overbearing perfume and oily texture.

Best examples: Alsace (France), Burgenland (Austria)

Grenache Blanc

As a relatively low-acid variety, grenache blanc might not seem to be the most obvious choice for long maceration, but somehow its generous fruit and soft 'come hither' nature create incredibly appealing and well-balanced orange wines.

Best examples: Languedoc, Rhone valley (France)

Sauvignon Blanc

Sauvignon's aromatics change character with prolonged skin contact, from fresh citrus and gooseberry to candied peel or ripe apple, but are no less intense. Great acidity is the perfect foil for the complex, structured character of orange wines made with this variety.

Best examples: Friuli Collio (Italy), Southern Styria (Austria)

ITALIAN VARIETIES

Malvasia di Candia Aromatica

It is no accident that you'll find so many great orange wines in Emilia-Romagna. The region's local variant of malvasia produces an intensely perfumed, prodigiously structured wine when macerated – and many producers in the region extend the maceration time to several months.

Best examples: Emilia-Romagna, Tuscany (Italy)

Malvasia Istriana / Malvazija Istarska

This generous, fruit-laden variety plays brilliantly well with long skin contact, which probably explains why the style has always had its fans in the variety's native Istria. The peachy aromatics provide character, the full-bodied, complex palate can be an absolute joy.

Best examples: Istria (Croatia), Istra (Slovenia), Carso (Italy)

Ribolla Gialla / Rebula

This regal variety can be pretty dull when vinified without the skins, but leave them in the ferment and the magical spicy, honeyed complexity unfolds. Ribolla gialla (or rebula as it is known in Slovene) is native to the Collio/Brda area, and has incredibly thick skins – so much so that they jam old-fashioned basket presses if they have not been macerated.

Best examples: Friuli Collio (Italy), Goriška Brda (Slovenia)

Trebbiano di Toscana

The humble trebbiano, aka France's ugni blanc, was once considered barely good enough for distillation, and is certainly not the most exciting when made as a simple white wine. But with skin contact, the picture changes completely, and some of northern and central Italy's top orange wines are based around trebbiano. Synonyms are myriad, and include trebbiano di Soave, procanico and turbiana.

Best examples (mostly in blends): Tuscany, Umbria, Lazio (Italy)

Vitovska

A hardy native of the rocky, windswept Carso, vitovska is capable of extraordinary elegance and persistence when made with long skin contact. Floral aromatics are intensified and entrancing, the structure always remains subtle without overbearing tannins and the terroir expression is peerless.

Best examples: Carso (Italy), Karst (Slovenia)

GEORGIAN VARIETIES

Mtsvane

The mtsvane grape of the eastern Georgian region of Kakheti is perhaps the thickest skinned, most tannic of all the country's popular white varieties. Although it demands longer ageing and careful treatment to avoid too much rasp, fantastic aromas of jasmine and poached pear emerge in good examples, along with full-bodied, attractive fruit and a pleasing nutty finish.

Best examples: Kakheti (Georgia)

Rkatsiteli

Georgia's most planted white grape really comes into its own when made as a traditional qvevri wine with six months of skin contact. Good examples will show wonderful floral aromas as well as ripe fruit and fresh acidity. Tannins can dominate if yields are not kept low, or the wine is over-extracted.

Best examples: Kakheti, Imereti (Georgia)

Tsolikouri

This yellow skinned variety is popular all over western Georgia. Made in the traditional qvevri style, it has a very distinctive earthy, mineral character, and can be quite lean or even austere. That leanness translates into a wine of real elegance and refinement in the best examples.

Best examples: Imereti, Kartli (Georgia)

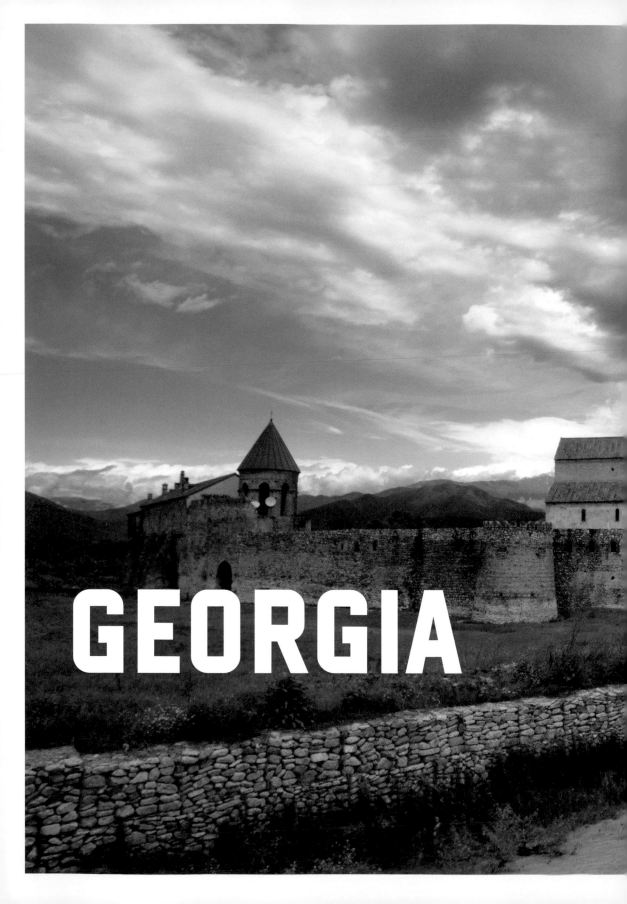

GEORGIA

Alaverdi Monastery, with the Caucasus mountains visible in the distance

May 2000

Thirteen years after his unwelcome Californian epiphany, Joško Gravner was finally able to keep the personal promise that he would journey to the cradle of wine. Georgia was no longer ravaged by civil war or its repressive Soviet over-lords. Better still, Gravner had met a Slovene-speaking Georgian who offered to facilitate the trip. His newfound friend Razdan acted as guide and translator, and even organised bodyguards equipped with Kalashnikovs.[32] Together, the group headed east of Tbilisi for Kakheti, the country's most famous wine region. Gravner's knowledge of the area's ancient winemaking traditions was thus far only academic. The burning question was whether anyone was still making wine in buried amphorae (qvevris)?

On 20 May 2000, with help of his guide, Gravner located a small cooperative cellar in the city of Telavi. In Georgian culture, guests are a gift from God, so the cellar's denizens were honoured and delighted to open a qvevri which had remained sealed since the previous year's harvest. Gravner was offered a generous serving from the *azarphesha*,[33] despite meekly protesting that he only wanted to taste the dark, amber-coloured liquid.[34]

Taking a sip of what he had expected to be a rustic and simple drink, Gravner quickly became besotted. "I was astonished by the result of this kind of produc-tion. It was heavenly." He would later remark that it was the best wine he ever tasted in Georgia. By the end of the trip, he had already ordered a batch of 11 qvevris for his cellar, convinced that there was no more perfect vessel for wine than these womb-like amphorae. Frustratingly, they did not arrive in Oslavia until November that year, just too late for the year's harvest. That wasn't the only problem – Georgia's few remaining qvevri makers had no experience of

---

32 Georgia was not a safe country for independent travel in the decade immediately after communism, especially outside the larger more westernised cities, and ambushes on the more isolated roads were common.

33 A traditional ceremonial ladle, made from silver, gold or even wood, from which wine is served or drunk.

34 The wine was a rkatsiteli (Georgia's most popular white grape).

shipping their wares such long distances, and the qvevris arrived on the back of a truck with scant protection. Only two of the 11 vessels had survived the journey in one piece!

Nonetheless, from 2001 onwards, Gravner gradually switched to qvevris for all his fermentations, burying them in a new, specially built cellar which created a contemplative and almost austere atmosphere all its own. It would take him another four years, and require the purchase of almost 100 of the vessels before he had 46 that were robust enough to survive the journey and not shatter once they were buried in the ground.[35] With the use of the qvevri came another shift in the winemaking. While Gravner had started out imitating his family's ancestral methods of a few days to a week's skin contact, he now kept the skins and the stems with the fermenting wines for a full six months as the Kakhetians did. Not only did the results astonish his customers at the time, they also drew back the curtain on an extraordinary and hitherto hidden culture. Gravner's first qvevri vintages (2001 and 2002) actually pre-dated wide availability of Georgian examples in the west. Almost 20 years on, Georgia's artisan winemakers still talk about Gravner with reverence, as one of the first westerners who allowed the world a glimpse of their precious secrets.

Major wine regions in Georgia

---

35 Gravner's Breg and Ribolla Gialla had the 'anfora' orange flash added to their labels from the 2001 vintage, even though these wines were not 100% fermented in anfora until 2003. Breg Rosso was not made in qvevri until the 2005 vintage. From 2007, the anfora indication was removed from all labels as the Gravner family decided there was no longer any need to provide this information.

7

The Russian Bear and the industrialists

H

Hermann John Thumm's youth was spent living in paradise – at least, that's how he describes it in his autobiography *The Road to Yaldara: My Life with Wine and Viticulture.* Born to German parents in December 1912 in Georgia, Thumm would go on to found the pioneering Chateau Yaldara in Australia's Barossa Valley in 1947, an estate that not only helped establish the region for quality wine but also for enotourism. By the time of his death in 2009, he had become recognised as an important innovator.

Thumm emigrated to Australia after the second world war, but his early years were spent in Georgia living in an expat community of some 12,000 Caucasus Germans.[36] He speaks fondly of the entirely German-speaking schools and universities, the mulberry trees and vines groaning with luscious fruit, and of the considerable privileges that were enjoyed by Germans in Georgia at that time.

Their influence on Georgia's winemaking culture is an annex of the country's history which is often neglected or ignored – the official chapter and verse,

---

36 Frustratingly he does not mention the location, however German communities in Georgia were well established in various parts of the country, including in the vicinity of Tbilisi and the nearby Kartli region.

Looking into a qvevri at Brothers Winery, Bolnisi

focusing on Georgia's 8,000 vintages of making wine in the traditional manner with buried qvevris, enjoys far greater prominence – even if it conveniently obscures how close Georgians came to losing their ancient traditions forever.

Although Georgia has been independent since 1991, it had previously spent almost two centuries under the rule of Russia and subsequently the USSR. The absorption into Russia was far from comfortable, mainly because Georgia is culturally and ethnically quite distinct, even compared to other ex-USSR nations such as Ukraine. Its language has a softly guttural, almost Asian cadence, and a similarly incomparable curlicue-filled script. Neither script nor language bear any relation to Russian, which has east Slavic roots. But it's not only language that sets Georgia apart from its neighbours and its erstwhile ruler: The country's traditional polyphonic singing, with its close harmonies, dissonance and exotic key changes is a potent symbol of its distinct heritage. Where there is singing, there will be food and celebration. And where there is food and celebration, there *must* be wine.

It is known that Georgian winemaking has a history that stretches back into the mists of time, or at least back to approximately 6,000 BC. But the very particular way it has been made since antiquity – grapes, skins, seeds and often stems all thrown into the buried qvevri, allowed to ferment and then sealed from any intervention for up to nine months – became so endangered as a tradition that UNESCO and the Slow Food Foundation for Biodiversity have both taken steps to help preserve it.

Those German expats surely didn't pause to think that they were disrupting a winemaking heritage dating back many millennia. Since the mid-1800s, when Swabian wine expert G. Lentz[37] relocated to the Kakheti region in eastern Georgia, there has been a documented history of German winemakers and coopers bringing their techniques and even vine-cuttings to Georgia. It would have delighted the anonymous author[38] of *The Wine-Drinker's Manual*, published in 1830, who noted Georgia's abundance of wine but lamented that,

---

37 His first name is not recorded in any document that could be traced by the current author.

38 The author is only identified by the phrase "In vino veritas" on the cover, and in the preface as "The Author", based in Richmond, UK.

Guram Abkopashvili, Brothers winery, Bolnisi, Georgia

"The Georgians have not yet learnt to keep their wine in casks, without which it is vain to look for any improvement in its manufacture. Yet the mountains abound in the requisite materials, and only a few coopers are wanted to make the commencement."

In contradiction, Lentz praised the qvevri as an ideal vessel for wine, but his words seem to have largely fallen on deaf ears.[39] By the time Hermann Thumm was born in 1912, the transformation to using large wooden barrels and pressing the white grapes directly had become deeply ingrained. Brothers Guram and Giorgi Abkopashvili have been using traditional qvevris in their small cellar in the village of Bolnisi[40] since 2014, but previously they produced what Guram calls

---

39 Noted by Teimuraz Ghlonti Doctor of Technical Sciences, Winemaking Adviser of Alaverdi Monastery, in the foreword to Giorgi Barisashvili, *Making Wine in Qvevri: a Unique Georgian Tradition* (Tbilisi: Biological Farming Association 'Elkana', 2011).

40 Bolnisi is situated in the Kartli wine region, about an hour's drive from the capital Tbilisi.

'European style' wines which were aged in large oak barrels. Guram remembers clearly how his grandfather, who lived in one of the German communities, followed the practice of making wine in the Teutonic fashion – and even though he and Giorgi are clearly proud of their newly installed qvevris, in a quiet moment he waxes lyrical about the German style and even admits to preferring it for his personal drinking. "I never tasted the great wines from Bordeaux", he muses, "but when I read the tasting notes, I imagine they taste just like our 'European wines' made here in Bolnisi."

Guram's neighbour just across the street is the tall and rather svelte Vakhtang Chagelishvili, whose wines are bottled under the brand Bolnuri. His story is similar to the Abkopashvilis – the family's wine cellar was built by German settlers, but he's just converted it to house a fleet of qvevris – the old wooden barrels now sit outside in a lean-to, looking a tiny bit dejected at their fall from grace.

Still, if the 19th-century German settlers certainly diluted Georgia's pre-existing wine culture, their effect was minor in comparison to the wholesale destruction that would follow during the Soviet era. Russia had always been thirsty for Georgia's superior wines, and after the formation of Stalin's Soviet Union in 1922 (into which Georgia was subsumed) it set about rationalising and industrialising wine production with scant regard for anything beyond quantity.

The Soviet state alcohol monopoly Samtrest was established in 1929, gradually becoming the owner of all Georgia's wineries and related distribution businesses. Over the following decades a utilitarian system was evolved which rode roughshod over any notions of individuality in the wine. Georgia's grape growers delivered their harvest to one of hundreds of 'primary wineries'. These fermentation factories processed the grapes and turned them into so called 'wine materials' – essentially, bulk wine. This mostly rather mediocre liquid was then delivered to a designated 'secondary winery', often located in Tbilisi or another big city. Here, the bulk product was aged, processed, bottled and labelled, before being shipped to its designated customers – again, a list supplied by the state.

As all Georgian wine was bottled under the Samtrest label, the winery's name did not appear on the bottle.[41] Differentiation was achieved through style or 'appellation'. Denominated areas such as Kindzmarauli, Khvanchkara or Mukuzani were popularised more as brands, each with a regulated stylistic signature. Khvanchkara – reputedly Stalin's favourite – was naturally semi-sweet, Mukuzani was oak aged, Tsinandali was a dry blend of rkatsiteli and mtsvane.

The homogenisation didn't stop with labelling. From the 1950s, further state reforms limited the number of grape varieties which could be grown to just 16, and in practice this further reduced to just two mainstays, white rkatsiteli and red saperavi. Disease-resistant hybrids (crossings of *Vitis vinifera* with American vine families as such *V. rupestris* or *V. labrusca*) also became popular during this period, known as 'non-treated vineyards' by their growers as they could be cultivated without the vast amount of pesticides and fungicides that were routinely sprayed on conventional vines.

Georgia has always been incredibly rich in indigenous grape cultivars, with a claimed 525 native varieties. In the 1930s, around 60 were still in common use, but by the end of the 20th century this had shrunk to as few as six. Literary critic, Georgian wine expert and author Malkhaz Kharbedia notes that prior

---

41 For the initiated, it was sometimes possible to deduce which winery had made the wine by looking at the lot number or other obscure codes which might appear on the label.

to the Soviet reforms, one could have enjoyed khidistauri, akhmeta-tetri, rachuli tetra, ikalto jananuri, tskhinvaluri, shavkapito, kvishkhuri, nagutneuli, tsolikauri obcha, saperavi sanavardo, kvareli nabegari, kardanakhi tsarapi, akhoebi saperavi, krakhuna sviri, ruispiri mtsvane, mtsvane nasamkhrali, argvetuli sapere, mukhranuli saperavi, aladasturi or gunashauri – many of these varieties are either lost to history or barely cultivated any more.[42]

It's no surprise that the qvevri tradition became another near-casualty of the Soviet period. Every Georgian homestead traditionally had its small *marani* (cellar) or even just a few qvevri buried outdoors, but the Soviet state regarded it as a worthless peasant custom and qvevri winemaking was marginalised and largely forgotten. Home production of wine was tolerated but selling was forbidden. Families focused on survival and delivering their grapes to the wine factories, with only a minuscule number who clung to the old tradition of making qvevri wine.

Zaza Remi Kbilashvili with freshly fired and lime coated qvevris

---

42 More recently the National Collection of Georgian Indigenous grape varieties held at the Scientific Research Centre of Agriculture has developed/rescued an impressive collection of over 400 indigenous varieties in its research vineyard near Tbilisi.

Disused qvevris at Alaverdi Monastery

Well-made qvevris can remain in active service for centuries, but as qvevri maker Zaza Kbilashvili sternly notes, they must be used every year or they become difficult if not impossible to maintain in a hygienic state. It's hard to imagine how many of these magnificent terracotta vessels were abandoned, destroyed or rendered useless by the 70-odd years of the USSR, but the monks at the orthodox Alaverdi Monastery in Kakheti have a better idea than most. The current monastery dates its origins back to the 11th century, although there is evidence of the existence of a wine cellar there dating from the 9th century. But this commanding complex, with its breathtaking backdrop of the Caucasus mountains, was almost completely destroyed and brutally ransacked during the Soviet era and the second world war. Some of its 50 historic qvevris were ruined by being used by Bolsheviks to store petrol, while many more were simply smashed into smithereens. The remains are littered around the monastery's grounds, some still reeking of petrol fumes to this day.

As the traditional way of making wine started to disappear from everyday life, so did the infrastructure it had supported. Qvevri-making is a very specialised form of pottery, which, like most other ancient knowledge, is typically passed down the family line from father to son.[43] Qvevri makers would have been common in almost every village a century or more ago, but by the time of the downfall of the USSR, there were perhaps a half dozen left in the entire country.

The Soviet state didn't just wreak havoc on the Georgian qvevri tradition. Polyphonic singing and the all-important oral tradition of passing songs down from one generation to the next was also greatly harmed, as the singers of the Ensemble Erthoba recount. In theory, the USSR placed a high value on folk traditions, at least so long as they were not overtly linked to Christianity, but the state's love of bombast and ever larger, grander choirs and ensembles was disruptive to the Georgian tradition, which is almost entirely informal and based around social gatherings. Traditional polyphonic songs have no formal notation, and it's estimated that many thousands have been lost or simply forgotten over the past 100 years, despite the efforts of a few individuals to

---

43 Georgia is still an extremely patriarchal culture, and to date I am not aware of a female qvevri-maker.

Singers at the New Wine Festival, Tbilisi, May 2017

record or transcribe them. Transcription presents a further challenge as there
is no official music notation system which expresses some of the microtonal
elements in the songs.

While qvevris remained empty, wineries such as Tbilvino (based in the capital
Tbilisi) produced as many as 18 million bottles a year in their heyday. But with
the arrival of Mikhail Gorbachev and Perestroika came a number of measures
to drastically limit the sale and consumption of alcohol. The period 1985–87
saw production volumes plummet and Georgia's wine factories start to struggle.
After the collapse of the USSR and Georgia's declaration of independence
in 1991, the giant wineries fell silent, suddenly stripped of their order books,
with no sales contacts and no marketable brand identity without the once
all-pervasive Samtrest.

Dr. Irakli 'Eko' Glonti at his house in Tbilisi

It's tempting to link the Georgian wine industry's recovery from those dark days with the surge of interest in its traditional winemaking, but the truth is far stranger, if less beautiful than a qvevri. The destruction of the Soviet way of life and the country's near economic ruin gave way at first to ambitious entrepreneurs and industrialists, and was shaped more by politics than culture. The modern wine industry emerged out of a scorched-earth scenario after the break-up of the USSR followed by years of civil war and Russia's devastating embargo on all Georgian wine between 2006 and 2013.[44]

Georgia's minister of agriculture Levan Davitashvili,[45] who worked at Schuchmann winery in 2010–12, recalls that every part of the supply chain was decimated after 1991: "It was a very difficult period, especially for agriculture. Most of the land was [re]distributed to farmers. People switched to growing cheap sustenance crops just to feed their animals. No-one cared about commerce, so the value chain was broken – including wine."[46]

This partly explains the extraordinary destruction of Georgia's vineyards. According to Irakli Cholobargia of the National Wine Agency (the successor to Samtrest), Georgia had around 150,000 hectares of vineyards during the Soviet era. By 2006, only 36,000 remained. "After the Soviet collapse, many of the farmers got rid of their vineyards and planted watermelons. It was a market economy-driven thing," Cholobargia explains. In fact, both vineyards and the rarer grape varieties had been disappearing ever since the 1920s. Many of Georgia's oldest wine-producing regions, such as Guria, Abkhazia and Adjara were rezoned for wheat or potatoes. Vines were pulled up, in some cases forever.

Those vineyards that survived were usually in a bad way, as a co-founder of Telavi Wine Cellar (also known as Marani) Zurab Ramazashvili recalls: "We started by renting vineyards from the government, but their condition

---

44 The embargo was declared on the grounds that there were large quantities of counterfeit Georgian wines entering the Russian market, although its true purpose was almost certainly more political than anything else, as Russia and Georgia have constantly disputed their borders since 1991.

45 As of 2017.

46 Told to the author in a phone interview, July 2017.

had been devastated by civil war and was generally very poor, with old vines, non-standard trellising systems and missing plants." Not to mention that those rows of supposed saperavi were just as likely to contain some undeclared isabella (a popular hybrid).

To exacerbate matters, Soviet viticultural expertise didn't extend much further than the systemic use of herbicides and fungicides. Irakli 'Eko' Glonti, a medical doctor turned winemaker and champion of sustainable, traditional viticulture, has been working with growers to restore these chemically dependent vineyards. He has found many issues in the soils, such as compaction and calcium deficiency. "There's no macrobiology," he says with regard to a plot in Kakheti, "there is nothing to help the roots consume minerals, and after the rain the water just runs away."

The art of making qvevri

In some ways the technique of building qvevris is like making a giant coil pot. The vessels are built up layer by layer until they reach the requisite dimensions. The process can take two to three months to complete, and the qvevri then needs to be dried for two to three weeks before it's ready to fire in a huge, outdoor wood oven. Qvevri maker Zaza Remi Kbilashvili says that the exact volume is approximate; it's all done by instinct, so no two qvevris will be identical.

The type of clay is important, with clay from Imereti being the most prized. Joško Gravner has often remarked that a clay with so few pollutants is almost impossible to find anywhere else in the world.

After a new qvevri is fired (for up to a week at between 1000°C and 1300°C), it is left for a few days to cool down. Then, when it is barely still warm, it is lightly sealed with beeswax inside. As qvevri winemaking expert and scholar Giorgi Barisashvili cautions in his book, *Making Wine in Kvevri – a Unique Georgian Tradition* (2011), the beeswax must be very sparingly applied. The aim is not to create an airtight seal, but merely to fill some of the larger pores. A lined qvevri where the wine is not in direct contact with the clay will not achieve the desired micro-oxygenation, nor lend the expected character to the wine.

Qvevris are sometimes coated on the outside with a white-grey lime wash, but as Kbilashvili confirms, most natural wine producers prefer their qvevris unlined.

Qvevris are always buried in the ground up to their necks, either outdoors or, more commonly these days, in a dedicated cellar (*marani*).

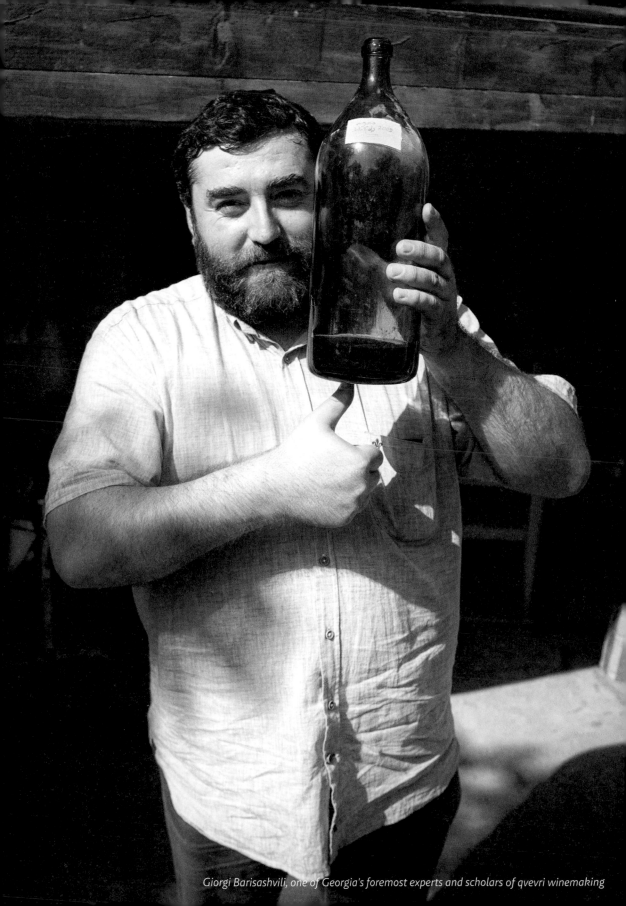

Giorgi Barisashvili, one of Georgia's foremost experts and scholars of qvevri winemaking

After the fall of the USSR, failing and bankrupt wineries were snapped up by the private sector, as entrepreneurs realised that Russia was still thirsty for Georgian wine. A string of JSCs (joint stock companies) sprang up in the late 1990s, including GWS (Georgian Wines & Spirits), Tbilvino, Telavi Wine Cellar and Teliani Valley. The names and company structures might have changed, but the product and its intended market largely had not. Corruption was rife, right up to government level and there was more than a grain of truth in Russia's accusations about adulterated or fake wine, a problem which has taken decades to stamp out.

Russian consumers were not clamouring for artisanal qvevri wines either. The bestsellers were and are mass-produced semi-sweet wines such as Alazani Valley (a generic style, even though it sounds like a producer) or Kindzmarauli. These styles currently represent about half of Georgia's total output, and Russia is still the biggest customer by far.[47]

Gauze covering qvevris at Bolnuri winery, Kartli

---

47 In 2017, approximately 60% of Georgia's wine exports by volume went to Russia, according to the Georgian National Wine Agency.

Ceremonial serving of a kisi wine at the New Wine Festival, Tbilisi, May 2017

Brothers Zura and Giorgi Margvelashvili were shareholders in Tbilvino, following independence in 1991. Their story is typical. Zura returned from a winemaking internship in California, inspired to work with wine. The brothers invested the family savings in a share buyout, taking control of Tbilvino in 1998. They have never disclosed the purchase price, but the chances are it was a bargain. As Giorgi recalls, "Tbilvino was not in very good shape in 1998 – it had close to zero production. Contact with former suppliers and customers was lost." So what had the brothers got for their money? Tbilvino didn't own any vineyards, but it did boast a winery. Occupying a vast five-hectare site in Tbilisi, the facility was in fairly good shape, albeit with outdated technology. And there was a bonus – the three million litres of bulk wine lying in the winery's cellars.

A cohort of international wine experts were summoned to assess these 'wine materials'. The advice was brutal: "It's rubbish, you should not bottle this". Still, it was a lifeline for the fledgling business. "We managed to sell the wine in bulk, and paid off a few debts," Giorgi remembers. "With the remaining cash we went and bought grapes in Kakheti in 1999, and made our first vintage."

From this unpromising start, the brothers built Tbilvino up with a radically different approach to its former Soviet function of blindly accepting and bottling bulk wine. The new strategy meant getting involved with the many different growers who supplied the grapes, taking an active part in the harvest and upgrading the quality of the wine. In 2006, the company lost around 52% of its business when the Russian embargo was imposed. It turned out to be a blessing in disguise. Most of the Tbilisi site was sold off to raise money, and a new, smaller, quality-optimised winery was built. By 2008, Tbilvino had recovered and was stronger than ever. Today the company produces around four million bottles a year and exports to 30 countries. Giorgi is disarmingly frank about the seat-of-the-pants running of the company during its first decade: "We were quite young, we didn't have much experience. We took all the challenges as normal occurrences. We didn't have much to lose, we didn't come into this business with a lot of money. It was challenging but it was also fun."

Many of Georgia's major wine producers agree the embargo was a critical turning point, as Tea Kikvadze, head of marketing at Teliani Valley JSC, confirms: "With Russia you could sell everything you had. But with Europe and other markets, you needed quality wine. The embargo was bad for companies, but it was good for Georgian winemaking, it forced winemakers to care about the quality. It has really changed a lot." The embargo also forced producers to aggressively court new markets such as China, Poland and the UK. Since 2013, Russia has come back into the fray, but its absolute dominance of Georgia's wine exports has reduced from 90% to 60%.

What was missing from this equation? None of these new private companies had Georgia's traditional qvevri style in their sights. Their white grapes were quickly pressed off the skins and fermented with aromatic laboratory yeasts to produce inoffensive, pale-coloured modern white wines. If anything, they became part of the continuum of European winemaking that had begun with Hermann Thumm's ancestors. Most even employed consultant winemakers from Europe or the new world to assist them in adopting the latest technologies. Outdated Soviet equipment was eagerly replaced by gleaming stainless steel tanks from Italy, or new oak *barriques* from France, as soon as funds permitted.

Qvevri winemaking became such a rarity that when American author Darra Goldstein wrote the first edition of her cookery book *The Georgian Feast: The Vibrant Culture and Savory Food of the Republic of Georgia* in 1993, she lamented that, "The only true Kakhetian wines you're likely to taste have been prepared at home". Joško Gravner could not have imagined how lucky he'd been back in 2000.

8

Peasants and their clay pots

When Ramaz Nikoladze welcomed

an old friend round to dinner at his house in 2004, he had no idea it would be a turning point for Georgia's artisan winemaking scene. His friend brought a guest, the Japanese food writer Natsu Shimamura. Entranced by the cuisine and the wine that Nikoladze decanted straight out of his backyard qvevri, Shimamura recommended him to the Italian Slow Food organisation, which has a special foundation tasked with protecting disappearing food and wine traditions worldwide.

Based in western Imereti, Nikoladze keenly carried on his parent's winemaking activities, even though the family did not possess a cellar. Instead, his qvevris were buried under the skies, with a ramshackle plastic sheet providing protection from the elements when required. This was winemaking with a DIY punk ethic – and appropriately enough punk is Ramaz's favourite soundtrack, as he munches whole chillies and holds court over a few glasses of his straightforward, timeless amber wines.

Nikoladze had never intended to become his country's ambassador, and he found his first visits to the slow-food event Terra Madre in Turin rather taxing having no English, never mind Italian. Still, visitors to the fair were as fascinated with these Georgians who made wine in clay pots, just as Shimamura had been

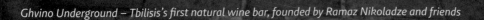

Ghvino Underground – Tbilisis's first natural wine bar, founded by Ramaz Nikoladze and friends

before them. Qvevri winemaking surely qualified for a Slow Food Presidium to be dedicated to it but the challenge was that there needed to be evidence of a movement, not just one producer. A few years later, Nikoladze met another experienced artisan winemaker from almost the opposite side of his country. Soliko Tsaishvili was based in Kakheti, and together with friends he had formed a company called Prince Makashvili Cellar in 2003. It would later be renamed to Chveni Gvino, or Our Wine as it is now better known.

Tsaishvili and his friends moved into the wine business for a very simple reason – to guarantee their own supply. They preferred traditional Georgian qvevri wine to the modern European styles that by then dominated the market, but living in Tbilisi it was close to impossible to find. Only people who were lucky enough to own vineyards or a homestead in the countryside could easily manufacture good qvevri wine. The five friends decided to purchase some land and a small building in Kakheti, initially buying in fruit and vinifying it traditionally in qvevris.

Ramaz had found the perfect partner for his quest in Soliko, and in 2007 the two began combing their respective regions for families who were practising organic viticulture and making good quality traditional qvevri wine. If they could just persuade a few more winemakers to start bottling and selling, the qvevri tradition would qualify for a Slow Food Presidium and potentially grow from its near terminal decline – and they could access funding to help them market their production. A small number of families were identified and persuaded to join the movement, and Georgian qvevri wine got its first big publicity boost with Slow Food's blessing in 2008.

For non-Georgians, it's easy to underestimate the significance of preserving this tradition. Wine is not regarded in Georgia merely as a beverage, nor does it suffer from the unfortunate Anglo-Saxon habit of regarding it as a drug or an intoxicant. It is life itself, imbued with a symbolism and heritage that is insepa-rable from religion or any other aspect of the country's culture. Qvevris are the most potent part of this tradition, often quite literally accompanying Georgians from the cradle to the grave. It is still popular to fill a qvevri with young wine at the birth of a child, where it will stay until the day they get married. Qvevris also have a more morbid function that is well documented in history – many Georgians have been buried in older vessels that were cut in half specially for the purpose. The symbolism works both ways – when wine ferments in the qvevri, the skins, stems and pips are called 'the mother', and just as a mother protects her child during the early years, so the pomace protects the wine during its first months of transformation from mere grape juice, lending it phenolic compounds that protect against oxidation and unwanted bacteria. Dr. Eko Glonti notes that etymologically in Georgian, "Wine is not made, rather it is born. We make a womb out of clay, then bury it in the soil like a goddess".

Iago Bitarishvili, aka The Chinuri Master, is not someone who shirks from hard work.[48] With his skinny frame, he looks as if he might have sat down long enough to eat a full meal sometime around 2003 – when he made his first vintage of qvevri-fermented chinuri. At that point, he'd already been working organically in the family's vineyards for five years. Just two years later he would receive Georgia's first official organic certification. "The war caused a lot of pollution in the countryside," he notes, "and back in 2003 there were only big companies making wine commercially, which didn't help." Iago was always fascinated by his family's qvevri, even if his father made chinuri in a more modern style without the skins. Finally in 2008, he decided to vinify the entire chinuri harvest with its skins in the family's 200 to 300-year-old qvevris. His father was furious, but a family friend was more supportive as he took Iago to one side, saying, "Your grandfather made wine like this, you know!"

Bitarishvili is modest to a fault. In 2009 he decided to organise a grand tasting with all the artisan producers of qvevri wines he could find. There were precisely five, "not including myself, of course", he shrugs, "I couldn't include my own wines when I'm organising the tasting." Those five were Alaverdi Monastery, Pheasant's Tears, Vinoterra (Schuchmann), Our Wine and Ramaz Nikoladze. The tasting was the forerunner of the annual New Wine Festival, which Iago has organised each May since 2010. The event now takes place in Tbilisi's Msatsminda Park and attracts over 10,000 visitors and 100 producers, almost all of whom offer traditionally produced qvevri wines. These days, Iago does include himself in the tastings.

---

48 Chinuri is a white grape variety indigenous to the Kartli region.

Iago Bitarishvili in the qvevri cellar

Pheasant's Tears – the original cellar, Signaghi

This sudden explosion of interest and rebirth of a traditional winemaking culture wasn't purely fuelled by Georgians. Interest from westerners such as Joško Gravner played a significant part in drawing attention to Georgia and its 'womb' for the wine. And so too did an American painter who arrived in 1995.

Looking for all the world like a Norse king with a ponytail, John Wurdeman is originally from New Mexico, and visited Georgia while he was a postgraduate art student at the Surikov Institute of Art in Moscow. It didn't take him long to fall in love with the country, and by 1997 he had bought a house in the mountain village of Signaghi, right in the middle of Kakheti. Fascinated by the polyphonic singing tradition, he became entranced one night hearing a singer outside his window. In a story that plays wonderfully to Georgia's spirit of romance and humanity, Wurdeman tracked the heavenly sound down to one Ketevan Mindorashvili, who two years later became his wife.

Together Wurdeman and Mindorashvili worked to promote traditional song and dance, while he also continued his work as a painter and they became parents. But a mutual friend in a nearby village had a different vision for Wurdeman's future. In a near legendary story which is beautifully and poetically told by Alice Feiring in her 2016 book *For the Love of Wine: My Odyssey through the World's Most Ancient Wine Culture*, Wurdeman encountered local winegrower Gela Patalishvili in the vineyards near his house in 2007. Patalishvili invited Wurdeman to his home that evening, as he said he had "some business to discuss".

An emotional evening followed, filled with copious amber libations. The young Georgian praised Wurdeman's work in promoting his country's culture, but pointed out that its authentic wine tradition was in at least as much danger if not more so: "Why are you neglecting the very pulse of our nation, the very heart, which is wine?" he demanded with tears in his eyes. His despair came from the fact that the new Georgian wine giants were all trying to ape European styles – the old knowledge was being lost. Patalishvili lacked money or market- ing skills, but he did have eight generations of winemaking heritage behind him, and had just spotted a prime vineyard site. Would Wurdeman care to help?

Wurdeman was strong-armed into helping vinify that year's harvest when Patalishvili literally arrived outside his door with a truck laden with grapes,

Gela Patalishvili, winemaker at Pheasant's Tears winery in Signaghi

and would not take no for an answer. Wurdeman accepted his destiny gracefully, and shortly after the pair founded the winery Pheasant's Tears. What started as a small operation grew into a mini-empire which now makes wine all over Georgia and has restaurants in both Signaghi and Tbilisi. The wines are available in every corner of the globe and have doubtless provided the first experience of amber wine for many.

Wurdeman (or Djoni as he's affectionately known in his adopted country) has since become a much loved and respected ambassador for Georgian culture, welcoming visitors, travelling the world and promoting far more than just Pheasant's Tears. In 2012, visitors to The Real Wine Fair in London could take in the somewhat surreal sight of the towering Wurdeman holding court next to Alaverdi Monastery's Father Gerasim, a winemaker and monk garbed in full habit and not a word of English. For many visitors to the fair, including this author, it provided the first mind-blowing taste of the qvevri style. Since neither Gerasim nor his bottles could tell the story, Djoni's fluent translations were invaluable.

Alaverdi Monastery

Father Gerasim, 2012

Alaverdi Monastery and its historic *marani* (cellar) were rebuilt between 2005 and 2006 and its pastor, Bishop David, felt that it should once again attempt to be as self-sufficient as possible, which meant the production of honey, yoghurt and wine. Five monks now work at the monastery, and Father Gerasim is the winemaker.[49] With his long, straggly beard and probing stare, Gerasim looks far more at home in the monastery's cellar than he did at the wine fair in London. In fact, winemaking was a dream come true for this humble monk, who had decided to give his life up to God even though it meant forsaking his passion for the qvevri and winemaking in general. Whether Bishop David was a good judge of character or Gerasim just got lucky is open to question, but either way it was a serendipitous moment when the bishop asked Gerasim if he wanted to take on the winemaking duties in the newly reconstructed cellar.

---

49 Gerasim works with a consultant winemaker from Badagoni, one of the country's largest wine producers. Production of the Alaverdi Monastery wines should not be confused with the more budget 'Alaverdi tradition' line, made from bought-in grapes and marketed by Badagoni rather than the monastery itself.

Father Gerasim, 2012

A monk tends the grounds at Alaverdi Monastery

Production at the monastery adheres to the most traditional Kakhetian methods possible, with six to nine-month macerations for the white grapes, with skins and stems included as is the custom in the region. For Father Gerasim, whether to treat the wines with sulphur or any other additive isn't a matter of choice. The imperative is simple. Any impurities in the finished product would render it unworthy in the eyes of God. That said, as only red wine is used in the monastery's religious ceremonies, the white wines are sometimes protected with a small amount of added sulphites.

The perfect vessel for fermentation

Because of their large mass and the tradition of burying them in the ground, qvevris provide excellent temperature regulation, cooling the fermentation but also maintaining a very stable temperature throughout the different seasons.

The larger the qvevri, the higher the fermentation temperature, thus there's a further subtle element of control if the winemaker has a selection of differently sized qvevri at their disposal. In general, qvevris used for fermentation rather than ageing will hold between 500 to 1,500 litres.

The egg-like shape of qvevris (and amphorae in general) is said to create convection currents as fermentation changes the internal temperature. This gently stimulates the lees, creating a kind of battonage* without the winemaker needing to be involved.

The sharp point at the bottom of the qvevri collects the lees (dead yeasts), skins and other solids (stems, if used) as they gradually sink to the bottom. Because the area of contact between the solids and the wine is so small, there is very little chance for reductive compounds to develop.

For as many months as the wine remains undisturbed there will continue to be a slow, gentle extraction of tannins and polyphenols – all beneficial to the stability of the wine.

The combination of long skin contact and qvevri allows for a method of wine-making which requires close to zero intervention from the winemaker, and certainly no additives of any kind.

---

* Stirring up of the dead yeasts to bring them into contact with the wine, enriching its texture and stability.

The monastery also fulfils its ancillary function as a place of learning and research, harbouring an experimental vineyard with some 104 indigenous Georgian grape varieties and hosting the first two editions of the International Symposium for Qvevri Wines in 2011 and 2013. It's a powerful and affecting place to visit, even more so now that refurbishments to the impressive chapel are complete. Perhaps inevitably, the experience is a little more touristic than it once was, with professional guides often substituted for the monks themselves, but that is testament to the increasing number of travellers worldwide who come to experience one of the most authentic sources of Georgian wine still in existence.

Giorgi 'Gogi' Dakishvili is a third generation winemaker from Telavi in Kakheti. His work with traditional qvevri winemaking has been every bit as pioneering as that of his colleagues. However, he took a different route, first perfecting his craft making western-style wines. Dakishvili began his career as the winemaker at Teliani Valley JSC, a major commercial winery that was privatised in 1997. His father had worked for the company's previous incarnation in Soviet times. Dakishvili had no intention of just sticking with Teliani's mainstream style. From 2002 he began to acquire small parcels of his own vineyards, and created a small winery which would become Vinoterra in 2005. Away from his day job, the goal was very different: to make traditional qvevri wines.

Sealed qvevris at Schuchmann winery, Kakheti

Qvevri cellar at Orgo/Telada winery, Kakheti

Dakishvili recalls that it was very difficult to sell the first vintages: "There was no amber wine category in 2003," he recalls, "so I just put 'white wine' on the label. But customers from outside Georgia found that very hard to understand." Nonetheless, by 2004 he'd started to export a small amount of wine as far afield as the USA. His genius was to harness modern winemaking knowledge with a deep love of the region's pre-existing traditions. The Vinoterra wines are accessible and consistent, remaining utterly authentic but subtly informed by Dakishvili's commercial understanding.

It wasn't until 2008, when German industrialist Burkhard Schuchmann decided to invest in the Vinoterra winery, that it really took off. Schuchmann bought the business and made Dakishvili a partner. Although Schuchmann Wines (as the business was renamed) now focuses on European styles, it has also scaled up its qvevri production (which remains under the Vinoterra label) to around 300,000 bottles a year. Boasting three cellars housing a total of 87 qvevris, Schuchmann is now comfortably the largest producer of qvevri wines in Georgia, and as most of those 300,000 bottles are made from white grape varieties (rkatsiteli, kisi and mtsvane), it's also arguably the largest orange wine producer worldwide.

Many of Georgia's largest producers have followed suit and added boutique qvevri lines to their ranges, partly out of national pride but also with a keen eye on this developing market. 'Boutique' in this context can – and does – still mean major quantities that would dwarf the output of a small family grower. Although Marani's qvevri range (Satrapezo) was launched in 2004,[50] the winery has a much longer history in this style of production, as Zurab Ramazashvili explains: "Our winery specialised in qvevri wine production during the Soviet period. We had more than half a hectare of qvevris in a half-underground cellar, but the state decided in the 1980s that qvevri production was too costly. They decided to remove most of the qvevris and sell them. When we arrived, there were still 40 qvevris left, but there was no soil any more!" He's proud that the Satrapezo range is now so in demand that it is frequently sold out and intends to increase production to around 100,000 bottles a year.

---

50 Initially only a saperavi was made in qvevri. From 2007, Satrapezo launched a qvevri-fermented rkatsiteli.

The Kakhetian qvevri wine method

Eastern Kakheti has always had a focus on white grapes, with the power trio of rkatsiteli, kisi and mtsvane reigning supreme in the modern age. It's here that the most intense and structured qvevri wines are made. At its most traditional, the method is simplicity itself:

▶ Healthy grapes are harvested and foot-trodden in a *satsnakheli* (long wooden trough) – a method resembling the port-wine tradition of using *lagares*.

▶ The grapes are transferred to the qvevris, with skins and stems.

▶ Fermentation starts spontaneously with the grapes' natural yeasts. The skins are regularly punched down (three to five times a day) to ensure they stay wet.

▶ After approximately two weeks, or whenever the fermentation is complete, the qvevri will be sealed with a stone or wooden lid and made airtight with earth piled on top.

▶ Around six months later (sometimes even longer), the qvevri will be opened to reveal a gloriously deep-hued yet clear liquid – which will then be bottled or decanted into clean qvevris for further storage/ageing.

In western Imereti, by contrast, stems are not traditionally used and the length of skin contact will be significantly less (around three months maximum).

Grape treading trough (or satsnakheli) at Alaverdi

When Tbilisi winemaker Tbilvino, which produces around four million bottles a year,[51] decided to start producing qvevri wines in 2010, its output was also ramped up quite quickly to 75,000 bottles and the company has plans to double that in the following years. Both Tbilvino and Marani make their qvevri ranges using broadly traditional methods and are achieving high quality. The phenomenon of relatively mass-produced wines made in this style is fascinating, because it is almost unprecedented anywhere else in the world.[52] Outside Georgia, the largest producers of what can broadly be termed 'orange wines' barely scrape 50,000 bottles a year, and all fit easily into the small, artisanal, independent category.

It should be clear that the passionate adherents, agitators and accidental ambassadors of the Georgian qvevri tradition, with its unparalleled heritage of macerating white grapes to produce dark amber wines, are the small guys. But for the efforts of Ramaz Nikoladze, Soliko Tsaishvili, Iago Bitarishvili, Gela Patalishvili, Giorgi Dakishvili and John Wurdeman, there might be not much of a legacy to write about. That said, the past decade (2008–18) has seen their initial striking of the match ignite into a satisfying blaze as the new corporate being of Georgian wine properly puts its shoulder to the wheel and gives it a very big shove.

Despite all the marketing and the hype within specialist circles, no-one's pretending that qvevri wines represent any more than a tiny slice of Georgia's total vinous output (which reached 76.7 million bottles on the export market in 2017). Nonetheless, the traditional qvevri sector appears to be expanding at least as fast as its more mainstream brother, rather than being in terminal decline as it was during the dark days of Soviet domination. It's a hugely important and symbolic reversal, because this iconic clay vessel and the potent amber liquid that it nurtures are as inseparable from the Georgian cultural paradigm as life itself.[53]

---

51 2017 figure.

52 Some of the larger Alentejo producers ferment significant amounts of wine in *talhas* (Portuguese amphorae).

53 Red wines are, of course, also made in qvevris, however for the purposes of this book I've just focused on the white grapes, or so-called amber wines.

Freshly fired qvevri in the oven at Zaza Remi Kbilashvili's workshop

Qvevri hygiene

If there's one issue above all that winemakers outside of Georgia complain about, it's the labour-intensive process of cleaning qvevris. They're certainly not as easy to maintain as a modern stainless-steel tank, with its multiple trap-doors and lid, but provided one brings a certain zen-like attitude to the task, it is doable.

Traditionally, qvevris are cleaned with a lime or ash wash, and then rinsed with hot water – a process which can take many hours for a large qvevri. The cleaning implement will be a brush made of St John's wort or a long pole with a sponge made of cherry bark; both have antiseptic qualities.

Sulphur may optionally be burned in the qvevri after cleaning, as an additional anti-bacterial measure.

This is one of the most important tasks in the winemaker's calendar. As Giorgi Barisashvili says, "Pouring wine into an unwashed qvevri is inadmissible!"

The traditional method of proving that the qvevri is properly clean is to drink the water used to rinse it out. If it tastes good, work is over!

Partially built qvevris at Zaza Remi Kbilashvili's workshop

Soliko Tsaishvili passed away in April 2018 after a two-year battle with pancreatic cancer. Georgia has truly lost one of its most important champions and pioneers of the modern qvevri renaissance.

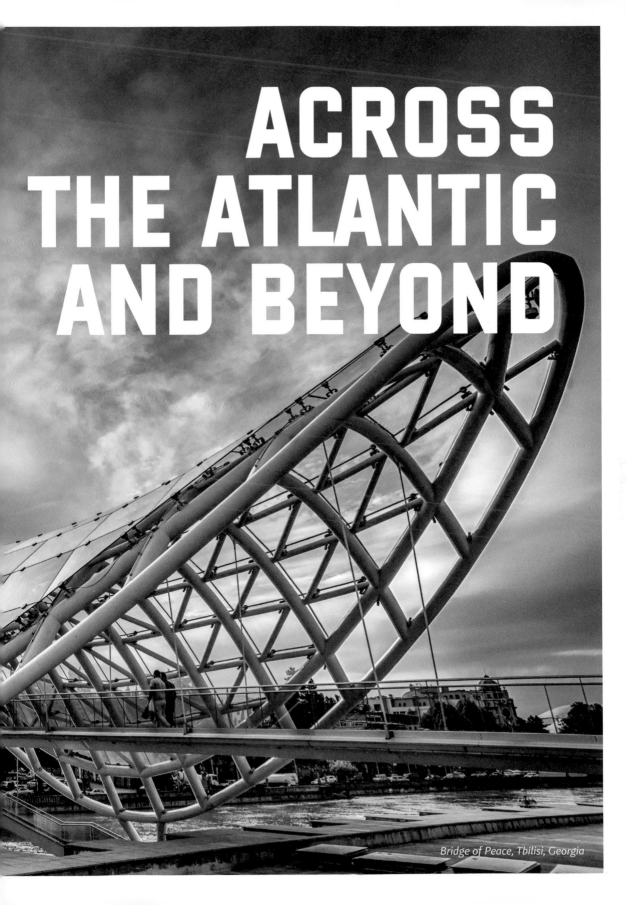

ACROSS THE ATLANTIC AND BEYOND

Bridge of Peace, Tbilisi, Georgia

May 2009

Nothing could have prepared Joško Gravner for the events of Saturday, 2 May 2009. Receiving a telephone call that his son Miha had been injured in a motorcycle accident, he immediately jumped in the car to make the four-hour drive to the hospital. It would be a fruitless journey. Miha died from internal bleeding in the ambulance, and Joško never saw him alive again.

If Joško had previously retreated from interaction with other local winemakers, and if he'd had to take a few knocks from Italian critics over the years, it was nothing compared with the level of isolation he now felt. Miha had been working alongside his father for a number of years and was gearing up to eventually take over the reins. He'd been pushing biodynamics as the next logical step in the vineyards. Joško hadn't the heart to continue the exploration without his son, and the adoption of Steiner's teachings would have to wait another half-decade before his younger daughter Jana dared broach the topic.

Joško retreated to his vineyards and his wines over the following years, becoming even less enthusiastic about receiving visitors than before. Whether *Gambero Rosso* or anywhere else published negative reviews of his wines no longer mattered. In interviews during those years, he would recite almost as a mantra, "I make wine for myself, what's left I sell", and it was a clear metaphor for the introversion and introspection that naturally followed such a cataclysmic personal event.

Little by little, Joško's daughters filled the void. Jana, who shares the same soulful intensity of her father, began to accompany him in the cellar and the vineyards, while the outgoing, ever-smiling Mateja – herself a trained winemaker – uprooted her new life in Alto Adige to step into the important role of the winery's front of house, becoming the public face of the operation from 2014.

Joško did not stand still either. If observers felt that his absolute conversion to qvevri and macerated wines was extreme and puritan, they were in for an even bigger surprise. Ribolla gialla had always been his favourite grape variety – the most well adapted, with its extensive local history of at least 500 years, and with the thickest, most flavoursome skins that could only give their all with many months of skin contact. Gravner's all-or-nothing logic was simple – if this was the best grape, why waste time on anything else? He began to grub up all the international white varieties in the vineyards, either returning the ground to nature or replanting with more ribolla if the site was of sufficient quality. The process was completed by 2012, and that autumn Joško made his last vintage of Breg, the white blend of chardonnay, pinot grigio, sauvignon blanc and welschriesling that had been a mainstay of the winery's output for some two decades.[54]

And while Joško applied these reductionist ethics to condense his production into its purest form, the world was gradually learning how to enjoy the wines.

Mateja Gravner, October 2017

---

54 The 2012 Breg will be released for sale in 2020.

9

I am kurious oranj

Bobby Stuckey's career was seriously

taking off as the new millennium began. A straight-talking, hard-working sommelier from Arizona, he'd just finished a five-year stint as wine director at The Little Nell restaurant in Aspen, Colorado. The awards had piled in, from the *Wine Spectator* to the James Beard Foundation and beyond. The year 2000 started with a change to a yet more prestigious position, as wine director at Thomas Keller's French Laundry, in Yountville in California's Napa Valley.

Since 2004, Stuckey has been one of only 249 individuals across the globe who hold the coveted Master Sommelier qualification,[55] which demands not only years of study and experience, but also a notoriously difficult set of exams and blind tastings. He's also a huge fan of Friuli's wines.

Stuckey had been buying the Collio's top wines since the early 1990s – and they didn't come any more lauded than Joško Gravner's barrel fermented cuvées. His task at The French Laundry was to transform the hitherto all-Napa list into a more all-encompassing smorgasbord that included European classics from Burgundy to Tuscany and all points in between. Ordering Gravner's just-released 1997s was a no-brainer – especially as they'd be sold out at the winery in a flash.

---

55 As of February 2018.

Gravner bottles

Stuckey's first experience of tasting Gravner's new wine wasn't even from his own stock – eating out at a nearby restaurant who had just listed the same vintage, he was about to have an almighty shock. "My first instinct was, 'it's oxidised'," he recalls, as he looked at the slightly hazy, russet-brown liquid in his glass. "My second instinct was, I need to call the importer!"

He marshalled his thoughts, mentally donning the sommelier's hat. The aromas didn't suggest a spoiled, oxidised wine, and neither did the flavour. It absolutely, definitely was not flawed. Clearly something else was going on. Stuckey knew he had to stick to his guns, but he was flying blind. In 2000, there were no wine blogs to fall back on, and producers like Joško Gravner were not contactable via email. Luckily, he had a wildcard to play.

George Vare Jr, a graduate of the Harvard Business School, became one of the Napa Valley's leading wine magnates from 1972 into the mid 1990s. In 1996 he set up the Luna winery to focus on growing Italian grape varieties in Napa. As retirement loomed in the late 1990s, Vare took his fascination with Italy's traditions and small family wineries a step further – he became increasingly obsessed with Friuli and befriended Joško Gravner, who gifted him a few precious ribolla gialla vines. Vare smuggled them back into the states and used them to foster a small vineyard. Bobby Stuckey knew that Vare could give him the inside track on Gravner – and he didn't disappoint.

Nonetheless, even armed with the knowledge about Gravner's turnaround, the wines weren't an easy sell. "Gravner was basically the biggest hit parade there was in Friulian wines back then", remembers Stuckey. "He was getting *tre biccheri* from *Gambero Rosso* every year.[56] It was really, really dramatic to do what he had just done." As predicted, not one bottle of Gravner's Ribolla Gialla or Breg 1997 would be sold at The French Laundry without a lengthy courtship from the sommelier.

Stuckey's challenge was partly the lack of a genre. Not only did it wreck established food matches – "we kind of had a playlist for what to pair with Gravner, but that didn't work anymore" – but also the wine was neither red, rosé nor white.

In 2004, a young wine importer from the UK travelled to Mount Etna in Sicily, to work as a 'cellar rat'[57] for radical Belgian winemaker Frank Cornelissen. The importer's name was David A. Harvey, and he would grapple with the same problem that Stuckey faced, but from a different angle. Cornelissen had moved to the mountain to start making wine in 2001, abandoning previous lives as a financial trader, mountaineer and fine wine broker. His aim was to "make fine wine with nothing added", in other words nothing apart from grapes – no selected yeasts, no added acids, not even any added sulphur dioxide.

---

56 Tre Biccheri, or three glasses, is the top award given by the annual Italian wine guide *Gambero Rosso* to an individual wine.

57 An assistant who works in the cellar, never seeing the light of day (like a rat).

Hues of maceration at Primosic

Cornelissen built a swift reputation as either a madman or a genius, depending on whether you liked his wines or not. Early bottlings were unpredictable to say the least, sometimes refermenting in the bottle, sometimes prematurely oxidised – but also captivating on occasion. He produces a single white wine, Munjebel Bianco,[58] fermented on its skins for 30 days, because he loves the simplicity of the skin contact method. Like Gravner, Cornelissen visited Georgia (coincidentally) in 2000, and also decided that qvevri were the perfect fermentation vessel – although in his case the love affair with amphorae would be more temporary.

Ageing orange wines

The great skin-macerated white wines of the Collio or Brda demand time in the bottle to show their best. Levi Dalton remarks that "the more people treat these bottles like Barolo, the happier they tend to be", and it's an excellent comparison. No-one expects a three-year-old Barolo to be singing and giving 100% of its best, and the same is true of ribolla gialla or many other varieties that have undergone long maceration times.

Sadly the economics of production and storage are such that many producers release their wines far, far too young. This is particularly the case with newer estates that haven't had time to build up their stocks or achieve financial stability.

Producers such as Radikon, Gravner, JNK and Zorjan, who age their wines for up to a decade before release, command my huge respect. They prioritise the enjoyment of their customers ahead of profits, not an easy thing to do.

The vast majority of producers release wines when they are one to two years old. Ideally, purchase at least two bottles of a wine that interests you and even if you can't resist popping the cork on the first, store the second in a cool, dark place for another year or two. The extra bottle age can make an extraordinary difference to a wine's equilibrium, complexity and drinkability.

Concerns are sometimes expressed about the ability of wines made with no added sulphur to endure. This isn't a problem with a well-made wine, but it is smart to pay attention to the storage temperature. Wine prefers an absence of light and a stable temperature that doesn't rise significantly above 16°C to 18°C. Corks are the weak point of any bottle, but storing wines on their sides and ensuring that the humidity of your storage area is higher rather than lower (80–90% is ideal) will help preserve the cork. All of these factors become yet more important when there's no added sulphur to protect the wine.

---

58 In more recent vintages, Cornelissen has added a Munjebel Bianco VA (Vigne Alte, or old vines), which is also macerated. He has reduced maceration times to only 1–2 weeks.

Harvey and Cornelissen were well matched – both strong willed, robustly intellectual and geeky to boot, just as happy with discourse as imbibement – or even better, both combined. Harvey recalls, "Harvesting and selecting grapes for Munjebel Bianco, we talked/drank Gravner, Radikon, Vodopivec, when a conundrum became apparent: there was no name for this emerging genre."

Harvey coined the term 'orange wine' by a process of elimination, as he later explained in *World of Fine Wine* magazine in 2011: "Candidates for names were macerated (technical), amber (obscure), yellow (taken[59]), gold (pretentious), and orange, which delightfully is the same word in English, French and German". He's since described the search for the right term as "an intense theoretical exercise to resolve the issues associated with the wines being called white, considering all the options and all the extant wine types or appellations that would preclude adoption of such a colour or technique name. For example, Vin Jaune or Rivesaltes Ambre."

Starting with Harvey's initial usage of orange wine as a descriptor in his sales newsletters and other writings, the moniker was gradually adopted by the industry and by consumers. Harvey also held tastings of the wines for Jancis Robinson and Rose Murray Brown MW, both of whom used the term in their newspaper articles in 2007.

Eric Asimov, long-standing wine critic for the *New York Times*, wrote about Gravner and his move to Georgian qvevri in 2005. He had no catch-all term to press into service. In 2007, he turned his attention to Radikon and Vodopivec, but again had no easy terminology at hand to categorise the wines, falling back on descriptions such as the "hazy pink, almost cidery" colours, and the notion of "aliveness". But by 2009, when Asimov once again riffed on the subject, he was happy to accept "what Levi Dalton, the Convivio sommelier, called orange wines, which seems as good a term as any for an otherwise heterogeneous group of white wines linked together by the technique of leaving freshly crushed juice in contact with the grape skins for a prolonged period." Asimov's laboured attempt to summarise the definition is clear evidence of the need for a short and memorable name.

---

59 Harvey here is referring to Vin Jaune, a deliberately oxidative style of savagnin from the Jura.

Levi Dalton had a name as one of the smartest, most creative sommeliers working on the east coast in the 2000s.[60] Working his way through three high-class establishments, Masa, Convivio and Alto, Dalton noticed that wine pairings became extremely challenging when guests chose their own dishes – and the order of those dishes, as they were able to do with Convivio's prix fixe menu. His solution was to utilise a whole string of more obscure Italian grape varieties and styles to bridge the gaps. Dalton's guests got an education in frappato, aglianico or malvasia di candia alongside their entrées.

They were also highly likely to be served a glass of his other developing passion – orange wine. Dalton had a slug of Gravner's Ribolla Gialla poured into his glass at a trade tasting in 2002 or 2003, courtesy of a wine distributor colleague named Chip Coen.[61] It wasn't love at first sight, but rather fascination, as he later recalled: "I'd like to say the heavens opened up, and that I fell to the ground in awe, stunned by the revelation. In reality, I was perplexed. I have found over time that this is a key facet for eliciting real interest from me. If I totally don't get it, then, of course, bring it on! More! The wine also had a nice label. A nice label helps. Anyway, I was smitten. How to get more, how to learn more about this sharp-clawed Hippogriff of a wine?"

Dalton wasted no time putting the wine on the list of the Boston-based restaurant where he worked at the time, but unsurprisingly it failed to sell. It wasn't until his stint at Convivio (2008–09) that he had the chance to start introducing his beloved Gravner and Radikon wines to a larger audience. He saw the wines as a "get out of jail free card", when guests at the same table chose a completely incompatible combination of main dishes, or tricky ingredients such as sea urchin or asparagus appeared on the menu. Dalton's new-found obsession quickly spread around Manhattan's wine world, especially after he organised a marathon

---

60 He has since traded in his profession as sommelier to become the presenter and producer of the podcast "I'll drink to that". Listen to it for free via www.illdrinktothatpod.com.

61 Dalton does not recall whether this happened in late 2002 or early/mid 2003, however it was before November 2003 in any case. On his blog www.soyouwanttobeasommelier.blogspot.com, he claims the vintage was 2000, however according to the Gravner family this would have been impossible, as the 2000 Ribolla Gialla was not bottled until 2004.

tasting dinner with 37 orange wines in May 2009. The attendees included Asimov and the wine critics and bloggers Tyler Colman (aka Dr. Vino) and Thor Iverson, all of whom wrote extensively about the event afterwards. Orange wine's secret was out – it was geeky, but it had a name, and fans in high places.

Wines tasted at the seminal orange wine dinner, Convivio, May 2009

Casa Coste Piane - *'Tranquillo' Prosecco 2006*
Cornelissen - *Munjebel 4 Bianco*
De Conciliis - *Antece 2004*
Monastero Suore Cistercensi - *Coenobium 2007*
Monastero Suore Cistercensi - *Coenobium Rusticum 2007*
Monastero Suore Cistercensi - *Coenobium 2006*
Paolo Bea - *Arboreus 2004*
Massa Vecchia - *Bianco 2005*
Cà de Noci - *Notte di Luna 2007*
Cà de Noci - *Notte di Luna 2006*
Cà de Noci - *Riserva dei Fratelli 2005*
La Stoppa - *Ageno 2004*
Castello di Lispida - *Amphora 2002*
Castello di Lispida - *Terralba 2002*
La Biancara - *Taibane 1996*
Kante - *Sauvignon 2006*
Damijan Podversic - *Kaplja 2003*
Damijan Podversic - *Kaplja 2004*
Radikon - *Jakot 2003*
Radikon - *Ribolla Gialla Riserva 1997*
Radikon - *Ribolla Gialla 2001*
Gravner - *Ribolla Gialla 1997*
Gravner - *Ribolla Gialla Anfora 2001*
Gravner - *Ribolla Gialla 2000*
Gravner - *Breg Anfora 2001*
Zidarich - *Vitovska 2005*
Zidarich - *Malvasia 2005*
Vodopivec - *Vitovska 2003*
Vodopivec - *Vitovska 2004*
Vodopivec - *Solo MM4*
Giorgio Clai - *Sveti Jakov 2007*
Movia - *Lunar 2007*
Vinoterra - *Kisi 2006*
Wind Gap - *Pinot Gris 2007*
Scholium Project - *San Floriano Del Collio 2006*

Choosing orange wines

The orange wine category is as varied as white, red or rosé.
Here are some tips for differentiating and finding your preferred style.

Lighter, more floral and refreshing oranges

Look for semi-aromatic varieties such as sauvignon blanc, or friulano where the skin contact has been kept to a week or less. Vitovska also fits this category, if the maceration time is kept short.

These wines are usually lighter coloured and may barely reveal their 'orangeness' until you taste them.

A number of younger estates in Australia, New Zealand and South Africa are perfecting this style. Here, maceration isn't really centre stage, but instead just gently supports the fruit of the wine, fleshing it out and lending some additional complexity to the proceedings.

Intensely aromatic oranges

Aromatic varieties such as muscat or gewürztraminer (and the semi-aromatic traminers) have their already powerful bouquet turbo-charged by a week's skin contact. They can play more to delicate floral notes or dominating perfumes. These are some of the most characterful orange wines out there, utterly unmissable, but inspiring a love-hate reaction if rose petal or lychee aromas are not your thing.

Medium-bodied oranges with soft textures

Wines made with two to three weeks of skin contact, but gentle extraction, can deliver a lot of aroma and flavour punch, while still behaving more like a white wine texturally. These wines are amongst the most versatile of all, drinking well on their own or with food.

The chameleon chardonnay often turns its hand well to this genre, as do the trebbiano-based oranges from much of central Italy (Lazio, Umbria and Tuscany).

Full-bodied, tannic, age-worthy oranges

Wines made with a month or more of maceration, from thick-skinned varieties such as ribolla gialla, cortese or mtsvane will deliver a full-on orange experience. These are often wines that need to be matured for a few years in bottle. They can do battle with serious, structured red wines, and should be treated in a similar way – serve them at room temperature and let them breathe.

Gravner, Prinčič and Radikon's Ribolla Giallas are the reference point here, as are the qvevri wines from Kakheti.

Elegant, complex wines with delicate texture

Skilled use of amphorae, qvevris or concrete eggs often results in a very gentle extraction, and equally gentle stimulation of the lees (caused by convection currents in the ovoid shapes of the vessels). Wines from Foradori, Iago Bitarishvili or Vodopivec have been with their skins for six months or more, yet emerge as subtle, silky beauties.

Pink skins and shocking colours

Some varieties that are commonly accepted as white varieties actually have pinkish skins (pinot grigio and grenache gris are notable examples). Fermenting on the skins can produce wines which are in appearance indistinguishable from a rosé, or sometimes even a light red. Pinot grigio, in particular, only needs a few days of maceration to give the wine a shocking pink hue.

Orange bubbles

There's no reason why you can't have bubbles in your orange wine; some producers in the Prosecco region or Emilia-Romagna wouldn't have it any other way. The revelation is that sparkling wine doesn't just have to taste like battery acid or sucking on a lemon sherbet. It can have all the depth and herby complexity of a still orange wine, plus the joyful effervescence. The pleasantly tannic wines from Croci are a benchmark here, as are the funky, earthy *col fondos* (naturally sparkling Prosecco) from Costadilà.

10
Haters
gonna hate

I n the late 2000s, wine critics and pundits

on both sides of the Atlantic weren't just grappling with the new genre-busting output from Gravner, Radikon and their disciples – they were also scratching their heads and trying to figure out what to make of the fast developing natural wine scene. Although this grass-roots sub-culture of small artisan producers and their fans had been bubbling under for well over a decade, it became steadily more vocal and visible as the new millennium advanced.

Natural wine as an idea incensed many of the wine world's more established figures, partly because it positioned itself as a rebel cry against what could only be implied were 'unnatural' wines – the mass-produced mainstream, in other words. The other issue was its innate slipperiness as a category. Organic and biodynamic growers had certification and thus legal obligations to fall back on, even if, like many small Italian producers, they chose not to apply for the rubber stamp. But natural wine had no firm definition, no regulation and no hard-and-fast rules. It's been compared to the punk movement, but a better analogy might be with emerging art styles. The artists Wassily Kandinsky and Piet Mondrian were two giants of abstraction in painting in the early 20th-century, but never met or exchanged ideas while they were alive. The style they helped create can only easily be defined from a retrospective point of view.

History may well look back on natural wine in a similar way. Although there is talk of regulation by the INAO,[62] and an increasing incidence of manifestos issued by wine fairs and independent producers, there is still no official definition of what constitutes a natural wine. The general tenets revolve around sustainability, adherence to tradition and the minimum possible intervention in both vineyard and cellar. This usually means:

▶ Vineyards are farmed organically or biodynamically, whether with certification or not

▶ Harvesting is manual

▶ Fermentation occurs spontaneously with indigenous (wild) yeasts

▶ No enzymes, corrections or other additives are used at any point (so no acidification or deacidification, no added tannins or colouring agents)

▶ Some proponents add that the fermentation temperature should not be artificially controlled, nor should the malolactic fermentation[63] be blocked, even in white wines

▶ Minimal or no added SO_2 at any point during the winemaking process, including bottling (this point is usually the most hotly contested)

▶ Unfined and unfiltered

▶ No other heavy manipulation (such as spinning cone, reverse osmosis, cryoextraction, rapid-finishing, ultraviolet-C irradiation)

▶ Some contend that any use of new oak or other barrels that leave a strong flavour in the wine is also inherently non-natural

One of natural wine's most passionate champions emerged blinking into the limelight in 2008. Flame-haired and about five-foot-nothing tall, Alice Feiring is the archetypal New Yorker – nervy, fast-talking and fiercely intellectual. With her 2008 book *The Battle for Wine and Love: Or How I Saved the World from Parkerization*, Feiring well and truly staked out her patch as the saviour of

---

62 The Institut National de l'Origine et de la Qualité is the body that oversees all regulations governing wine and viticulture in France.

63 The second non-alcoholic fermentation which usually occurs naturally in all wines, if the producer does not intervene to prevent it. It converts sharp malic acids into softer lactic acids, hence malolactic.

artisanal wines. Her strong stance against homogenisation in winemaking and the 100-points culture that rewarded pumped-up, high-alcohol cuvées defined her quickly as the darling of the natural wine world, and the go-to resource on its best producers.

Feiring's initial focus was overwhelmingly French, and neither of her first two books devotes any space to the concept of orange wine. However, her avowed love letter to Georgia and its wine culture, *For the Love of Wine* (2016), preached the gospel of skin contact in both white and red.[64] Still, Feiring is a cautious advocate of long skin fermentation, and one senses it is not always her favourite technique – as evidenced in this summary published on her site in February 2017:

> Back in something like 2006 the first skin contacts started to arrive on our shores. Many weren't successful. Some had dried, starched fruit and aggressive tannins. But over the past decade, as the skins were more understood as a way to make wine without addition, when the use of clay for fermentation spread (grape juice takes to clay as butter takes to toast), and winemakers learned to do less, great 'orange' wines have proliferated. Not because they were a style, but because they had a purpose.

In the UK in summer 2011, Isabelle Legeron MW (France's only female Master of Wine to date) teamed up with the country's biggest importer of natural wines Les Caves de Pyrene to organise London's first dedicated Natural Wine Fair. A few thousand eager wine lovers and professionals packed out the three-day event at the historic Borough Market arches, and press coverage both on and offline was considerable. It was a pivotal moment which clearly divided the wine world's commentators. Some, such as Tim Atkin MW, Robert Joseph and Tom Wark, were sceptical or even overtly anti-natural, claiming that the movement was just an excuse for faulty, badly made wines – a case of the emperor's new clothes. Others, including Jancis Robinson, Jamie Goode and Eric Asimov, were excited by the variety and boldness of what natural wine had to offer.

---

64 The original title of the book, when it was first published as a pamphlet
  (in collaboration with the National Wine Association of Georgia) in 2014,
  was *Skin Contact*.

Skerk bottles

The Natural Wine Fair partnership didn't survive, and in 2012 Londoners had two competing events to choose from, Les Caves' Real Wine Fair and Legeron's Raw Wine Fair. Both have gone on to become huge successes, both for the trade and the ever-increasing number of wine consumers who have latched onto the natural wine movement as a path to more sustainable and adventurous drinking.

Unlike Feiring, Legeron is an unabashed lover of skin contact in white wines. In 2011, she collaborated in the making of a qvevri-fermented amber wine with Dr. Eko Glonti, a Georgian medical doctor who had decided to change career. The resulting Lagvinari Rkatsiteli helped launch Glonti as one of the country's best winemakers and was unveiled in a masterclass at Raw Wine Fair 2013.

Orange wine became the favourite touch-point for critics of the natural scene, as it is in some ways the most extreme manifestation of difference when compared to mainstream whites. The idea of what was ostensibly a white wine sometimes having spiky tannins proved close to impossible for some traditionalists to square.

Many established writers and experts just couldn't get past the colour – "Orange wines? They're just plain oxidised", would be the riposte. Amber, russet, gold or orange colours were seemingly hardwired with the notion of a white wine that had spoiled, at least within professional circles.

Frédéric Brochet has a cast-iron grasp of this presumption based on visual cues – the French academic conducted a study on a roomful of 52 oenology students in 2001, where he offered two wines to be tasted. One was a white wine, the other a red. The students came up with descriptors for the white wine such as "floral", "peach" or "honeyed" – all quite sensible, as the wine they had in their glasses was actually a Semillon/Sauvignon blend from Bordeaux. Once they had the red wine in their glasses, the descriptors changed to notes like "raspberry", "cherry" or "tobacco". The kicker? Brochet had taken the same wine and added some tasteless, odourless red dye before serving it.

His admittedly sneaky experiment demonstrated just how much aesthetics affect the perception of wine. Just as Bobby Stuckey had to do a mental double-take in 2000 when he first tried an orange wine, so wine lovers and professionals alike were often thrown into confusion when they were confronted with a bottle of Radikon's Oslavje or Zidarich's Vitovska. Some were able to shake off their presumptions, others weren't.

Stephen Browett, chairman of venerable London wine merchant Farr Vintners, and Malcolm Gluck, the famously outspoken and now retired English wine critic of 'Superplonk'[65] fame, were two who clearly couldn't. At a specially convened 40th anniversary Judgement of Paris[66] tasting at the Sager + Wilde winebar in June 2016, a group of wine professionals including Gluck, Browett, Stephen Spurrier, Julia Harding MW and this writer were served six flights of wine blind.

---

65 Malcolm Gluck's weekly roundup of supermarket wines in the *Guardian*, a 1980s phenomenon which lead to a number of identically titled books which were published well into the 2000s.

66 A now legendary blind tasting of Californian and French wines conducted by Stephen Spurrier in 1976 in California, which caused outrage at the time when some of the Californian wines triumphed over their much more famous Bordelaise peers. It was dramatised in 2008 as the film *Bottle Shock*, with Alan Rickman playing the part of Spurrier.

Each flight consisted of two wines – one Californian, the other French. While the professionals deliberated on the mezzanine level, a packed room full of 50 young and enthusiastic natural wine lovers was tasting the same flights down below.

Flight number three pushed the envelope far beyond what had been tasted at the original Judgement of Paris event in 1976. The dynamic, positively effervescent Michael Sager had chosen two amber-hued wines, Scholium's Prince in his Caves 2014 and Sébastien Riffault's Sauletas 2010.[67] Gluck could barely contain his disgust – "I wouldn't serve these wines to someone I didn't like at a funeral", he gagged – presumably not finding the tannins, the colour or the oxidative components of Sauletas to his liking. Browett signalled agreement, as did Gluck's neighbour at the table Michael Schuster. Buoyed by their encouragement, Gluck waited until the hapless Sager was perched at his shoulder before going in for rhetorical kill: "I bet you can't actually find me a single person in this place who actually enjoys these wines!"

Sager is rarely nonplussed, but he had no printable response at that instant. He gestured limply towards the packed house, before two of the young sommeliers around the professionals table also put their hands up. Gluck has of course built an entire career on making incendiary statements and getting the wine industry's back up, as he most famously did when he published his final book *The Great Wine Swindle* in 2008. However, his comments and the unquestioning support they yielded were a clear demonstration that the more entrenched strata of the wine world still find the idea of orange wine (or indeed anything else that differs violently from the established mainstream) difficult to get to grips with. For every open-minded advocate such as Bobby Stuckey or Michael Sager, there are 10 more hidebound members of the profession who either consciously or unconsciously radiate a message to the wine drinking public that orange wines are somehow difficult, faulty or worse, just plain disgusting. Haters gonna hate, as they say.

---

67 Despite its deep amber colour, Riffault's wine is made without skin contact and *does* get its colour from deliberate oxidation. Riffault made his first ever skin-contact wine in 2013, the Auksinis (Skin Contact). Prince in his Caves is a skin-fermented sauvignon blanc.

Robert Parker's views on orange wine are not specifically recorded in print anywhere, but one suspects they would not be complimentary, judging by his outburst in the famous 'Article of Merit' published on the Wine Advocate website in 2014. Parker railed bitterly against natural wine "crusaders", as he referred to them, and their insinuation that many of the established fine wines such as top Bordeaux or Burgundy were industrial and manipulated. He lumped all natural wine into one metaphorical spit-bucket and condemned them as "oxidized, stale, [stinking] of fecal matter as well as [looking] like orange juice or rusty ice tea". While his rant had a frustrated and bitter tone, it also spoke for his generation, many of whom were cheering Parker on from the aisles.

His A-list wine critic equivalents in the UK have generally been more open-minded. Jancis Robinson and her colleague Julia Harding MW have always given orange wines a fair hearing, and any criticism dished out is normally as equitable and fair as it would be to wines of any style, colour or creed. Robinson rated a large number of Slovenian wines in a long article published in 2008. She noted, "The real point of difference for some producers is their unusual fondness for keeping their baby wines in contact with the grape skins", but had no issue with heartily recommending some of the results – classics such as Batič's Zaria and Movia's Rebula were singled out for praise, although others excited her less so.[68]

If there is anyone who could top Robinson's extraordinary level of experience and catholic taste, it would be Hugh Johnson. Eleven years Jancis's senior, Johnson started writing about wine in December 1960 (in the UK edition of *Vogue* magazine, no less), and has always positioned himself as being immune to fashion – whilst also demonstrating a wide-ranging, inclusive attitude to whatever happens to cross his path. However, when interviewed for the *Washington Post* in 2016, he professed irritation with the emerging genres of natural and orange wine. "Orange wines are a sideshow and a waste of time", he said. "What's the point of experimenting? We know how to make really good wine. Why do we want to throw away the formula and do something different?"

---

68 She did not use the term 'orange wine' anywhere in the article. which was originally published in the *Financial Times* in 2008, but is now available at www.jancisrobinson.com/articles/slovenia-land-of-extreme-winemaking

Wanting to understand what had prompted this dismissive attitude towards a style of wine with such massive historical interest, I challenged Johnson to a dialogue. Via a mutual friend (the ever diplomatic Justin Howard-Sneyd MW), a meeting was arranged at London's 67 Pall Mall club. I selected eight wines for us to taste together, with the aim of showing that extended skin maceration in white wine was not only a broad church, but also an important theme in the modern wine world, and certainly rather more than a sideshow.

Our opinions on the wines were mostly quite divergent, but the more interesting discourse was around the term orange wine itself. It transpired that Johnson had come to the session without a clear idea of what it meant. Dave MacIntyre, the journalist who interviewed him for the *Washington Post*, had mentioned the thorny topic of natural wine. Johnson immediately bristled and went in for the kill, dragging orange wine into the crossfire, even though it was not the technique of extended skin maceration which had so got his goat. He was quite familiar with Joško Gravner's wines, and a bottle of Gravner's Ribolla Gialla 2007 proved to be the highlight of the tasting. We parted as friends, and Johnson seemed genuinely appreciative of the opportunity to dig deeper into the sub-genre of maceration.

Hugh Johnson contemplates a glass of Gravner's Ribolla Gialla 2007

Where serious wine hacks felt they had to take a strong line either pro or anti all things orange, the popular press and the blogosphere suffered from no such hang-ups. Increasing numbers of pithy articles about the new wine trend sweeping fashionable winebars started to appear in both online and offline publications across the globe from around 2015. Many were poorly researched with garbled factoids – but *Vogue*'s summer 2015 exhortation to "Never mind white, red or rosé – you should be drinking orange this fall" namechecked seven excellent wines and quoted the redoubtable Pascaline Lepeltier MS. Times were clearly changing.

It wasn't only the critics who started discovering orange wines during the 2000s. As Slovenia increased in popularity as a tourist destination, and the cheap airlines added direct routes to Ljubljana, increasing numbers of European wine and food lovers were beating a path to the cellars of its artisan growers and falling in love with macerated rebula or malvasia. The *Rough Guide* latched onto the phenomenon in 2014 and published an article about Goriška Brda's orange wine tradition, although it is not specifically mentioned in the current edition of their guidebook. Somewhat surprisingly, the last place that macerated wines are promoted strongly is Slovenia itself. Most of the country's wine drinkers want little to do with a style of wine which they see as a throwback to the past, a piece of rustic memorabilia but not what sophisticated Europeans ought to be drinking. Almost every Slovenian producer of macerated wines laments that the Slovenian market is close to insignificant for them. Perhaps a population that only escaped the shackles of communism in 1991 is still too fond of modern innovation to yet be enthusiastic about the 'back to the roots' ethic implicit in the culture of orange winemaking.

Unlike its Italian and Austrian neighbours, Slovenia has no dedicated organisation for promoting its wine and wine growers, so this job falls to the Slovenian Tourist Board. While the STO is increasingly cognisant of the draw that its artisan growers have for natural and orange wine fans outside the country, they remain rather coy in mentioning it by name. The tourist board's marketing talks about the "strong, dry wines of Primorska" (surely code for 'macerated') but stops short of name-checking orange wine itself.

The exception to Slovenia's nonchalance about its most traditional of wine styles is a clutch of high-end restaurants who keenly promote the nation's best artisan growers. Locations such as the fêted Hiša Franko (whose chef Ana Roš was crowned world's best female chef in 2017[69]) and Hiša Denk offer extensive collections of the country's best macerated wines, showcasing how great they are in complex food pairings. Mention must also be made of Boris and Miriam Novak, the driving force behind the Orange Wine Festival, a popular and exuberant tasting and celebration which happens twice a year, in Izola (Slovenian Istra) and in Vienna. It's typically attended by over 60 winemakers from Slovenia and the surrounding countries.

Producers in the Collio, Brda and Georgia began discovering unexpected markets for their wines in the 21st century – the Japanese palate seemed perfectly adjusted for the more savoury, almost umami notes in many macerated white wines, and Asian markets in general developed a passion for orange wines that no-one could have predicted. Japanese cuisine includes a greater range of bitter and umami flavours than most western tables, and these often proved to be the perfect match. A strong natural wine sector in the Nordic countries (in particular Denmark, Sweden and Norway) also began to clamour for orange wines during the mid-late 2000s. In one case, a Danish importer even requested that one of his signings start producing orange wines to satisfy his clients' demands. Based in Austria's Kamptal region close to the Danube, the young Martin Arndorfer and his wife Anna were open to experimentation but might not have decided to create a whole line of skin-macerated white varietals if it hadn't been for this surprise intervention. Not only was there a market for orange wines – it was thirsty!

It wasn't just Denmark that was clamouring for more orange wines. As a younger, millennial audience started to discover that wine could be exciting and even rebellious, orange wines started springing up on the lists of new natural-wine bars and restaurants across the globe. Now well established locations such as Racines and The Four Horsemen in New York, Terroirs, The Remedy or Sager + Wilde in London didn't need any conversion to orange wine. The young entrepreneurs, wine geeks and sommeliers who launched and staffed these businesses had no hang-ups about whether their white wines were actually amber or orange – and to a large extent, neither did their clientele.

---

69 The award was given by The World's 50 Best Restaurants, an initiative of William Reed Media. There have been many comments that the idea of a separate award for women is outdated and even insulting – but none the less, it is extremely prestigious.

Misconceptions

"Orange wines are oxidised"

It's quite surprising how many wine experts make the immediate pronouncement that macerated white wines are oxidised, merely by looking at the colour. Visual cues can be hard to shake off, but anyone who tastes with their palate rather than their preconceptions will realise that well-made orange wines from Collio, Brda or Georgia have a lively zestiness that balances their complexity.

Some producers in countries such as France, Greece or Portugal have made orange wines that aim to be more oxidative, but this has never been the goal in the countries that have the strongest traditions of macerating their white grapes.

"Orange wines are natural wines"

The term 'orange wine' just describes a process, a winemaking technique. 'Natural wine' describes a much broader philosophy. Although most orange wine producers happen to sit within the 'natural' category, it doesn't follow that all do. Some more mainstream wineries have experimented with skin contact in the context of conventional winemaking (selected yeasts, temperature control, fining and filtration). The individual has to make their own mind up about whether they consider these to be true orange wines or not.

"Orange wines are made in amphorae"

Some are, some aren't. Orange wines can, and have been made in stainless steel tanks, barriques, large oak barrels, cement tanks, plastic tubs and clay vessels of all kinds.

"Orange wines can't express terroir"

A popular snub made by orange wine haters is that macerating white grapes erases any sense of place or characteristics of the grape variety. Since the winemaking technique is identical to that used in red wine, one wonders if these commentators feel that red wines also don't show their origins?

"Orange wines all taste the same"

This is a bit like saying "all hip-hop music sounds the same", "all Bollywood films have the same plot" or "all wine tastes the same". All styles and sub-genres require a little exploration before their depth of variety and subtle gradations become clear.

Challenges and faults in orange wines

Haters love to say that all orange wines are faulty, oxidised and volatile. While this is nonsense, there are challenges with this hands-off method of winemaking – and not all the resulting wines could be said to be fault-free.

Volatile acidity

One of the biggest challenges with orange wine making is to avoid too much volatile acidity. Volatile acidity (essentially acetic acid) gives aromas of vinegar or nail polish remover. The risk can occur when skins rise to the top of a fermenting vat, dry out and become exposed to oxygen. Regular punchdowns or other cap management techniques are essential to avoid this occurring.

That said, a certain amount of volatility can add lift and drive to a wine. It's all a matter of balance. Older vintages of the classic Chateau Musar, from the Lebanon, are famous for their relatively high volatility levels. Radikon's wines play with volatility, as a key component that gives the sensation of freshness and excitement. In the right proportions, it can work wonders.

Brettanomyces

A rogue yeast that can join the party, unwanted, during a wild yeast ferment. Its presence is less likely when laboratory yeasts are used, as these are strong, predictable yeasts that accomplish fermentation much more quickly than wild yeasts, knocking everything else out of their way.

As most orange wines are spontaneously fermented, brettanomyces can be an issue. It also lives deep in the pores of oak barrels – and once a barrel becomes infected, there is little option but to throw it away.

Brettanomyces manifests itself at low levels with aromas of clove or Elastoplast. At higher levels, the nose will smell of farmyards or manure, and can destroy or mask any sensation of fruit in the wine.

Mousiness

Poorly understood and often confused with brettanomyces, mousiness is a separate taint which can develop in the presence of lactobacillus bacteria – but these in turn can end up in the wine alongside brettanomyces (aka dekkera), making it difficult to separate the two.

Mousy taint develops easily in wines where the pH is high (usually meaning the acidity is low), and when there is sufficient warmth and oxygen. A tiny sniff of sulphur is enough to knock it sideways – so this problem tends only to manifest itself in wines made with no added sulphites.

The taint isn't volatile at the standard pH of wine and can't be detected by smell. When wine tasters say that a wine "smells mousy", they are usually describing brettanomyces, whether knowingly or not. When a mousy wine is tasted or drunk, the liquid mixes with the taster's saliva, the pH is raised and the taint's disgusting "dog breath" or "stale popcorn" flavour is released. Often this arrives as a sensation in the mouth, some 10 to 20 seconds after the wine has been imbibed. It can be shocking and surprising, especially in a context where many wines are tasted in quick succession, and the culprit may not be easily identifiable.

Furthermore, sensitivity to mousiness varies widely. An estimated 30% of winemakers cannot detect it, even at high levels.

It should be noted that none of the above problems are exclusive to orange wines. However, for wines made with minimal intervention and low or no sulphur, they are more common.

11

Ceci n'est pas un blanc

Orange wine's challenge hasn't only

been acceptance by the more traditional backwaters of the wine industry, but also an ongoing identity crisis. If it wasn't difficult enough that these deep hued beverages are often muddled up with conventional white wines in retail environments and restaurants, it's also often assumed that the term orange wine is somehow synonymous with natural wine. Why is it that the two are so often merged into one nebulous category?

Properly speaking, 'natural wine' refers to a movement or a philosophy about wine – there are of course natural wine producers making red, white, rosé, orange and sparkling wines. 'Orange wine', at least in the view of this author, refers to the wine produced from white grapes which have been fermented with their skins. While the style's roots lie in tradition, and all of its major proponents fit broadly into the natural wine

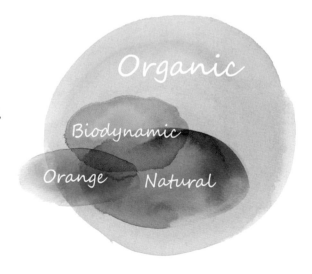

canon, there are plenty of exceptions which cloud this temptingly simple picture. In reality, the orange wine category is a subset which overlaps heavily with natural wine, but is not entirely contained within it.

Tony Milanowski takes this confusion to heart. He's got a certain gruffness about him, the no-nonsense antipodean quality of someone who's been around the block at least once. Following a classical winemaking career that took in Hardys (Australia) and Farnese (Italy), he's currently programme manager and lecturer for the winemaking faculty at Plumpton College in Sussex, UK. Milanowski is an unlikely promoter of orange wine, but one of the few who is very clear about the defining line between technique and ideology. He visited Saša Radikon in Friuli to find out more about the family's winemaking methods, before attending an orange wine masterclass at Raw Wine London fair in 2013. It left him feeling unsatisfied – "I was a bit disgruntled in a way as I felt they were just advocating one way of using skin contact (the ultra-natural, low-intervention way). The Raw version isn't the only idea. That's why I thought I'd get the students to do it."

True to his word, Milanowski added fermentation of white grapes with the skins to the syllabus, and has now presided over two vintages of the college's orange wine (2015 and 2016), made in a squeaky clean, modern fashion, with laboratory yeasts, temperature control and sterile filtration.[70] The results are fascinating, if muted, because they demonstrate that extended skin contact is indeed just a technique, and one which loses a lot of its romance and vitality if it is treated in this more scientific, clinical fashion.

Winemaker Josh Donaghay-Spire is a Milanowski protégé who now works at Chapel Down, one of the UK's largest and most successful wineries. Inspired by his experience of the macerated white wine style, he made the Chapel Down Orange Bacchus in 2014 – a bottling that became the UK's first commercially available orange wine. Again, the Orange Bacchus demonstrates that extended skin contact during fermentation can become almost imperceptible if it is combined with more interventionist practice. Donaghay-Spire was concerned that after only 10 days of

---

70 The college has installed some Georgian qvevri and, starting in 2018, will also be experimenting with a more 'natural' style of winemaking.

skin contact, the wine was becoming rather astringent, so he decided to just use the free-run juice,[71] which in turn was aged in oak barrels for nine months. The end result was then fined with bentonite and filtered.[72] It is utterly inoffensive, but for anyone who has enjoyed the regal qualities of Oslavia's macerated ribolla gialla or the magical elegance of Carso's skin-contact vitovska, the Orange Bacchus falls a bit short on its bacchanalian promise. Still, Chapel Down's 2015 and 2016 Orange Bacchus are both being made with inclusion of the press-juice and more extended maceration (15 and 21 days respectively), and Donaghay-Spire notes that the first vintage did at least give him the confidence to push the boundaries further.

Where to buy

Supermarkets are mostly a dead loss when it comes to small production, artisanal wines, and that accounts for 99% of all orange wines. In any case it's better to give your hard-earned cash to a local business if you possibly can.

Independent wine merchants are the go-to resource here, especially those who have a focus on natural, organic and biodynamic growers. Make friends, visit often and ask if they ever have tastings where you can try before you buy.

Smaller wine importers or distributors in many parts of the world (excepting the US or countries with alcohol monopolies) are often willing and able to sell direct to individuals. If you have a favourite wine, it's usually not too hard to discover who imports it to your corner of the world – if in doubt, contact the winery and ask. Then contact the importer and ask if you can buy.

Natural wine bars and restaurants frequently offer off-sales as a possibility. Expect a small discount from the bar price if you buy to take-away. An increasing number are adopting the enoteca model, where you can drink a glass on-site and buy a bottle from the shop on the same premises. This is optimal.

Buying online is a viable option for many of the rarer wines and producers mentioned in this book. Use search engines or specialised sites such as wine-searcher.com or Vivino to track down a supplier. If you live within the EU, it's usually not too expensive to have a few bottles shipped from one EU country to another.

----

71 The juice that drains freely from grapes in a crusher or from a fermentation vessel, without pressing.

72 Both of these processes are absolutely run of the mill for mass-produced, mainstream wines, but very seldom if ever used by traditional orange wine producers in Italy, Slovenia or Georgia.

Batič wines

There are plenty of commentators who would suggest that the efforts of people like Milanowski and Donaghay-Spire are precisely what is needed to provide an entry point for orange wines. Then there is the opposing view, that the whole concept of orange wine is of a natural, traditionally made product with very minimal intervention in the cellar. And maybe, just maybe, the great unwashed don't actually need orange wine to be dumbed down in order to understand it. In 2015, UK supermarket Marks and Spencer listed an unfiltered Georgian qvevri wine for the first time.[73] The retailer has said that it sold "amazingly well", and several years later it's still part of the range. Austrian customers of the Aldi chain (called Hofer in Austria) could buy a small-production 'orange' Sauvignon Blanc in December 2017,[74] even if the checkout clerks viewed the slightly cloudy, russet-orange contents with suspicion while ringing up the purchase.

Key to the success of these offerings was probably that they were clearly sign-posted as unusual (at least where the supermarket's standard customer-base was concerned). No hapless customer could have bought Hofer's Orange Sauvignon Blanc mistaking it for a conventional white wine – the word 'orange' was inscribed boldly on the brightly coloured label. A more cynical observer might also point out that, at its price point of € 9.99, it was one of the most expensive bottles in Hofer's stores.

Clear signposting is unfortunately often still lacking in a large part of the retail and restaurant sectors. With the huge growth in high-end restaurants special-ising in natural wine, there are now plenty of 'oranges' to be found on lists from Paris to London to New York and all points in between. The challenge is that they are not always categorised as such. It helps that since 2004 there is a convenient name (orange wine) that can be pressed into service, but old habits die hard, and those establishments that take the plunge and add an orange section between their white, red and rosé are still in the minority.

Saša Radikon has always been adamant about the need for a separate category. "Orange wine may not be the perfect name," he says, "but it is important to put these wines in their own section. If someone orders one of our wines from the white wine section, then it turns up and it's this strange colour, they're going to be surprised or even disappointed." The counter-argument goes that orange wines are such an insignificant niche that they will always require the explana-tion and curation of a knowledgeable sommelier or wine merchant, and never be accidentally purchased by an unwary consumer.

---

73 The wine was an M&S own-brand bottling of Tbilvino's Qvevris Rkatsiteli. The winery confirmed that the contents of the bottle are identical to their Tbilvino branded version.

74 Made by Weingut Waldherr in Burgenland.

Both arguments obscure the crux of the problem, which is the often extremely backward nature of the institutions managing appellation control or its lingual equivalents in other countries. Given that Italy can claim the birthright for modern orange wines, one might think that its quality-wine classification laws would include options for producers who want to bottle them, but it has been steadfast in its rejection of macerated white wines from almost every DOC and DOCG[75] across the country. The only legal option open to many Italian producers is to bottle their orange wines as basic Vino Bianco. While this just about passes muster for a wine such as La Biancara's Pico or Vodopivec's Solo (both of which are relatively light in colour), it is plainly ridiculous for Radikon or Prinčič's deep russet-coloured Ribolla Giallas, or La Stoppa's luminescent copper Ageno.

Colour and cloudiness are generally issues which fall foul of many quality-wine designations, meaning that the vast majority of orange wines are bottled as lowly table wines. After repeated requests from Stanko Radikon and Damijan Podversic, the Consorzio Collio finally changed its rules to allow macerated wines to be bottled as DOC Collio wines from the 2005 vintage. It meant a subtle annexing of the *disciplinare* wording, "wines must have an elegant straw-yellow colour". However, there is still no legal way of showing on the bottle that the wine was made with extended maceration. In any case, by 2005 many of Oslavia's top producers had run out of patience with the Consorzio. To date, Gravner, Radikon[76] and Prinčič all bottle under the broader and theoretically less prestigious Venezia Giuli IGT classification, which does not penalise wines for overly vibrant pigmentation.

---

75 The Denominazione di Origine Controllata and Denominazione di Origine Controllata e Garantita are Italy's two highest wine classifications, typically used for wines from delimited areas made in specific styles.

76 It is commonly presumed that Radikon's wines were and are refused the Collio DOC designation due to their colour, but it has also been suggested that their relatively high levels of volatile acidity are an additional issue. The Consorzio Collio however claims that it merely enforces EU limits for volatile acidity, which are 18 milliequivalents per litre (18 mEq/L).

Even this option has become trickier since the 2017 vintage, as Friuli's producers gained a new classification called Della Venezie DOC. The new category allows varietal pinot grigio[77] made from almost anywhere in north-eastern Italy to be elevated to DOC level, but it also simultaneously removes the possibility of designating a more lowly IGT pinot grigio in these areas. Thus, Radikon's Pinot Grigio, which would not qualify for the DOC, has now had to become a table wine (vino bianco) with the quasi-fantasy name "Sivi".[78] Saša Radikon is philosophical if clearly frustrated about the issue, which has merely added another mountain of paperwork to the already groaning dossiers that are required by Italy's chamber of commerce and *consorzi*. And there is little if any benefit to the end consumer in all of this – apart from wondering why their favourite wine has suddenly changed its name.

Slovenian wine labelling laws also offer no ideal solution. Wine must be either white, red or rosé. There is no orange or amber option, despite the growing proliferation of producers making macerated white wines. The Ministry of Agriculture of Georgia has very recently introduced an official labelling scheme for qvevri wines, however it does not enforce any skin maceration, so wines made from white grapes could theoretically be made with no skin contact at all and still qualify. Still, there's a good chance that a Kakhetian[79] bottle of rkatsiteli, mtsvane or kisi with a qvevri symbol on the label will deliver the expected amber experience.

At the time of writing, there are just two locations in the world which have official labelling schemes for orange wines, Ontario and South Africa. Both are recent and demonstrate that there are at least some classification bodies who listen to their members and react accordingly. South Africa's Wine & Spirits Board (WSB) did not know what to make of the new-style wines from producers

---

77 A number of other grape varieties are included in the Delle Venezie DOC *disciplinare*, but it is overwhelmingly focused on pinot grigio, the Veneto and Friuli's biggest cash cow after Prosecco.

78 Sivi pinot is the Slovenian name for pinot grigio. Table wines cannot state either grape variety, region or vintage on the label.

79 Other regions of Georgia, particularly towards the west, have a tradition of less skin contact than in Kakheti.

such as Craig Hawkins of Testalonga winery and Jurgen Gouws of the Intellego label, and between 2010 and 2015 denied export licences to many white wines which were cloudy, obviously macerated or made with full malolactic fermentation. Hawkins' 2011 Cortez was a notable example, a wine that had been pre-ordered by many European importers that was denied its passport to leave the country.

Hawkins teamed up with a number of other alternative winemakers in Swartland (Gouws, Eben Sadie, Chris and Andrea Mullineux, Callie Louw, and Adi Badenhorst), and together the group suggested a number of new categories for addition to the board's existing classifications. These included skin-fermented white, methode ancestrale, and alternative white/red – basically, a natural wine, made with minimal sulphur and allowed to complete malolactic fermentation.

The WSB's definition of skin fermented white, which was enshrined in the regulations in late 2015, is as follows:

1. *The product shall be fermented and macerated on its skins for at least 96 hours (4 days).*
2. *The product shall complete malolactic fermentation.*
3. *The sulphur dioxide content of the product shall not exceed 40.0 mg/L.*
4. *The residual sugar content of the product shall not exceed 4.0 g/L.*
5. *The product shall be anywhere from light golden to deep orange in colour.*

Ontario might not yet be up there with Burgundy or Napa Valley, but its regulatory board is also clearly more open-minded and nimbler on its feet than the sluggish administrations of more famed appellations. The area also boasts at least six wineries which produce orange wines. One of them is Southbrook Vineyards, whose head winemaker Ann Sperling petitioned the Ontario Vintners Quality Alliance or VQA to introduce a classification for her 'Skin fermented Vidal'. On 1 July 2017, the VQA passed new regulations which added the category 'skin fermented white' to its list of permissible styles. It offers the following guide to what such a wine entails:

▸ Mostly still wines, typically dry to medium dry. Made from white or pink grape varieties, fermented in contact with the grape skins for a minimum of 10 days. This skin contact fermentation results in wines with more tannins and herbal notes with restrained fruit flavors and tea-like characteristics. These wines are labelled "Skin Fermented White".

A brief glance at some of the labelling stipulations provides a fascinating glimpse into the absolute pedantry that goes with the territory of wine classification and regulation:

▸ Skin Fermented White shall be declared in a type size at least as large as the varietal declaration on the principal display panel and not less than 2 mm based on the smallest letter.
▸ Nothing shall be written between the grape variety name and Skin Fermented White.
▸ Where no grape varieties are declared on the principal display panel, the term Skin Fermented White shall be declared in a type size not less than 3.2 mm based on the smallest letter.
▸ The terms Amber Wine, Orange Wine or Vin Orange may appear at the producer's discretion.

Still, these two classifications are vital for the producers concerned, and also provide a great deal more transparency for wine drinkers who want to know what they're buying. There's been very little fanfare in either case, but it's fair to say that these classifications represent a turning point – orange wines are a thing, a valid category, with a clear definition and a market.

What does the future hold? Orange wines are now made in every wine-making country of the world, even if only experimentally. It's difficult to estimate the total number of producers who made at least one commercially available orange wine in 2017, but the figure definitely runs into thousands. Most of these bottlings are made in small quantities and sold at premium prices. Orange wine is not destined to become a mainstream style sold for peanuts on supermarket shelves, but it is slowly but surely taking its place alongside other niche offerings such as sherry, English sparkling wine or Etna Rosso. Still, ideally it should be considered not as a niche style, but more as the fourth wine colour. The variety of hues, aromas and flavours in orange wines is easily as broad as those in red, white or rosé, and their versatility at the table is peerless. As the age-old technique of extended maceration finds new fans amongst winemakers across the globe, the protagonists are starting to divide into two clear factions – the dabblers, and those who truly believe in the style. In the former camp, many of the larger, more mainstream wineries have introduced experimental cuvées to allow their winemaking staff the opportunity to experiment and play with the orange technique. The results vary, but are often produced as a one-off, or a micro-vinification that is barely commercial. Domäne Wachau, one of Austria's biggest producers and certainly the largest in its region, has produced an excellent skin-macerated riesling for the last few years, but the quantity available is so small and the style so distinct from anything else produced at the winery that it is not even offered to their distributors. Visitors to the estate are able to purchase one of the 1,500 or so bottles produced each year.

Then there are the true converts who tend to come from the 'natural' side of the table. They're generally growers who realise that the inclusion of skins in white ferments allows them a great deal more latitude when it comes to doing without other additives such as sulphur. Growers such as Theo Coles at The Hermit Ram in New Zealand, the aforementioned Craig Hawkins, or Philip Hart of AmByth in Paso Robles use skin contact for a large part of their production, out of a true love for its textures, flavours and ability to express vineyard character. It's winemakers such as these who are properly taking the baton from the ancient traditions of Collio, Brda or Georgia, and running with it.

Given the continued growth of interest and consumption of natural wines, particularly by a young and emerging audience, orange wines seem to have hitched a free ride. The arguments about how they should be categorised and what they should be called will probably continue as long as the discussions about whether wine is actually good for us or not. There will doubtless continue to be strongly worded criticism of the style, both from those who can't get past classed growth Bordeaux or the more guarded commentators who damn with faint praise ("It's interesting but I don't think I could drink a second glass"). Meanwhile, enthusiastic drinkers filling natural wine bars and fairs have increasingly drowned out the voices of the naysayers. For those without the baggage of the previous generation or a surfeit of perceived wine knowledge, orange wine is just another genre to discover, not something to fear or ridicule. It's a far cry from the last days of the 1990s, when Joško Gravner and Stanko Radikon were considered to be madmen rather than pioneers.

Is Gravner surprised by quite how popular macerated white wines have become? "Yes, because everyone was so against it at first!" Still, it's the nature of revolutions that they force everyone outside established comfort zones. The amber revolution has challenged producers, drinkers, legislators and retailers, but it has also permanently enhanced wine's spectrum. It will be honoured not just in the history books, but ever more thirstily in our glasses.

Sign at The Klinec Inn, Medana, Slovenia

Serving and food matching

Orange wines sit right in the middle between white and red. Their lively acidity and fruit is often reminiscent of white wines, but textually and structurally the reference is closer to red. This makes them incredibly versatile when it comes to food pairing. It is quite possible to drink only orange wines over the course of an entire menu, should you wish.

The ideal serving temperature depends a lot on the specific style of the wine, from lighter and softer textured, to heavier and more tannic. For the lighter styles, try chilling down to 10°C to 12°C and then let the wine warm up a little more if it feels too muted. For heavier more structured wines, 14°C to 16°C is a better bet to unlock all the flavours. The spiky prickle of tannins often dominates if the serving temperature is too cold.

Decanting or carafing young wines is a great way to oxygenate them quickly and get them to open up a little faster than they will in your glass. Many producers also recommend shaking or upending the bottle before opening, to mix any sediment or lees evenly into the wine. This is a matter of personal taste – if you prefer things to be a little less cloudy then let the bottle stand upright for a few hours before serving.

Personal taste also comes into play with glassware. Wide-bowled glasses of the shape classically used for pinot noir often allow heavier more complex orange wines to express themselves best. Several winemakers in Friuli and Slovenia have designed their own custom stemware to suit their wines, notably Gravner and Movia.

Here are some sample wine and food matches to stimulate the tastebuds. If in doubt, just open up your favourite bottle with dinner and enjoy! Sometimes serendipity achieves the most heavenly combinations without any help from experts.

Dishes at a Georgian supra, with various cheeses and khachapuri

▶ **Raw oysters or sea urchins**

With their salty, umami burst of minerality, these creatures adore being paired with both lighter and heavier orange wines. Nino Barraco's Catarratto works wonders, as would Elisabetta Foradori's Nosiola or anything from Sato.

▶ **Charcuterie or rillette**

What better to have with your aperitivo than orange bubbles? Croci's De Campedello or Tomac's Amphora Brut have that marvellous combination of acidity and grip, just perfect for freshening the taste buds between each delicious slice of salami or Pršut.

▶ **Spicy Indian, Thai or Indonesian food with aromatic herbs and flavourings such as cumin, kaffir lime leaf or pandan**

Orange wines made with an aromatic variety such as gewürztraminer or muscat work really well with spicy cuisine, especially if they have a slight touch of sweetness (technically, a few grams of residual sugar that has not been fermented to dryness). The sweetness and the aromas moderate the spices on your palate and ensure that the wine doesn't get lost.

▶ **Gnocchi and pasta dishes with rich, cheesy sauces**

Try heavier orange wines from Tuscany or Emilia-Romagna, such as La Stoppa's Ageno, Vino del Poggio's Bianco or La Colombaia's Bianco.

▶ **Gnocchi and pasta with tomato-based sauces, or pizza Margherita**

Dario Prinčič's wines have an abundance of fresh acidity and red fruit that is a match made in heaven with tomatoes. Craig Hawkins' Mangaliza Part 2 also works wonders here, particularly given some bottle age.

▶ **Pork and clams, or any casserole or stew made with a fattier cut of pork**

There's nothing better than the sharp, almost sour twang of Radikon's Jakot to slice through the fat of a pork dish. Tom Shobrook's Giallo or Intellego's Elementis are also recommended.

▶ **Semi-sweet desserts made with beetroot or carrot**

Esencia Rural's Sol a Sol Airen has significant residual sugar in some vintages. Try it with dessert and you might be surprised how well it works. Thanks to Figo Onna from Choux Restaurant in Amsterdam for this inspired pairing.

▶ **Cheeseboards**

Almost anything is up for grabs. Orange wines that are big on structure and tannins can work very well with strong, aged hard cheeses such as Comté, Remeker or Pecorino. For soft, stinky or blue cheeses, try a wine with more opulent fruit and aromatics – Il Tufiello's Fiano or Ambyth's Priscus are the winners here.

Epilogue

W

riting about orange wine is one thing, but making it is quite another. Due more to luck than judgement, I've had two opportunities to try my hand at it while I was planning and writing this book. It began in July 2016 with a seemingly innocent question from the ever charming Portuguese winemaker Oscar Quevedo: "Simon, do you know how to make an orange wine?". Oscar isn't stupid, he knew damn well I'd have something to say on the subject.

We were sitting in the tasting room at Quevedo, a port and still wine producer in the Cima Corgo sub-region of the Douro valley, on a typically roasting-hot July day. The question came completely out of the blue. "Well, theoretically yes. I've never made one, but I've visited and talked to maybe 100 producers who have."

Fast forward one hour, and I'd blurted out just about everything I could think of, mostly recycled pearls of wisdom from luminaries such as the Radikon or Gravner families. Oscar revealed his intention to try making an orange wine, as the year's side-project to try something new at the winery. I offered my questionable consultancy services to come and help.

Two months later I was back in S. João da Pesqueira, with approximately 10 days to collaborate with Quevedo's winemaking team to make their first ever skin-contact white wine – perhaps even the Douro's first.[80] The aim was 1,000 bottles. No marketing plan, first see how the wine turns out.

Journalists, writers and bloggers such as myself may think we know a thing or two about production. We make intelligent-sounding comments about malolactic fermentation or the use of battonage to impress winemakers that our technical chops are sound. But do we really know what we're talking about? No, we don't. As I discovered, making wine involves a whole series of decisions, logistics and other factors that never enter into the head of most outsiders, not even, I suspect, seasoned wine critics.

The first challenge was to decide what blend of grapes to use. We wanted our Douro 'Orange' to have something to say about the region, so as with most traditional Douro wines it would be a blend of indigenous varieties. After much deliberation, we decided that the aromatics of rabigato might pair well with viosinho (good acidity). Searching for a thick-skinned variety, we settled on síria (aka codega, aka roupeiro aka many other things).

Then came the first issue. Quevedo buys in most of its white grapes, and the rabigato didn't show up when expected. We had síria from two different growers, harvested on the same day but very different (one with good acids and the other a bit flat), plenty of viosinho (borderline ripe but excellent acidity), but no rabigato. Oscar had the solution – some gouveio had also just been harvested, so our blend quickly mutated into 50% síria, 25% viosinho and 25% gouveio.

Our next decision was whether to destem. A quick taste of the síria stems revealed that we definitely should – they were bitter and unripe, although the grapes tasted good. A small destemmer was located, but there was no way to automate the loading. Quevedo's larger destemmer was not only far too huge for the job, but also too rough – we wanted to keep as many grapes whole as we could. (In the end we also included about 10% of the gouveio stems as they tasted great.)

---

80 As I now know, this achievement properly goes to Bago de Touriga's Gouvyas Branco Âmbar 2010.

Selecting grapes at Quevedo

30 minutes later, with a small jerry-rigged destemmer perched atop some wooden pallets, we were off, hand-loading eight cassettes of grapes into the hopper, a tedious and time-consuming task. Thank goodness for Mario and his colleague (assistants at the winery), a string of students, Teresa and Ryan Opaz, who all pitched in at various points during this five-hour slog.

Quevedo's winemaker Teresa wanted to add some SO_2 to the must at this point. I wasn't too happy about it. Her line of reasoning was that we had the grapes in open vats, and they'd be at risk of oxidation until fermentation started. She persuaded me by pointing out that all of the SO_2 would be consumed by the fermentation. We added a small dose to each tank (500ml @ 6% solution per 750 Kg grapes).

Finally, by around 10 PM, 1,880 Kg of grapes were settled in two 1,000 litre open steel vats, looking for all the world like some kind of weird olive porridge. Oscar arrived right on time with pizza. I finished with a late-night ceremonial punchdown (very important for skin contact wines), using a wonderful wooden implement that Teresa discovered somewhere deep in the bowels of the winery. I'm fairly sure it had been a museum piece for decades.

There was no sign of fermentation the next day, so Oscar and I jumped into the vat (with carefully washed feet, of course) to foot-tread the grapes, Douro style. It's quite bizarre to feel the different temperature zones and the soft squish of the grapes breaking underfoot. But it didn't make one jot of difference to the fermentation, which stubbornly refused to start. I spent the next six days in mortal fear that the end result would be an oxidised cake of nothingness, despite constant reassurance from Claudia Quevedo and Teresa.

My final 48 hours in the Douro were looming, and there was precisely nothing happening. That evening, Oscar and I went out to eat dinner. As we parted company close to midnight, a luminescent full moon beamed down. I looked up. "This will be it, I'm sure!" And sure enough, the next morning my two tanks were in full flow, the skins pushed up to the top by the CO_2 and a happy bubbling emanating from within. I spent an enjoyable day punching the tanks down every three hours, finally feeling like more than a spare part.

The last evening was supposed to be spent visiting another winemaker friend an hour's drive away. Fermentation aromas had surely addled my mind because I crashed the car that Oscar had lent me just metres down the road from the winery. No-one got hurt but I almost wrote off the vehicle and made a dent in the neighbour's wall. It wasn't a great way to finish the week, but at least we had wine and not oxidised grape juice.

The rest of the wine's development happened largely without my presence, albeit with plenty of back-and-forth via email and phone. The fermentation completed nicely, we had 12% of alcohol, almost no sugar and about 21 days of skin contact. It was pretty tannic, so the obvious choice was to put the wine into used oak for a while. Quevedo is a busy winery and didn't have any spare barrels, so two second-hand *pipas* (600-litre port barrels) that had previously been used to store *aguardiente* were purchased and cleaned. Our wine spent almost a year in barrel, before finally being bottled (with a pinch of sulphur) in December 2017. As I speak, it still feels a little prepubescent, albeit expressive on the palate.

The following year there was another random request. My wine importer friend Marnix Rombaut in Amsterdam wondered if I'd like to help him make an orange wine at a small organically certified winery in the south of the Netherlands. I confirmed that I would like, very much.

Ron Langeveld has a few hectares of vineyard that are probably unique in the Netherlands, if not the world. Focusing only on disease-resistant hybrid grape varieties (the so-called PIWIS), he not only farms organically but also without any copper or sulphur sprays. Over the period of a decade or so, Ron has isolated those varieties that can really handle the Dutch climate without the need for any treatments of any kind. All he does is prune, making his vines some of the most beautiful I've ever seen. There is none of the white powdery coating that is commonly found even in biodynamic vineyards after they've been sprayed with sulphur.

Ron's fruit may be as naked as it can possibly be, but the wines he makes at Dassemus are made in a modern and fairly technical fashion – selected yeasts, chaptalisation[81] if needed, filtration and so forth. Our mission was to do the polar opposite and make a wine that was unchaptalised, spontaneously fermented and free from any additions whatsoever. We'd selected a parcel of souvignier gris for the experiment. Souvignier gris is a hybrid, a crossing of cabernet sauvignon and solaris (itself a hybrid crossing). It has the most beautiful rose-pink skins, despite being ostensibly a white variety, and a ton of acidity, plus rather thick skins. It ought to be perfect, we thought.

Harvest day was set for 15 October, as the variety is late ripening. The weather was idyllic, and a small team of friends and family went out into the vines. The first plot of souvignier gris was picked in the morning, but we hit a snag – analysis showed the grapes to have a mere 10.5% alcohol. Ron wasn't happy, especially as we were adamant about not chaptalising. But he had the solution – an older plot of souvignier gris which also needed picking. Sure enough, the slightly more mature vines had more concentration. We'd pushed our potential alcohol level up to a majestic 11% and some change.

---

81 The addition of sugar, or grape must to a ferment, to raise the potential alcohol level of a wine – a practice in common usage in many parts of northern Europe where grapes don't always ripen optimally, although generally avoided by natural winemakers.

We destemmed and lightly crushed the fruit into a small metal vat. Unlike my experience in Portugal, this baby started bubbling practically by the time Ron left the winery to go inside for his dinner. Two weeks later, it had completed its business. We let it have another three days of skin contact before Ron and Marnix started getting fidgety. The wine was racked into another tank to age.

It's now March 2018. Our wine is definitely in a teenaged phase, a little gawky and bad tempered, yet full of fruit and acidity and all the other good things needed for survival. We'll have to see how it turns out. I'm hoping Ron may discover a spare barrel somewhere, as I have a sneaking suspicion our pinky-orange juice needs fattening up a little.

It's far too early to say whether either of these experiments can be considered a real success, but they have been real learning experiences. My key take-away was that although viticulture is a year-round sport, winemaking happens once a year, and it involves a surprising number of decisions all compressed into the space of hours or days. A wrong decision might not produce vinegar but could make the difference between sublime or swill.

Risk enters the equation at every step of the way. What if the wine doesn't turn out well, or customers don't like it? Will it be too different to last year? At least our risk was limited to a barrel or two. It's hard to imagine the angst that growers like Stanko Radikon or Joško Gravner must have had in those first years, wondering if anyone would ever buy their wines again – or the nagging doubt that Iago Bitarishvili or Ramaz Nikoladze may have suffered. Wouldn't their lives have been easier if they just planted watermelons and potatoes like their neighbours? Perhaps Branko Čotar or Joško Renčel wondered from time to time whether they'd have to forsake tradition and fall in line with more modern fashions – or risk never selling another bottle.

To all these single-minded characters, with their mix of obstinacy, foolhardiness and blindingly clear vision: I salute you.

Harvesting at Dassemus, with Ron Langeveld

RECOMMENDED PRODUCERS

Sunset on the Collio/Brda border

Recommended producers

T
he number of wineries worldwide who
are having a go at making orange wine is now easily into four figures, even
if this has sometimes taken the form of one-off experiments. The selection
of producers included below is therefore not in any sense a complete listing,
but rather an unashamedly personal selection of acknowledged masters and
upcoming new talent.

I adopted a number of criteria for inclusion. These are:

▶ A track record in making orange wines (multiple vintages, consistent quality).

▶ Commitment to the technique, either making their entire range of white wines
with maceration or at least a substantial proportion. Note that if a winery only
makes one white wine, but it is a macerated marvel, that qualifies.

▶ Using the traditional technique with integrity – which means wild yeasts/ spontaneous fermentation, no temperature control during fermentation, no fining, no or light
filtration and minimal use of sulphur dioxide (*a small number of producers included
do not work exclusively in this way. Specific exceptions are noted in the text*).

▶ Certified organic or biodynamic viticulture is strongly preferred, however uncertified
organic practices/no use of synthetic pesticides, fungicides or herbicides in the vineyards is also acceptable. Orange wines are fermented with the skins, remember!

▶ I personally enjoy the wines and feel they are accomplished within their region.

▶ I have visited the property or talked with the grower, or at the very least have tasted
the wines on multiple occasions.

Having set these rules, it was inevitable there would be a need to break them. Some countries with developing wine cultures are yielding fascinating orange wines, but there is little or no track record. Rather than just ignore them, I've listed a few innovators and newcomers who are worth watching.

Since this book focuses overwhelmingly on those countries which have the oldest and most well-established cultures of producing macerated white wines, a disproportionate number of recommended producers are from Italy, Slovenia and Georgia. I make no apology for this bias. Winemakers in these countries are often the most accomplished and experienced with the technique. There's a kind of unspoken collective confidence with extended maceration in these parts of the world. However, growers from 20 countries in total are included, but this omits many important winemaking nations. Here are a few words about the more notable absences.

Serbia has a growing core of natural winemakers who are experimenting with orange wine, but at the time of writing next to nothing was commercially available – it is simply too early to pronounce on the wines or the probable high-flyers. Many other eastern European countries fall into a similar category. There are surely interesting experiments underway in Romania, Hungary and Moldova, but these countries are very much under the orange radar in comparison to their Adriatic cousins.

There is little doubt that growers in Greece, Turkey and Cyprus would have macerated their white grapes in pre-technology times, but these traditions have been virtually obliterated by the march of progress. A small number of Greek producers are starting to experiment within the orange wine oeuvre, and I have even tasted a macerated retsina, which was more of a curiosity than anything else, but certainly intriguing. Santorini's high quality assyrtiko grape could well hold huge potential here.

Winemaking in the Middle East (especially Israel and the Lebanon) is developed on a small scale, but very much follows the French model stylistically and in terms of the mostly red grape varieties. A winemaker named Jacob Oryah has made an Israeli orange wine. Along with Armenia, all these countries could theoretically challenge Georgia's claim as the cradle of wine, but none has the same unbroken line of tradition.

South America harbours many interesting and ancient winemaking methods, but thus far its modern-day production has been overwhelmingly focused on large estates and mainstream styles. Chile has produced at least one orange wine, as has Peru. All of these countries have venerable traditions of rustic viniculture, and inevitably in the absence of presses or de-stemming machines, white grapes would have been fermented with their skins and some of the stems,[82] if they were separated out from the red grapes at all. As more artisan growers establish themselves in this corner of the world, we can expect some fascinating macerated wines alongside a general increase in variety.

Winemaking in Asia is experiencing a boom period, with China leaping from nowhere to being the fifth biggest wine producer (by volume) in the world.[83] It would be absolute folly to claim that there are no orange wines being made in India, China or Japan, because by the time this book rolls off the printing presses, someone will have rendered that statement inaccurate. For now, though, an exploration of Asian 'oranges' will have to wait for a second edition.

New discoveries are posted regularly on www.themorningclaret.com so even if your favourite orange winemaker isn't listed here, don't despair.

---

82 In Chile, a *zaranda* was traditionally used to destem grapes. It's a set of wooden poles mounted on a frame, with holes in between them that are just big enough to let grapes pass through. Inevitably, some of the stems and all of the skins end up in the ferment with this process.

83 The 2014 figure, according to the Food and Agriculture Organization, a department of United Nations.

Key

Organically certified viticulture
(may or may not be stated on the bottle)

Biodynamically certified viticulture *(Demeter or equivalent certification bodies, eg. BiodyVin in France, may or may not be stated on the bottle)*

No SO₂ is added during the winemaking or bottling *(but note that wines may still contain naturally occurring sulphites which are produced by the fermentation process, at typical levels of 10–20 mg/L)*

Expert This producer uses skin maceration in all their white wines and is one of the foremost exponents of the style worldwide

Australia

The nation that precipitated a revolution in modern, technical winemaking is finally beginning to breed a new generation of growers keen to explore more minimal intervention and move away from the technology. With this has come a swift growth of experimentation with skin maceration for whites. So far there are few experts, but those growers who are prioritising freshness and early picking are the winners, at least to this author's tastes.

Australia's wine labelling laws allow considerable latitude when compared with those of most European nations, thus orange wines can theoretically be classified as quality wines with a statement of origin. That said, the joker in the pack is the cool climate Orange wine region in New South Wales, which has been vocal about its disapproval of the term orange wine. The Orange GI[84] association has on occasion threatened to prosecute Australian winemakers in other parts of the country who use the term on their labels, suggesting that 'skin fermented white wine' or 'amber wine' would be a better alternative. They have a point.

---

84 'Geographical Indication', the legal classification system used for delimited Australian wine regions.

AUSTRALIA / BAROSSA

Shobbrook Wines

The ball of maverick energy that is Tom Shobbrook has properly shaken up Australian winemaking, ever since he returned to Barossa in 2007, following a six-year stint in Tuscany. Ceramic eggs are his weapon of choice for white wines, many of which are made with extended skin maceration. Giallo (a blend of muscat, riesling and semillon) and Sammlon (just semillon) are two tasty examples. These are wines that turn the notion that Australia only does big, heavy wines right on its head.

Address PO Box 609, Greenock, South Australia, 5360 Tel +61 438 369 654
Email shobbrookwines@gmail.com

AUSTRALIA / MARGARET RIVER

Si Vintners

This first-generation winemaking couple (Sarah Morris and Iwo Jakimowicz) returned from winemaking experience in Spain to Margaret River, and by good fortune found a perfect old vineyard (planted 1978) for sale in 2010. Two white cuvées are made with skin contact, including the concrete-egg fermented Lello (semillon/sauvignon blanc) and Baba Yaga (sauvignon blanc with a smidge of cabernet sauvignon added for extra fruit lift). The wines are bursting with fruit and speak exuberantly of their terroir. The pair are also once more making wine in Spain, in Calatayud.

Address N/A Tel N/A Email info@sivintners.com

AUSTRALIA / VICTORIA

Momento Mori Wines

Kiwi Dane Johns cut his teeth working for various wineries across Australia. He cites the pivotal moment when he first drank a glass of Radikon as the inspiration to use skin contact. The first Momento Mori wine was made in an amphora buried in his back garden, but together with his wife Hannah, he's now acquired some old vineyards and built a small winery with four amphorae made from Australian clay. The subtle, featherweight Staring at the Sun blend is a surprise outcome for a three-month maceration, but shows the considerable talent of this winemaker. One to watch.

Address Gipsland Tel N/A Email momentomoriwines@gmail.com

Austria

Proximity to Slovenia and northern Italy has surely been a factor in developing Austrian winemakers' love for orange wines. The Schmecke das Leben group of five winemakers[85] based in Styria are in many ways the leaders, with over a decade of experience in extended maceration. Producers in every corner of this small, landlocked nation have added skin contact to their skillsets, with even the massive Domäne Wachau turning its hand to an amphora-fermented riesling.

Bernhard Ott is certainly one of the pioneers in Lower Austria (which includes Wachau) with a qvevri-fermented grüner veltliner which has been made every year since 2009. He is not included below, as this is the only such wine in his range. There are many excellent Austrian growers who produce a single orange wine, but this selection focuses on those who have specialised a little more.

---

85   Andreas Tscheppe, Sepp Muster, Strohmeier, Tauss, Werlitsch.

Arndorfer

In an amusing case of the tail wagging the dog, Martin and Anna Arndorfer were encouraged by their Danish importer to experiment with skin ferments. His hunch that the Kamptal region's loamy terroir could produce excellent orange wines appears to have paid off. The three wines in the Per Se line offer an excellent mini-masterclass in the characteristics of different varietals (müller-thurgau, grüner veltliner and neuburger in this case) made with maceration. The Per Se wines were first made in 2012. The Neuburger is the most successful in my opinion.

Address Weinbergweg 16, A-3491 Strass/Strassertal
Tel +43 6645 1570 44 Email info@ma-arndorfer.at

Winzerhof Landauer-Gisperg

Franz Landauer was inspired by Joško Gravner to acquire some Georgian qvevri, which he uses to make one white and one red blend. Amphorae Weiss is complex and thrilling stuff, sometimes exceeding quality levels of anything else produced at this winery, situated in the flatlands of the Thermenregion. The blend varies from year to year but is always rotgipfler-dominated. Franz's son Stef is increasingly taking control of the winemaking and has added the tasty skin-macerated traminer Wild to the range (fermented in stainless steel).

Address Badner Straße 32, A-2523 Tattendorf Tel +43 2253 8127 2
Email wein@winzerhof.eu

Loimer

Fred Loimer's operation is sizable, now including not just 30 hectares in Kamptal, but also parcels in Thermenregion and across Lower Austria. Vineyards from the last of these provide the fruit for his Mit ACHTUNG range of five orange wines, a style he's been producing since 2006. That experience and confidence is demonstrated in spades here – the Mit ACHTUNGs are varietally typical, elegant and rather moreish. The Gemischter Satz (traditional field blend) is particularly successful, with three to four weeks of skin contact subtly amplifying the texture and the fruit character.

Address Haindorfer Vögerlweg 23, A 3550 Langenlois Tel +43 2734 2239 0
Email weingut@loimer.at

Andert Wein

Brothers Michael and Erich Andert farm a 4.5 hectare parcel biodynamically, right on the Austro-Hungarian border. It's a proper farm, with hens, sheep, arable crops, production of cured meats and vermut into the bargain. "The vines always got the least attention, so they went a bit wild", Michael explains. After 14 years in business, the wines are gaining an international following. Their Pamhogna Weiss blend, Ruländer (pinot grigio) and the mysterious 'PM' all receive skin contact. They're vibrant and spicy, deserving more bottle age than the brother's release schedule allows. Some wines are bottled without sulphites, to my occasional consternation.

Address Lerchenweg 16, A-7152 Pamhagen **Tel** +43 680 55 15 472
Email michael@andert-wein.at

Claus Preisinger

Despite his youthful looks, Claus has been making wine a long time – since 2000, when he took on his dad's three-hectare estate. Now, there's an impressive modernist winery and the estate extends to 19 hectares. In 2009, Claus began fermenting white grapes in Georgian amphorae, and was one of the first Austrians to do so. There are now three oranges in the range, including the Edelgraben Grüner Veltliner and Weissburgunder. These are textural, exciting and hugely accomplished wines. Some trivia: Claus's partner is Susanne Renner, of Rennersistas fame.

Address Goldbergstrasse 60, A-7122 Gols **Tel** +43 2173 2592
Email wein@clauspreisinger.at

Gsellmann

Andreas Gsellmann was inspired by a visit to the Carso in 2010 to start using 14-day skin macerations, initially with the estate's traminer and pinot blanc. Since 2011 he macerates almost all white wines in the range, as he finds that this coaxes greater typicity from the varieties. Standouts include the Traminer, Chardonnay Exempel and Neuburger Exempel – but everything at this quality 21-hectare estate radiates purity, excitement and focus. Viticulture is biodynamic, but some vineyards are still in conversion and the estate has organic certification only.

Address Obere Hauptstrasse 38, 7122 Gols **Tel** +43 2173 2214
Email bureau@gsellmann.at

AUSTRIA / BURGENLAND
Gut Oggau

Originally from a winemaking family in Styria, Eduard Tscheppe and partner
Stephanie Eselböck moved to Oggau in 2007, to breathe new life into an old
estate comprising 14ha of vines and a massive beam press from 1820. Their
fictional family of wines (spanning three generations in ascending seniority and
complexity) have become much loved worldwide for their purity and joie de
vivre, as have the couple themselves. A proportion of Timoteus and Theodora
are skin fermented, while grandmother Mechtild rests entirely on her peels for
8–10 days. Since 2011, no sulphites have been used in any of the wines.

Address Hauptstrasse 31, A- 7063 Oggau Tel +43 664/2069298
Email office@gutoggau.at

AUSTRIA / BURGENLAND
Meinklang

One of Europe's largest biodynamically certified farms, the family-run,
border-straddling Meinklang extends to 700 hectares but only a small part
is under vine. Experiments with skin contact in white wines began in 2009,
as Niklas Peltzer explains: "We have good spiciness, fruit and depth but
sometimes miss texture and tightness, for that the skin fermentation gives
a great balance". Macerated wines now include the joyful Graupert Pinot Gris
and the more substantial Konkret, both fermented in concrete eggs. The
Graupert vineyard is completely unpruned, which surprisingly doesn't result
in chaos, but rather smaller grapes with more concentration.

Address Hauptstraße 86, A-7152 Pamhagen Tel +43 2174 2168-11
Email np@meinklang.at

AUSTRIA / BURGENLAND
Rennersistas

Stefanie and Susanne Renner make a range of natural wines under the
Rennersistas label, differentiated from the family's more classic Renner
line. Everything comes from the same 13-hectare vineyards around Gols.
Internships with Tom Lubbe (Matassa) and Tom Shobbrook provided
inspiration to use extended skin contact with all white grapes. The wines
have incredible vivaciousness and purity, plus possibly the cutest label ever.
Since 2016, the sisters manage the entire estate. Based on their first two
vintages (2015 and 2016), expect great things.

Address Obere Hauptstraße 97, 7122 Gols Tel +43 2173 2259
Email wein@rennerhelmuth.at

AUSTRIA / STYRIA

Ploder-Rosenberg

Fredi and Manuel Ploder were inspired by travels through Georgia to purchase several qvevris, which are now buried in front of their property. Four amber wines are produced, three fermented in qvevri and one in oak. Aero, a blend of sauvignon, traminer and gelber muskateller is always my favourite. Stylistically the amphora wines are hard to pin down, ranging from thrilling to occasionally a little bizarre. There is no faulting the passion and enthusiasm for innovation at this estate, which is also experimenting with a number of disease-resistant hybrid varieties (PIWIs).

Address Unterrosenberg 86, 8093 St. Peter a. O. Tel +43 3477 3234
Email office@ploder-rosenberg.at

AUSTRIA / STYRIA

Tauss

The smallest of the five Schmecke das Leben members (6ha) is going from strength to strength. Roland Tauss is a man of few words, but they are not needed if you're lucky enough to be in his cellar – the wines do the talking perfectly well. Grauburgunder, Sauvignon Blanc and Roter Traminer are macerated for around 10 days to create superbly differentiated, exciting wines. Sustainability runs through the whole estate, including the peaceful and very comfortable agriturismo, which includes a yoga studio and a solar-heated pool. Biodynamic since 2005.

Address Schloßberg 80, 8463 Leutschach Tel +43 3454 6715
Email info@weingut-tauss.at

AUSTRIA / STYRIA

Schnabel

This tiny estate (5ha) produces three tasty macerated bottlings – a chardonnay (known locally as morillon), rhine riesling and the Silicium blend of both, all with around 14 days of skin contact. The farm has been certified biodynamic since 2003, and the white grapes have always been skin fermented – the Schnabels find it creates additional complexity and livliness. Karl Schnabel's initial inspiration for winemaking came from visits to Burgundy in 1997 and 1998, and despite his relatively low profile internationally, he was probably one of the first to make orange wines and eschew the use of sulphur in Styria.

Address Maierhof 34, 8443 Gleinstätten Tel +43 3457 3643
Email weingut@karl-schnabel.at

AUSTRIA / STYRIA

Sepp Muster

Muster was inspired to start using long skin macerations after blind tasting Gravner's Breg 2001. Since 2005, he makes two orange wines, Gräfin and Erde. Gräfin is 100% sauvignon, left on its skins for 2–4 weeks, but my favourite is the more substantial Erde. A blend of 80% sauvignon and 20% chardonnay with six months skin contact in used oak barrels, plus further ageing in distinctive clay bottles. Sepp was won over by biodynamics during a visit to India in 1998. He is one of the linchpins behind the Schmecke das Leben group.

Address Schlossberg 38, 8463 Leutschach Tel +43 3454 70053
Email info@weingutmuster.at

AUSTRIA / STYRIA

Strohmeier

Health issues resulting from pesticide usage caused Franz and Christine Strohmeier to radically rethink their estate's direction a decade ago. No longer specialising in sparkling wines, they have been working biodynamically and completely without added sulphites since 2010. Their orange wines (initially labelled as Orange No. 1, Orange No. 2, etc) were inspired by other producers such as Sepp Muster, Radikon and Giorgio Clai. Wein der Stille is one of Styria's top macerated sauvignon blancs, a majestic wine with a full 12 months on the skins. Even if no longer the main event, the Sekts are also wonderful.

Address Lestein 148, 8511 St. Stefan o. Stainz Tel +43 6763 8324 30
Email office@strohmeier.at

AUSTRIA / STYRIA

Andreas Tscheppe

Possessing a wickedly dry humour, Andreas Tscheppe is deadly serious about his winemaking. As with his colleagues in the Schmecke das Leben group, vineyards are cultivated using biodynamic principles. Erdfass (Earth Barrel), produced since 2006, could be considered his nod to the Georgian qvevri tradition. A large barrel is buried underground during the winter, to benefit from the lifeforces below the surface. It's one of the greatest skin macerated wines on the planet, a massive riot of texture and flavour but beautifully balanced too. Schwalbenschwanz, his macerated gelber muskateller, is also exceptional.

Address Glanz, 8463 Leutschach Tel +43 3454 59861
Email office@at-weine.at

AUSTRIA / STYRIA
Werlitsch

Ewald Tscheppe shares a cellar with his brother Andreas but has his own high-trained vineyards. The estate's synonymous macerated Werlitsch cuvée is now labelled Glück, and the Amphorenwein which was originally made in qvevri (2007–10) is renamed as Freude. The latter spends a whole year with skins and stems and is perhaps the most powerful and structured orange wine made in the entire region. Tscheppe never really got comfortable with his qvevris, hence the move back to large barrels. For me, these two macerated gems often achieve greater consistency than the Ex Vero line.

Address Glanz 75, 8463 Leutschach **Tel** +43 3454 391
Email office@werlitsch.com

AUSTRIA / STYRIA
Winkler-Hermaden

A family estate with three generations working in the winery and its associated restaurant. Christof Winkler-Hermaden was inspired by Bernard Ott to purchase two Georgian qvevri in 2010, and the Gewürztraminer Orange was born in 2011. It's a superb effort, a six-month maceration with more balance and freshness than some of the later vintages. The qvevris were abandoned from 2013 in favour of stainless-steel fermentation, oak ageing and much shorter skin contact (about one month). A new wine Zunder was produced in 2016 with three days' skin contact. A vertical tasting affords a fascinating study in macerated traminers.

Address Schloss Kapfenstein, an der Schlösserstrasse, 8353 Kapfenstein 105
Tel +43 3157 2322 **Email** weingut@winkler-hermaden.at

Bosnia and Herzegovina

The predominantly Christian region of Herzegovina is this Balkan nation's winemaking stronghold, and it harbours the indigenous white gem žilavka. At the time of writing, the country only boasts one acknowledged natural winemaker who is profiled below, but mention should also be made of the winery Vinarija Škegro which added an excellent macerated žilavka to its otherwise more mainstream range in 2015.

There's a frustration that so much more could be happening in this country which is still split by ethnic tensions and hindered by the lack of a serious wine appreciation culture. As with most Balkan and Adriatic regions, skin maceration was the norm for whites and reds when wine was produced for home consumption.

BOSNIA AND HERZEGOVINA / MOSTAR

Brkić

It takes some balls to convert your vineyards to biodynamic farming in Bosnia, but that's what the audacious Josip Brkić initiated in 2007. Based in Čitluk in the heart of the country's Christian bible-belt (Medjugorje is nearby), he's one-of-a-kind in Bosnia for the moment. All three white wines are made with some skin maceration, a technique that his grandfather also used to help start fermentation. Mjesečar (or Moonwalker) is the highlight, an absolute gem showing indigenous žilavka's floral charm, but adding depth and complexity from the nine-month skin contact.

Address K. Tvrtka 9, Čitluk, 88260 **Tel** +387 36 644 466
Email brkic.josip@tel.net.ba

Bulgaria

Following disastrous land redistribution schemes post-communism, Bulgaria's wine industry is finally experiencing a resurgence. But mostly that has meant foreign investment, and rather old-fashioned ideas about super hi-tech wineries and new French *barriques* being the path to success. There's a small but growing clutch of producers working in a more authentic, artisanal way and, so far, just a couple of experiments with macerated white wines. The style doesn't appear to have any documented history here.

BULGARIA / THRACE

Rossidi

The dynamic and creatively garbed Edward Kourian has now made two vintages of what he terms "Bulgaria's only proper orange wine". Citing his influences as giants like Gravner and Radikon, he's very faithfully applied their hands-off methodology, first to chardonnay (2015) and then gewürztraminer (2016). These are good wines that really need time, so it's a shame that they are released so young. A larger Bulgarian producer, Villa Melnik, has also released a skin-contact sauvignon blanc, but it's a more watered-down affair – a sort of 'Orange-lite'.

Address Southern Industrial Zone, Sliven 8800 **Tel** +359 886 511080
Email info@rossidi.com

Canada

Who would have thought that Canada would be responsible for one of the world's first regional orange wine classifications? But it is, and the Ontario VQA for 'skin fermented white wine' is testament to a small but growing contingent of passionate growers who work in a sustainable fashion, with minimal intervention in vineyards and cellars. Thanks partly to climate change, Canada is no longer just home to hybrids and ice wine. Macerated white wines have no obvious pre-existing heritage, but the country's well-educated winemakers are taking to the technique from west (British Columbia) to east (Ontario), using both hybrids and more classic French varieties.

CANADA / BRITISH COLUMBIA

Okanagan Crush Pad

Christine Coletta imagined a small retirement project back in 2005, but her husband Steve had grander ideas. Their Okanagan Crush Pad now operates a "custom crush" business making wine for other labels, but also has its own "Haywire" line including several oranges – the lively Free Form (sauvignon blanc) and Wild Ferment, a pinot gris with eight months of skin contact. Kiwi winemaker Matt Dumayne has been at the helm since the beginning and utilises huge concrete tanks for fermentation and ageing. Some wines are bottled without added sulphur. Christine doesn't seem too miffed that she never got her retirement!

Address 16576 Fosbery Rd, Summerland, BC V0H 1Z6 **Tel** +1 250 494 4445 **Email** winery@okanagancrushpad.com

CANADA / BRITISH COLUMBIA/ONTARIO

Sperling Vineyards / Southbrook Vineyards

Ann Sperling's winemaking record in Canada goes back to the 1980s. She's also now working in Mendoza, Argentina. Fascinated by the idea of using all elements of the grape, including stems, she took inspiration from Gravner and Matassa and transplanted their techniques to Ontario. Her Orange Vidal from Southbrook in Niagara is a stunning, no-holds-barred tribute to the Collio style, while the Sperling Pinot Gris from Okanagan is shyer but every bit as brilliant. Both properties are farmed biodynamically, Southbrook is Demeter certified. Sperling was also the driving force behind the new Ontario skin fermented white wine VQA category.

Address 1405 Pioneer Road, Okanagan Valley, Kelowna, BC V1W 4M6 **Tel** +1 778 478 0260 **Email** a.sperling@sympatico.ca

CANADA / ONTARIO
Trail Estate

Purchased by retirees Anton and Hildegard Sproll in 2011, this innovative estate is now run by their children and winemaker/vineyard manager Mackenzie Brisbois. She's a fan of texture and started experimenting with skin maceration in 2015. Her skin-contact gewürztraminer has terrific precision, while the rather more bonkers ORNG with 355 days of maceration also emerges feeling restrained and not overdone. The gewürz is made in a more conventional fashion, with blocked malolactic fermentation and sterile filtering. I'm hoping for some wines that sit in-between these two extremes in the future.

Address 416 Benway Road, Hillier Tel +1 647 233 8599
Email alex@trailestate.com

Croatia

Although skin fermenting white wines was once the norm in all parts of Croatia, the modern tradition has coalesced in Istria, where malvazija istarska (literally Istrian malvasia) has proven that it takes to extended maceration like a duck to water. Istria has the greatest sophistication when it comes to both food and wine, and the Italian influence is clear to see. The Croatian Uplands focuses on white wine production, but producers rarely scale the heights of their Istrian neighbours.

Properly Mediterranean, southern Dalmatia has always been more focused on red grapes, however there are pockets of interest for the maceration lovers, and many rare native grape varieties to explore. Wine producing islands abound all down Croatia's abundant coastline, often harbouring not just precious rare grape cultivars but also older, more rustic wine traditions. Korčula, Vis, Hvar and Brač are the most important for wine.

CROATIA / ISTRIA
Benvenuti

A small, long-established estate situated in the inordinately pretty mountain village of Kaldir (looking over the valley to Motovun). Brothers Alfred and Nikola make two very fine malvazijas, one conventional and the other (Anno Domini) fermented on the skins for 15 days. The latter is a great example of how the variety works so well with maceration, intensifying its character and creating a rich, satisfying wine.

Address Kaldir 7, 52424 Motovun Tel +385 98 197 56 51
Email info@benvenutivina.com

 **CROATIA** / ISTRIA
Clai

After nearly 40 years working in Trieste as a restaurateur, Giorgio Clai decided to follow his dream to move back home and make wine. The first commercial vintage was 2002, and since then Clai has set the benchmark for Istrian natural wines. He's adamant that he just makes the wines he likes to drink, and that means skin maceration during the entire fermentation for the two whites, the formidable Sveti Jakov with malvazija and the Ottocento blend. Following a spate of ill health, he's now assisted in the winery and the vineyards by the very able Dimitri Brečević (see Piquentum).

Address Brajki 105, Karstica, 52460 Buje **Tel** +385 91 577 6364
Email info@clai.hr

 CROATIA / ISTRIA
Kabola

Kabola is one of very few Croatian wineries to have made the extra effort to gain organic certification, which garners my respect. Their amphora-fermented and aged malvazija is also unique in the region. Spending seven months on the skins, it's a substantial, structured effort that still has plenty to say about the grape variety. It's been a reliable fixture over a number of years and thus is worth mentioning here – even though the rest of the winery's output is more conventional. The winery is very scenically situated – a visit is recommended. The amphorae are buried outdoors.

Address Kanedolo 90, Momjan, 52460 Buje **Tel** +385 52 779 208
Email info@kabola.hr

 **CROATIA** / ISTRIA
Piquentum

Raised and trained as a winemaker in France, but with Croatian heritage, Dimitri Brečević returned to his father's homeland in 2006 to set up his own winery. His Piquentum winery is situated in a 1930s bunker built by the Italians as a water storage facility. Struggling to get his white wine fermentations going naturally, he realised after observing family and colleagues that using the skins was key. His Piquentum Blanc (the estate's only white wine, 100% malvazija) has been made with a few days of maceration ever since. Since 2016, Dimitri has also made the wine at Giorgio Clai.

Address Cesta Sveti.Ivan, Buzet 52420 Croatia **Tel** +385 95 5150 468
Email dimitri.brecevic@wanadoo.fr

CROATIA / ISTRIA

Roxanich

Mladen Rožanić created this estate in 2003, with the stated aim of focusing on traditional varieties and traditional winemaking. All white wines are macerated, for periods of up to 180 days (Antica Malvazija). The Ines u Bijelom ('Ines in white') blend of eight varieties is perhaps Roxanich's outstanding wine, made with 100 days of maceration. Its lively fruit and expansive character are perennially crowd-pleasing. The Milva chardonnay is also recommended. Wines are aged for six years before release. Some varietal bottlings are made for earlier release, typically with two days of maceration.

Address 52446 Nova Vas, Kosinožići 26 **Tel** +385 91 6170 700
Email info@roxanich.hr

CROATIA / PLEŠIVICA

Tomac

Tomislav Tomac has transformed this 5.5 hectare family winery into its current and innovative form. Following a trip to Georgia, he and his father installed six qvevris which have been used since 2007. Berba and Chardonnay are both excellent, but most unique is the Tomac Brut Amphora, produced from a hotchpotch of ancient local varieties plus some chardonnay, fermented and macerated for six months in amphorae, oak aged for a further 18 months and then finally bottled for its second fermentation. After all that, it emerges utterly fresh, lively and intriguing. Impressive.

Address Donja Reka 5, 10450 Jastrebarsko **Tel** +385 1 6282 617
Email tomac@tomac.hr

CROATIA / DALMATIA

Boškinac

This winery off the coast of northern Dalmatia is worthy of mention for a local curiosity, the gegić grape variety, which only grows on the island of Pag. Boškinac makes not only a fresh version but also a traditional macerated bottling, Ocu, which is macerated for 21 days and aged one year in oak. It's a fascinating link back to a style of wine that Boris's father remembers very well, and thus a historical gem. And a tasty one, too.

Address Škopaljska Ulica 220, 53291 Novalja – Island of Pag
Tel +385 53 663 500 **Email** info@boskinac.com

Vinarija Križ

It's very unusual to find the rare grk grape variety outside its native home on the island of Korčula, and even more so to find it skin fermented. Denis Bogoević Marušić dubs himself 'modernity' and his weather-beaten father Mile 'tradition'. It's a combination that seems to work well, and this orange grk (the micro-estate's only white wine) stays true to its rich, honeyed character with the skin contact adding texture and depth. The family has a serious commitment to sustainability, being one of the first in the region to achieve organic certification. They're also members of the Slow Food movement.

Address OPG Denis Bogoević Marušić, Prizdrina 10, 20244 Potomje
Tel +385 91 211 6974 **Email** vinarija.kriz@gmail.com

Czech Republic

There's a fast-growing scene of alternative young producers based in Moravia, the country's largest and most important wine growing region, which borders Austria and Slovakia (part of the same country until the split in 1993). Given its proximity to Austria, the popularity of varieties such as grüner veltliner, müller-thurgau and welschriesling is no surprise. Resistant crosses and hybrids are also popular in a country which is at the northern limits, at least classically, for grape ripening. It is interesting to note that both growers listed here were inspired by Aleš Kristančič (Movia)

CZECH REPUBLIC / MORAVIA

Dobrá Vinice

Who would suspect that a first-generation winemaking couple from Moravia now have their wines in three of London's Michelin-starred restaurants? But this is what Petr and Andrea Nejedlík have achieved, after being inspired by a visit to Aleš Kristančič of Movia in 2000. Their two qvevri-fermented whites, produced since 2012, are impressive wines, combining structure, freshness and fruit purity. It's a very worthy homage to Joško Gravner, who inspired the move to amphorae. Vineyards are on the edge of the Podyjí national park, a forested area with a mix of sandy, granite and limestone soils.

Address Do Říčan 592, Praha 9, 190 11 **Tel** +420 724 026 350
Email dv@dobravinice.cz

CZECH REPUBLIC / MORAVIA

Nestarec

Milan Nestarec studied with Aleš Kristančič before starting to make wine with the eight hectares his father planted in 2001. His Antica wines walk on the wild side, with long macerations (up to six months) and no sulphur additions. The range and the style seem to be evolving, but the staples of the macerated range are Tramin (aka gewürztraminer) and the charmingly named Podfuck (pinot grigio). Nestarec is a risk taker, and some vintages have been more successful than others, but he is definitely one to watch.

Address Pod Prednima 350, 691 02, Velke Bilovice **Tel** +420 775 072 624
Email m.nestarec@seznam.cz

France

Some may be surprised at the paucity of French producers listed here. While the south of France has long had a tradition of making rustic wines with maceration for the table, there is no obvious orange wine tradition in the north. In the south, there's no shortage of wineries making a single macerated wine, but there are few real experts. Furthermore, the relative lack of acidity in some of the south's most popular white varieties (grenache blanc, marsanne, rousanne) can make it challenging to produce a balanced and palatable macerated wine.

A number of producers in the Loire, Savoie and Jura use oxidative ageing as a deliberate component in their white wines. This is often confused with skin maceration but is stylistically different. Seminal Sancerre grower Sébastien Riffault is a good example, although he recently added a properly skin-macerated wine to his otherwise oxidatively produced range.

FRANCE / ALSACE

Laurent Bannwarth

Stéphane Bannwarth's fascination with qvevris began with a visit to Georgia in 2007. Sensing that this was the perfect way to make wine with the least possible intervention, and the logical next step on from biodynamics, he set about buying eight qvevris – a process that took four years before they were delivered! Their range of precise, delicious qvevri wines, including the wonderful Synergie blend, has now been joined by two macerated white wines not made in qvevri (Red Bild and La Vie en Rose). More qvevris are also on the way. These guys have well and truly got the orange wine bug.

Address 9 route du Vin, Rue Principale, Obermorschwihr, 68420
Tel +33 389 493 087 Email laurent@bannwarth.fr

FRANCE / ALSACE

Le Vignoble du Rêveur

The vineyard of the dreamer (to translate) is the precious plot inherited by Mathieu Deiss (son of the famous Marcel Deiss) from his grandfather. Now rejuvenated and converted to biodynamic agriculture, it provides the material for Deiss's experimental and often thrilling series of wines, some of which are fermented in amphora. Top picks include the amphora-fermented gewürztraminer (Une Instant sur Terre) and Singulier, a carbonic fermentation of riesling and pinot gris. The varietal precision and focus show a decidedly Alsatian twist on orange wines. One to watch.

Address 2 Rue de la Cave, Bennwihr, 68630 Tel +33 389 736 337
Email contact@vignoble-reveur.fr

Recrue des Sens

Judging by the constant price increases, Yann Durieux might be suffering from over-hype. But then again, quantities are minuscule, and this is a problem all over Burgundy. Les Ponts Blanc, one of three macerated whites, takes aligote and skin ferments it for two weeks. It's a sensational reading of the variety, full of elegance and poise and just that little bit more complexity and grip. The youthful, dreadlocked Durieux worked at Domaine Prieuré-Roch before creating his domaine in 2010. His vineyards are a stone's throw from Domaine de la Romanée-Conti, which certainly won't help the price situation!

Address 11 Rue des Vignes, 21220 Messanges Tel +33 380 625 064 Email N/A

FRANCE / SAVOIE

Jean-Yves Péron

Péron's wines have achieved cult success. He's pretty much one of a kind in the Savoie, having chosen to use whole bunch fermentation for all of his white and red wines since the first vintage in 2004. He cultivates small plots of indigenous varieties such as jacquère and altesse. Côtillon des Dames is one for the acid-freaks but it achieves an impressive level of complexity given some age, and it is pretty much immortal. Les Barrieux is slightly more full-bodied due to the rousanne in the blend. Péron favours fairly oxidative winemaking and typically bottles without added sulphur.

Address N/A Tel +33 683 585121 Email domaine.peron@gmail.com

FRANCE / LANGUEDOC

Domaine Turner Pageot

Emmanuel Pageot has been using orange wine techniques, as he terms them, for a decade, making him one of the pioneers in the region. His Les Choix is 100% marsanne with about five weeks of skin contact. It's a big, muscly wine that demands air and bottle age to show its best. Emmanuel also uses a proportion of macerated grapes in both Le Blanc (a wonderful and complex blend of rousanne and marsanne) and his exceptional sauvignon blanc Le Rupture. Viticulture is uncertified biodynamic, including the use of herbal tisanes in place of conventional sprays.

Address 1 & 3 Avenue de la Gare, 34320 Gabian Tel +33 6 77 40 14 32
Email contact@turnerpageot.com

Matassa

New Zealander Tom Lubbe created this estate together with consultant Sam Harrop in 2002, following a stint working at nearby Domaine Gauby. One suspects that Harrop's insistence on filtering the wines may not have been in line with the winery's eventual direction as Matassa has since become iconic in natural wine circles. Two muscat-based wines are made with maceration: Cuvée Alexandria (35 days maceration) and Cuvée Marguerite. There's no doubt that these wines come from a hot climate, however their typically salty tang adds all important freshness.

Address 2 Place de l'Aire, 66720 Montner Tel +33 468 641 013
Email matassa@orange.fr

Georgia

It would have been quite possible to list 100 commercial producers of qvevri wine in this book, had space permitted. That figure is incredible when one considers that just five years ago, there were less than half this number making or bottling qvevri wines. There is a certain amount of bandwagon jumping, as former grape growers or even just entrepreneurs realise there's a gravy train about to depart. I've selected a mixture of the most iconic and established producers, the true pioneers who mentored so many others, plus some of the most promising newcomers.

Winemaking during the Soviet era was concentrated in Kakheti and phased out in many other regions. Growers are now slowly starting to expand back into some of the Western areas such as Guria, Samagrelo and Adjara, but for the time being production of white grapes (and thus amber wines) is still centred around Kakheti, and to a more limited extent in central Kartli and western Imereti.

I have no qualms about listing a select few of Georgia's larger wineries as their qvevri ranges are excellent, often well priced and much easier to track down than some of the more boutique outfits.

Georgia's Ministry of Agriculture has introduced an official qvevri wine classification from the 2018 vintage. Sadly, the classification does not enforce any form of traditional winemaking, requiring only that the wine is fermented in the qvevri, with or without skins and with or without yeast or other additions. Still, it is a clear sign that qvevris are part of Georgia's future, not just its past.

GEORGIA / SAMEGRELO AND IMERETI

Vino M'artville

Grower Nika Partsvania and winemaker Zaza Gagua created this estate in a part of Georgia where wine production had almost totally ceased post-USSR. As well as championing their indigenous ojaleshi (a red variety), they're also making some interesting qvevri wines from fruit grown in neighbouring Imereti. So far, a tsolikouri-krakhuna blend has been most successful, but time will tell. Since 2014, they have been planting new vineyards in Samegrelo. The first vintage was 2012, and vineyard holdings are 0.5 hectare at the moment.

Address Martvili Municipality, Village Targameuli Tel +995 599 372 411
Email vinomartville@gmail.com

GEORGIA / IMERETI

Ének Peterson

This slight 23-year-old musician from Boston in the USA (but somehow with a Hungarian first name) travelled to Georgia in 2014 and never managed to board the return flight home. Familiar to regulars at Ghvino Underground, where she works behind the bar, she's now making her own qvevri wines with great precision and sensitivity. The first vintage was 2016 and includes a tsolikouri-krakhuna blend made two ways, with and without skin contact. Perhaps it shouldn't come as a surprise to learn that the skin contact version is the more successful!

Address Fersati, Imereti Tel +995 599 50 64 27
Email enek.peterson@gmail.com

GEORGIA / IMERETI

Nikoladzeebis Marani / I am Didimi

Ramaz Nikoladze is one of the cornerstones of Georgia's burgeoning natural wine scene. Co-founder of Tbilisi's first natural wine bar Ghvino Underground, and president of the Georgian chapter of Slow Food, he's been there since the beginning of the qvevri renaissance. Nikoladze's wines are the real deal – good, honest qvevri winemaking, often with long skin macerations more akin to Kakheti than Imereti. Until 2015, the wines were made in qvevri buried under the stars. Now he's upgraded to a basic winery, with running water and electricity. Ramaz also now makes the wines for his elderly father-in-law Didimi Maghlakelidze.

Address Village of Nakhshirghele near Terjola Tel +995 551 944841
Email georgianslowfood@yahoo.com

Gotsa

Winemaking was always in Beka Gotsadze's family, but communism stamped it out. In 2010 he decided to cease working as an architect and created his winery on the site of the family's summerhouse in Kartli. Gotsa focuses on traditional varieties, such as tsolikouri, tsitska and khikvi, of which there are a total of 15 in his vineyards. After some inconsistencies in the early vintages, the wines at this estate are starting to be really accomplished. My top pick is the Tsolikouri, but the Rkatsiteli-Mtsvane blend is also recommended.

Address G. Tabidze str, village Kiketi, Tbilisi **Tel** +995 599 509033
Email bgotsa@gmail.com

GEORGIA / KARTLI

Iago's Wine

Iago Bitarishvili has earned his nickname 'The Chinuri Master'. He's devoted his winemaking solely to Kartli's indigenous gem. Bitarishvili's father made modern-style wines and was apparently furious when Iago produced his first skin-contact qvevri wine in 2008. Moral support came from a friend who told him, "your grandfather made wine like this!" Iago makes chinuri both with and without skin contact (both in qvevri). It's a fascinating opportunity to compare and contrast – both are peerless wines in their purity and structure. He actively promotes Georgia's qvevri wine culture and organises the new wine festival in Tbilisi every year.

Address Chardakhi, Mtskheta 3318 **Tel** +995 599 55 10 45
Email chardakhi@gmail.com

GEORGIA / KARTLI

Marina Kurtanidze

Marina Kurtanidze's Mandili Mtsvane is an absolute joy, showing the wonderful aromatics of this variety but keeping its prodigious tannins under control. This wine was the first commercially produced in Georgia by a woman, when it was first released in 2012. Fruit is bought in, but from a trusted source with low yields. She also happens to be Iago Bitarishvili's wife, making this one of the Georgian qvevri scene's real power couples.

Address Chardakhi, Mtskheta 3318 **Tel** +995 599 55 10 45
Email chardakhi@gmail.com

Alaverdi Monastery *"Since 1011"*

Although there's been a monastery on this site since well before 1011, dark times consumed the premises and put a stop to the winemaking for centuries. The cellar was rebuilt and started operating again in 2006, with financial and expert support from the Badagoni winery. The head winemaker is Father Gerasim, a monk who had always had a calling to make wine. These are some of the greatest traditional Kakhetian wines, often tannic and impenetrable in youth but always worth the wait. A more mass-produced line labelled Alaverdi Tradition is made from bought-in fruit and sold by Badagoni.

Address 42.032497°N 45.377108°E (Zema Khodasheni-Alaverdi-Kvemo Alvani)
Tel +995 595 1011 99 **Email** mail@since1011.com

Gvymarani

Georgia is full of surprises. Yulia Zhdanova was born in Russia, trained as a winemaker in Moscow and France, and now has a day job at a very high-profile winery in Ribera del Duero. But having spent some of her childhood in Georgia, she fell in love with the country and has created her own side project in Kakheti. She specialises just in mtsvane from the village of Manavi. It's extremely good too, imposing and made in a very traditional style without compromises. The first vintage was 2013.

Address Tsichevdavi Village, GG19 **Tel** N/A **Email** info@gvymarani.com

Kerovani

Archil Natsvlishvili is a young software developer who started making wine as a hobby in 2013. Together with winemaker cousin Ilya Bezhashvili, the pair were able to pool a few small parcels of vineyard redistributed by the local government and have built a dedicated qvevri cellar. The old vineyards are not planted as mono-varietals, so Kerovani vinifies their output as a field blend. I prefer their scented, structured pure rkatsiteli so far. As Archil says about his return to the land, "It's a cry of blood!"

Address D. Agmashenebeli 18, Signaghi **Tel** +995 599 40 84 14
Email ilya_bezhashvili@yahoo.com

Niki Antadze

Antadze is one of the pioneers of Georgia's qvevri renaissance and has been rescuing interesting old vineyards and making qvevri wine since 2006. His rkatsiteli and mtsvane are textbook examples of traditional Kakhetian qvevri wines, with depth and complexity but also an unhampered rustic charm. A collaboration with Jura-born Laura Seibel produced two vintages of the more experimental Tsigani Gogo and Mon Caucasien.

Address Sagarejo District Village Manavi **Tel** +995 599 63 99 58
Email nikiantadze@gmail.com

Okros Wines

Based in Sighnaghi (along with Pheasant's Tears and many others), John Okruashvili's operation had humble beginnings when he decided to return to his homeland in 2004, abandoning a career in technology that had taken him to the UK and Iraq. From the first production of a few hundred litres in 2004, he now owns 4.5 hectares of vines and makes a range of wines from rkatsiteli, mtsvane, tsolikouri and saperavi. Comparing the 2016 mtsvane bottlings with and without skin contact provided a clear demonstration that no sulphur winemaking is much safer with the skins included.

Address 7 Chavchavadze Street, Sighnaghi **Tel** +995 551 622228
Email info@okroswines.com

Orgo / Telada

Orgo is the personal project of one of Kakheti's most established qvevri winemakers. Giorgi Dakishvili has been head winemaker at Schuchmann Wines/Vinoterra since its inception, and established his personal winery just a stone's throw away in 2010. Dakishvili is a superbly accomplished qvevri winemaker, and it shows in these beautifully judged efforts, made from the family's own eight hectares of vines. Totally estate grown and bottled is still very rare in Georgia. Rkatsiteli receives the whole six-month treatment in qvevri, but without stems. A sparkling mtsvane and saperavi are also produced. Telada was the original brand name.

Address Kisiskhevi, Telavi **Tel** +995 577 50 88 70
Email g.dakishvili@schuchmann-wines.com

GEORGIA / KAKHETI
Our Wine

Founded by five friends as the Prince Makashvili Cellar in 2003, then later renamed to Our Wine, this iconic label and its driving force, the late Soliko Tsaishvili, is truly one of the pioneers of the new qvevri era. The initial motivation was merely to be able to drink good quality traditional Georgian wines, which were albeit unavailable in Tbilisi at the time. The collective produces mainly rkatsiteli and saperavi from a number of vineyard parcels which are worked organically and increasingly biodynamically. The wines are expertly made in a no-holds-barred Kakhhetian style.

Address Bakurtsikhe Village **Tel** +995 599 117 727
Email chvenigvino@hotmail.com

GEORGIA / KAKHETI
Pheasant's Tears

The story of how American painter John Wurdeman came to Georgia and was persuaded to found a winery (in 2007) with grower Gela Patalishvili is now the stuff of legend. Pheasant's Tears has evolved into a significant operation, boasting a winery and multiple restaurants in Sighnaghi and Tbilisi. Wines are made in an ultra-traditional manner, with fruit from Kakheti, Kartli and Imereti. Sometimes quality control seems to be strained over such a distributed organisation and wines can vary from sensational to occasionally rather rustic. Still, Georgia owes a huge debt to Wurdeman in his role as unofficial cultural ambassador.

Address 18 Baratashvili Street, Sighnaghi 4200 **Tel** +995 599 53 44 84
Email jwurdeman@pheasantstears.com

GEORGIA / KAKHETI
Satrapezo (Telavi Wine Cellar)

Satrapezo is the boutique qvevri line of Telavi Wine Cellar (aka Marani), one of Georgia's largest wine producers. Excellent qvevri wines have been produced since 2004, although interestingly the pre-existing winery, which was acquired by Marani in 1997, was one of very few that specialised in qvevri wines during the Soviet era. Its vast qvevri cellar has capacity for up to 75,000 litres. A generous Mtsvane is particularly worthy of praise, although traditionalists may grumble as it's partly aged in oak after a traditional qvevri fermentation.

Address Kurdgelauri. 2200. Telavi **Tel** +995 350 27 3707
Email marani@marani.co

GEORGIA / KAKHETI

Shalauri Wine Cellar

Shalauri was created in 2013 by David Buadze and friends, with the aim of specialising in traditional winemaking with only qvevri wines being produced. The winery is located near the village of the same name. Their Mtsvane has been worthy of note in both 2014 and 2015, as a no-holds-barred Kakhetian style, with considerable structure and complexity. So far, I'm less enamoured with the Rkatsiteli, but it is early days. The first vintages were made with bought in fruit, but two hectares of vineyards with rkatsiteli, mtsvane, kisi and saperavi have been planted.

Address 2200 Shalauri Village, Telavi Tel +995 571 19 98 89
Email shalauricellar1@gmail.com

GEORGIA / KAKHETI

Tbilvino

Brothers Giorgi and Zura Margvelashvili bought this near-bankrupt winery in 1998 and have grown it into one of Georgia's largest producers. Although most of their output is western-style wines, a small but growing range of traditionally made qvevri wines has been produced since 2010. Tbilvino has the distinction of getting a rkatsiteli with six months of skin contact onto the shelves of UK supermarket Marks and Spencer. In terms of bang-for-buck, their qvevri wines are simply unbeatable. Production of the qvevri line is about 75,000 bottles (from a total of 4 million).

Address 2 David Sarajishvili Avenue, Tbilisi Tel +995 265 16 25
Email levani@tbilvino.ge

GEORGIA / KAKHETI

Vinoterra (Schuchmann Wines)

Schuchmann Wines was created by German industrialist and investor Burkhard Schuchmann in 2008. Giorgi Dakishvili has worked as head winemaker since the start, incorporating his existing winery Vinoterra (which makes traditional qvevri styles) into Schuchmann as a sub-brand. There is nothing second-rate about the Vinoterra line, and their pricing and availability worldwide has made the genre significantly more accessible. Some wines, such as the Saperavi, are aged in oak after their passage in qvevri, which may not suit all tastes. Their Kisi and Mtsvane can be exceptional with age. Production of qvevri wines now exceeds 300,000 bottles per year.

Address Village Kisiskhevi 2200 Telavi Tel +995 7 90 557045
Email info@schuchmann-wines.com

GEORGIA / KAKHETI

Viti Vinea

This is the label of Temuri and Daviti Dakishvili, Gogi Dakishvili's sons. Their first vintage was produced in 2010, and the range includes an outstanding kisi made in the tradition Kakhetian manner. It could be said that Viti Vinea and Orgo blend slightly into one – the family's vineyards are the source for all the fruit, and the wines are made in the same winery. The sons have definitely benefitted from their dad's peerless winemaking skills and experience – it'll be great to see them blossom.

Address Village Shalauri, Telavi District 2200 **Tel** (+995) 577 50 80 29
Email info@vitavinea.ge

GEORGIA / KAKHETI AND KARTLI

Doremi

This *marani* located just outside Tbilisi was created in 2013 by three friends (Giorgi Tsirgvava, Mamuka Tsiklauri and Gabriel). Organically grown fruit is sourced from Kartli and Kakheti. Winemaking is non-interventionist, with no additions or filtration. The pure, aromatic qualities of their Kisi, Rkatsiteli and Khikhvi are a great demonstration of what is possible with attention to detail, and great fruit. The labels feature wonderful hand drawn designs which were created by Giorgi's wife.

Address Gamargveba village, near Tbilisi **Tel** +995 14 44 91
Email doremiwine@yahoo.com

GEORGIA / KAKHETI AND KARTLI

Papari Valley

Nukri Kurdadze purchased his first vineyards in 2004, but only started bottling his own qvevri wines in 2015. He clearly knows a thing or two about it. His Rkatsiteli and Rkatsiteli-Chinuri blend are two of the most precise, thrilling young qvevri wines I've yet tasted. The vineyards are on a steep exposition and look out onto a breathtaking view of the Caucasus mountains. The cellar is built on three descending terraces, each with qvevris, allowing wines to pass through initial fermentation and then ageing via gravity.

Address Village Akhasheni, Gurjaani Municipality **Tel** +995 599 17 71 03
Email nkurdadze@gmail.com

GEORGIA / KAKHETI AND IMERETI

Monastery Wines (Khareba)

This huge property, which manages 745 hectares of vines, has made qvevri wines since 2010, under the label Monastery Wines. The name reflects the original use of the building which is now used as a winery. The labels are terrible, but the wines are very good, and traditionally made. Mtsvane (from fruit grown in Kakheti) is particularly recommended, Tsitska (Imereti) is made according to Imereti's traditions with only 50% on the skins. The range comprises a total of nine wines.

Address D. Agmashenebeli 6 km, Tbilisi Tel +995 595 80 88 83
Email info@winerykhareba.com

GEORGIA / KAKHETI AND TBILISI

Bina N37

Installing 43 qvevris on the terrace of an 8th-floor apartment in the middle of Tbilisi sounds pretty nuts. And it is, but somehow ex-medical doctor Zura Natroshvili has made it a reality and opened a restaurant on the premises into the bargain. Trucking in fruit from Kakheti and then winching it up to the 8th floor doesn't sound ideal, but his first vintage (Rkatsiteli 2015) offers a typical, enjoyable qvevri wine. Saperavi was less successful. Just in case this doesn't sound bonkers enough, a further nine qvevris in larger sizes are installed nearby at his brother's house.

Address Apartment N37, Mgaloblishvili street N5a, Tbilisi 0160
Tel +995 599 280 000 Email zurab.i.natroshvili@gmail.com

GEORGIA / VARIOUS

Lagvinari

Making your first vintage (2011) in collaboration with Isabelle Legeron MW is quite an entrance. Ex-cardio-anaesthesiologist Dr Eko Glonti brought a lifelong fascination with geology, and a clear commitment to organic viticulture to the table. Working with local farmers, he's revitalised parcels of vines in every corner of Georgia, and produced sensational Krakhuna, Tsolikouri and Aladasturi (to name but three). Glonti is without doubt one of the country's most considered and articulate winemakers.

Address Upper Bakurtsikhe, Kakheti 1501 Tel +995 5 77 546006
Email info@lagvinari.com

Germany

Of all the major European wine nations, Germany has shown itself to be the most conservative and slowest to embrace the movement towards less intervention in winemaking, and thus also for orange wines. There's a small niche in Franconia, where some producers macerate silvaner. So far, I have not been blown away by the results, so the solitary listing here is for a truly exceptional wine from further west.

Germany's most important white variety riesling is a tricky customer when it comes to maceration. In its best-known guise, as found in the classic sweet and off-dry wines from the Mosel, malolactic fermentation is avoided or even blocked, to ensure that the familiar aromatics and acidic drive remain. Traditionally skin-fermented riesling will have both a higher fermentation temperature and increased likelihood that it undergoes full malolactic fermentation, mutating into a more substantial style that not all winemakers (or their customers) appreciate.

GERMANY / PFALZ

Eymann

Vincent Eymann has developed a particular way of producing his tasty skin fermented gewürztraminer. It's aged in a solera system after four to six weeks of skin contact, so the current release (MDG #3) contains wine from three years. This is a very clever technique to get around the ageing problem, so even though the wines are released young, their complexity and drinkability is excellent. The first bottling was 2014.

Address Ludwigstraße 35, D-67161 Gönnheim Tel +49 6322 2808
Email info@weinguteymann.de

Italy

Since the late 1990s, Italy's winemakers have returned to skin maceration by storm, fanning out from the north-east to cover every corner of the country. Friuli Collio and the Carso still have the strongest, most confident traditions, and remain almost the only part of the country where it's common to find a winemaker who makes exclusively macerated whites. However, with its aromatic malvasia di candia, Emilia-Romagna is beginning to challenge that dominance, as are the central regions of Lazio, Umbria and Tuscany. Native white varieties are relatively thin on the ground, but what bonds most of central Italy together is trebbiano di Toscana (often under a plethora of local synonyms) – a neutral variety that has nonetheless proved its worth time and time again in macerated styles.

Sicily and Sardinia both seem to cultivate and foster single-minded and highly individual winemakers, making them fertile grounds for natural and thus orange wine producers.

There's a fairly obvious divide between Italy's larger, more corporate producers – especially those in big ticket areas such as Barolo or Chianti – and smaller, artisanal or family outfits. The bigger wineries have barely dipped a toe in the amber waters of maceration, perhaps because it tends to make DOC and DOCG classification much harder to obtain. Italian wine law often enshrines colour, flavour and aromatic profiles of regional wines into the *disciplinari* which form the regulations, and this inevitably results in many orange wines being downgraded to theoretically less prestigious classifications such as IGP[86] or even the basic table wine category Vino Bianco, which doesn't permit either year or grape variety to appear on the label.

---

86 Indicazione di Origine Protettiva, often still referred to as IGT (Indicazione Geografica Tipica)

ITALY / PIEDMONT

Cascina degli Ulivi

Stefano Bellotti has championed biodynamic agriculture since converting his farm in 1984. He's also brought wine back into the frame – Cascina degli Ulivi had a mere one hectare of vines remaining when he began working in 1977. Skin maceration is used in several white wines, notably A Demûa which is made from an intriguing blend of timorasso, verdea, bosco, moscatella and riesling. Bellotti appears at length in Jonathan Nossiter's 2015 film *Natural Resistance*. He's one of natural wine's more compelling orators, and a true proponent of community values.

Address Strada della Mazzola, 12 Tel +39 0143 744598
Email info@cascinadegliulivi.it

ITALY / PIEDMONT

Tenuta Grillo

Guido and Igiea Zampaglione have 17 hectares of vines in Monferrato, plus another 2.5 hectares of fiano in Campania (Il Tufiello). Guido is a fan of very long maceration times, usually between 45 and 60 days. He's also one of the very few who actually release wines when they're properly ready. Their wine Baccabianca's current vintage is 2010, and it's certainly built to last with super cortese structure and herbal complexity. My current favourite is the fiano from their Il Tufiello estate, bottled as Montemattina and made in the same way as the Piedmontese wines. It's zesty, and packed with typical character.

Address 15067 Novi Ligure Tel +39 339 5870423 Email info@tenutagrillo.it

ITALY / TRENTINO ALTO ADIGE

Eugenio Rosi

Rosi is one of 10 artisan winemakers in Trentino who together make up the I Dolomitici group. After gaining experience in local cooperative cellars, he commenced his own project in 1997 with two hectares of rented vineyards. The nosiola-heavy white blend Anisos has wonderful texture, freshness and precision. Nosiola is becoming an increasing focus at the estate, as older chardonnay and pinot bianco vineyards are replanted. Viticulture is uncertified organic.

Address Palazzo Demartin Via 3 novembre, 7 38060 Calliano
Tel +39 333 3752583 Email rosieugenio.viticoltore@gmail.com

ITALY / TRENTINO ALTO ADIGE
Foradori

Starting with her first vintage in 1984, the elfin Elisabetta Foradori has an extra-ordinary record of achievement and innovation. She initially focused on improving the biodiversity of Trentino's indigenous teroldego. In 2002 she converted the 28-hectare estate to biodynamic agriculture, and in 2008 she discovered the joys of fermenting in amphorae. Like COS, she uses small Spanish tinajas. Fontanasanta Nosiola, first made in 2009, is extraordinary for its elegance and delicacy, demonstrating the perfection of clay for long skin contact. It has been joined by a manzoni bianco and a pinot grigio, both also made with skin contact.

Address Via Damiano Chiesa, 1 38017 Mezzolombardo **Tel** +39 0461 601046
Email info@elisabettaforadori.com

ITALY / TRENTINO ALTO ADIGE
Pranzegg

Martin Gojer took over this estate in 2008, and promptly converted it to biodynamic agriculture. His dramatic terraced vineyards are high-trained using the pergola system, a decision that surely comes from experience – he used to work for Simonit & Sirch, perhaps the world's premier (and only?) vine pruning consultancy. White blends Tonsur and Caroline are made with a major proportion of the grapes fermenting on the skins, while GT is a skin-macerated gewürztraminer. The wines have the purity and focus of great Alto Adige, plus the extra added power that skin contact brings to the mix.

Address Kampenner Weg 8, via campegno 8, 39100 Bozen
Tel +39 328 4591961 **Email** info@pranzegg.com

ITALY / VENETO
Costadilà

Ernesto Cattel was one of the first to re-popularise *col fondo*, the ancestrale style of prosecco made with a natural second fermentation and bottled with the dead yeasts. Much of the flavour is in the cloudy sediment, so shake it up and cheerfully pour it into the glass! 280 slm (the name refers to the altitude of the vineyards) is made with 25 days of skin contact since 2009, 450 slm with just a few days. These wines are joyful and dangerously gluggable, gentle on the system with their low alcohol and no added sulphites. The first vintage was 2006.

Address Costa di là, 36 – Tarzo **Tel** N/A **Email** posta@ederlezi.it

ITALY / VENETO

La Biancara

With a background in making pizza, Angiolino Maule created his La Biancara domaine in Gambellara (neighbouring Soave) in the late 1980s, at the same time participating in regular discourse and tastings with Joško Gravner and his colleagues. His genius has been to assimilate skin fermentation into expressions of garganega that are subtle, elegant and complex. Some wines are produced without added sulphites. Maule founded the VinNatur Association of 130 natural-wine producers in 2006, which organises the annual Villa Favorita natural wine fair.

Address Località Monte Sorio, 8 – 36054 – Montebello Vicentino
Tel +39 444 444244 **Email** biancaravini@virgilio.it

ITALY / FRIULI COLLI ORIENTALI

Le Due Terre

This uncertified organic estate might be microscopic (just five hectares), but Le Due Terre's wines have a cult following worldwide, and justly so. Their sole white wine, Sacrisassi Bianco, is a friulano-ribolla gialla blend made with a traditional maceration of eight days. The fermentation is regulated to ensure it does not go higher than 20–22°C, and the wine is lightly filtered. Natural wine fans may shake their fists, but most drinkers will just enjoy this elegant, understated beverage from a winemaking family that cares far more for quality than fashion.

Address Via Roma 68/b, 33040 Prepotto **Tel** +39 432 713189
Email fortesilvana@libero.it

ITALY / FRIULI COLLI ORIENTALI

Ronco Severo

Jovial, outgoing Stefano Novello rejected his conventional winemaking education in 1999 when he changed style and started to macerate all of his white wines. His smart label depicting a boy balancing on a chair represents this risk-taking attitude – most of his existing clients abandoned him. Novello macerates his white grapes for between 28 and 46 days. Ribolla Gialla, Friulano and the Severo Bianco blend are all excellent, bold but balanced. The style is reminiscent of Dario Prinčič. Uncertified organic viticulture.

Address Via Ronchi 93, 33040 Prepotto **Tel** +39 432 713340
Email info@roncosevero.it

ITALY / FRIULI COLLIO

Damijan Podversic

Damijan Podversic does not lack dedication. Impressed with Gravner's work in the late 1990s, Podversic decided in 1999 to reject his classical winemaking education and focus on macerated wines. A bitter feud with Podversic's father ensued, resulting in a ban from the family winery. After years of vinifying his wines in a shared cellar in Gorizia, Damijan is now building the winery of his dreams, right next to his vineyard. "Maceration isn't what makes a good wine", he cautions. But his precise, pure Ribolla Gialla, Malvasia, Friulano and the Kapjla blend implement the technique with absolute perfection.

Address Via Brigata Pavia, 61 - 34170 Gorizia **Tel** +39 0481 78217
Email damijan@damijanpodversic.com

ITALY / FRIULI COLLIO

Dario Prinčič

If Gravner's wines represent a brooding intellect, and Radikon's are revolution and free love, Prinčič's are somewhere in between – deep-hued, joyful and just demanding to be drunk. Neither shy, nor over the top, his Ribolla Gialla (macerated 35 days), Jakot, Pinot Grigio and the Trebez blend (18–22 days) are all exceptional. Prinčič came to viticulture in 1988 and switched to making macerated white wines in 1999 with encouragement from his close friend Stanko Radikon. His two sons are gradually taking over production duties.

Address Via Ossario 15, Gorizia **Tel** +39 0481 532730
Email dario.princic@gmail.com

ITALY / FRIULI COLLIO

Francesco Miklus

Mitja Miklus has now created this completely separate brand for his excellent macerated wines. More mainstream offerings are produced under the Draga label. The Miklus range is expanding and now includes the Ribolla Gialla Natural Art (30 days' maceration), Malvasia (seven days), Pinot Grigio and (newly) Friulano. My favourite is inevitably the Ribolla. Mitja was inspired by tasting the wines of his uncle Franco Terpin, resulting in the first Miklus vintage of macerated wines in 2006. One to watch.

Address loc. Scedina 8, 34070 San Floriano del Collio **Tel** +39 329 7265005
Email mimiklus@gmail.com

Gravner

Joško Gravner is truly the father of the modern-day amber/orange/macerated wine movement. His brave, unprecedented rejection of modern winemaking in 1997 has had untold influence not just in Italy but worldwide. His travels to Georgia and subsequent adoption of the qvevri as the perfect fermentation vessel (in 2001) lifted the lid on Georgia's ancient winemaking traditions, inspiring a whole generation after him to explore it. Breg (the final vintage is 2012) and Ribolla Gialla, both made with around six months of skin contact in qvevri and released after seven years' ageing are some of the world's greatest wines.

Address Località Lenzuolo Bianco 9, 34170 Oslavia **Tel** +39 0481 30882
Email info@gravner.it

ITALY / FRIULI COLLIO

Il Carpino

The best part of tasting at Franco and Ana Sosol's 17-hectare estate, just up the road from Radikon, is the opportunity to compare the same grapes vinified with and without maceration. Franco makes a fresh line of wines (Vigna Runc) for customers who don't yet appreciate their amber cousins. Ribolla Gialla, vinified in *botti* with 45–55 days of skin contact, is age-worthy and typical. He's crystal clear about which style he prefers: "With skin maceration, I feel like it's the real wine, because we don't intervene, we just let it express itself".

Address Località Sovenza 14/A, 34070 San Floriano del Collio
Tel +39 0481 884097 **Email** ilcarpino@ilcarpino.com

ITALY / FRIULI COLLIO

La Castellada

In 1985, La Castellada evolved from a tavern to bottling its own wine. Brothers Giorgio 'Jordi' and Nicolò Bensa were part of the 'Gravner Group' in the 1980s and 1990s, although they moved more cautiously in adopting his extended maceration ideas. By 2006, they settled on a 60-day maceration for their Ribolla Gialla, which is one of Oslavia's finest. Friulano and Bianco di Castellada (both four days) are also often excellent. The estate is largely run by Nicolò's sons Stefano and Matteo. In a piece of historical symmetry, Jordi left to run a local *osmiza* (tavern).

Address La Castellada 1 - Località Oslavia 34170 **Tel** +39 0481 33670
Email info@lacastellada.it

ITALY / FRIULI COLLIO

Paraschos

Evangelos Paraschos relocated from Greece to the Collio in 1998 and was inspired by Joško Gravner to adopt not only the credo of natural winemaking but also the use of amphorae and maceration. The family uses small Cretan amphorae for their Amphoretus wines, which often have a wonderful nervosity and vitality. Other bottlings such as the excellent Ribolla Gialla or the Orange One cuvée are made in the now classic open-top wooden fermenters (à la Radikon and many others). No sulphur or any other additives have been used at the winery since 2003.

Address Bucuie 13/a, 34070 San Floriano del Collio **Tel** +39 0481 884154
Email paraschos99@yahoo.it

ITALY / FRIULI COLLIO

Primosic

Although Silvan Primosic made a macerated pinot grigio as an experiment in 1997 (it wasn't a success and most customers returned it), it wasn't until 2007 that his son Marko made a true macerated ribolla gialla, which is now made every year. The Primosic family has always been at the heart of Collio – Silvan released the fledging DOC's very first bottle in 1967, and Marko was instrumental in setting up the Associazione Produttori Ribolla di Oslavia (with Saša Radikon) which promotes Oslavia's special terroir for ribolla gialla.

Address Madonnina d'Oslavia 3, 34170 – Oslavia **Tel** +39 0481 53 51 53
Email info@primosic.com

ITALY / FRIULI COLLIO

Radikon

Stanko Radikon rests in peace after 36 vintages, leaving a bright future with son Saša at the helm. Since the eureka moment in 1995 when he first macerated ribolla gialla, this estate has focused entirely on orange wines. The Oslavje blend, Ribolla Gialla and Friulano (all made with three months' skin contact) have been made without added sulphites since 2002, when Stanko realised that long skin contact created wines of such stability that it wasn't needed. Slatnik and Pinot Grigio (one to two weeks' maceration) were introduced by Saša as a lighter style redolent of what grandfather Radikon might have made.

Address Località Tre Buchi, n. 4, 34071 – Gorizia **Tel** +39 0481 32804
Email sasa@radikon.it

ITALY / FRIULI COLLIO

Terpin

There's not an ounce of pretension about Franco Terpin's wines. Made from grapes grown on the brittle ponca soils around San Floriano del Collio, the wines are produced in a now classic Collio style: about one week's maceration in open-topped oak vats, further ageing in botti and then released onto the market when they're good and ready to drink, at anything up to 10 years old. The Quinto Quarto line, made with a shorter maceration (three days) represent outstanding value for money. Franco started bottling in 1996 but didn't switch to the macerated style until 2005.

Address Localita Valerisce 6/A, San Floriano del Collio, 34070 **Tel** N/A
Email francoterpin@vergilio.it

ITALY / FRIULI ISONZO, COLLI ORIENTALI AND COLLIO

Bressan Maistri Vinai

Nine generations of Bressans have made wine at this estate straddling three Friuli sub-regions, Isonzo, Colli Orientali and Collio. All three white wines (the Carat blend, a rich, dry Verduzzo and a Pinot Grigio) are macerated between two and four weeks depending on the vintage. Nereo Bressan (now in his 80s) vinified without the skins prior to his son Fulvio taking over in 1995. The current proprietor may be a controversial figure, but the wines are spectacular.

Address Via Conti Zoppini 35, 34072 Farra d'Isonzo **Tel** +39 0481 888 131
Email info@bressanwines.com

ITALY / CARSO

Skerk

Softly spoken Sandi Skerk has been a vital force for natural winemaking in the Carso, since his return to more traditional vineyard and cellar practices in 2000. His elemental stone cellar, which elevates gashes in the Carso rock to architectural features, is used to coax stunning expression from vitovska, malvasia, sauvignon blanc and pinot grigio. The Ograde blend (of all four) is frequently sensational. Maceration times are around a week, and these are wines that can win over orange 'haters', such is their elegance and balance. The vineyards, mostly alberello pruned, are certified organic.

Address Loc. Prepotto, 2034011 Duino Aurisina **Tel** +39 040 200156
Email info@skerk.com

Skerlj

This idyllically situated estate developed from a humble *osmiza* (tavern) post-second world war, to a fully blown agriturismo in 1996. Matej Skerlj decided to start bottling wine (which has been made for consumption on the premises for generations) in 2004, taking inspiration from Benjamin Zidarich for longer maceration times (two to three days were normal previously) and less intervention in the cellar. His Vitovska, macerated for three weeks, is a superbly aromatic, elegant expression of the variety. Malvasia is also recommended. Some of Matej's vines are still traditionally high-pergola trained.

Address Sales, 44 – 34010 Sgonico **Tel** +39 040 229253
Email info@agriturismoskerlj.com

ITALY / CARSO

Vodopivec

If there is a more magical expression of vitovska than the wines of Paolo Vodopivec, I have yet to taste it. Vodopivec's operation is an exercise in minimalism, focusing purely on this native of the Carso, vinifying some plots in Georgian qvevri (since 2005) and others in large wooden *botti*. Working with very long maceration times of up to a year, the wines emerge with incredible subtlety and elegance. The publicity-shy Vodopivec doesn't feel that his wines fit in to the category of orange or amber, but nonetheless maceration is a key element in their production.

Address Località Colludrozza, 4 - 34010 Sgonico **Tel** +39 040 229181
Email vodopivec@vodopivec.it

ITALY / CARSO

Zidarich

Benjamin Zidarich has built one of the Carso's most dramatic cellars (completed 2009), tunnelled into the impenetrable local limestone. It's put to good use vinifying the output from his eight hectares of vines, tended with some biodynamic practices. White grapes are all fermented with their skins, for around two weeks or more, in open-top wood fermenters. Zidarich also makes one cuvée vinified and aged in a specially designed stone vat (hewn from local rock, of course). His Vitovska and the Pruhlke blend are both recommended for their rich, spicy yet mineral character.

Address Prepotto, 23, Duino Aurisina – Trieste **Tel** +39 040 201223
Email info@zidarich.it

ITALY / TUSCANY

Colombaia

Tuscany as a region has been slow to embrace natural winemaking and orange wine, so it is great to see estates like Colombaia. Dante Lomazzi and Helena Variara's Colombaia Bianco can be quite spectacular in some vintages (it's the only white wine made at the property). A blend of trebbiano and malvasia with four months of maceration, it is an apt demonstration of how the humble trebbiano reveals hidden depths when its skins are invited to the party. A pinch of sulphur might improve the staying power of some of the wines.

Address Mensanello, 24, Colle Val d'Elsa, 53034-Siena **Tel** +39 393 36 23 742
Email info@colombaia.it

ITALY / TUSCANY

Massa Vecchia

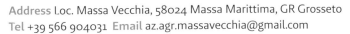

Francesca Sfrondrini has run this estate since she took over from her parents in 2009. Situated in the mountainous Maremma, there are no plumped-up super-Tuscan wines here. The delicious white (or rather, orange) wines, made from blends of vermentino, malvasia di candia and trebbiano, are all macerated for two to three weeks in open oak and chestnut vats. They're full of herbal and nutty complexity, but with real refinement and freshness too. Vines are worked using uncertified organic and biodynamic practices.

Address Loc. Massa Vecchia, 58024 Massa Marittima, GR Grosseto
Tel +39 566 904031 **Email** az.agr.massavecchia@gmail.com

ITALY / EMILIA-ROMAGNA

Cà de Noci

Brothers Giovanni and Alberto Masini began converting their seven-hectare vineyard to organic viticulture in 1993, leaving the local cooperative shortly afterwards. Notte di Luna is an understated classic in the world of macerated wines. A blend of malvasia de candia, moscato giallo and spergola (one of the most prized lambrusco grapes), it has 10 days of maceration. Their naturally frizzante Querciole is also made with a few days of skin contact.

Address Via Fratelli Bandiera 1/2 località Vendina, 42020 Quattro Castella
Tel +39 335 8355511 **Email** info@cadenoci.it

ITALY / EMILIA-ROMAGNA

Denavolo

When not working at La Stoppa, Giulio Armani makes his own wines under the Denavolo label. The three different macerated wines are variously Denavolo (six months' maceration), Denavolino (made from the lower part of the Denavolino vineyard, otherwise the same) and Catavela (seven days' maceration). All are blends centred on malvasia di candia aromatica, marsanne and ortrugo. The style is very reminiscent of La Stoppa's Ageno, with rich, heady aromas and full-bodied texture.

Address Loc. Gattavera - Denavolo 29020 Travo PC **Tel** +39 335 6480766
Email denavolo@gmail.com

ITALY / EMILIA-ROMAGNA

La Stoppa

Ageno, named after the lawyer who originally owned the La Stoppa estate, has become one of the classics of the macerated wine world, and Elena Pantaleoni is its current grand dame. With its rich blend of malvasia di candia, ortrugo and trebbiano, macerated for 30 days, this is a defiant, full-on orange wine – deeply coloured, tannic and big hearted in every way. Some vintages flirt more with volatility and brettanomyces, others are cleaner. But it's always delicious and moreish. The winemaker is Giulio Armani (see also Denavolo).

Address Loc. Ancarano di Rivergaro 29029 PC **Tel** +39 0523 958159
Email info@lastoppa.it

ITALY / EMILIA-ROMAGNA

Podere Pradarolo

Alberto Carretti and Claudia Iannelli migrated from more industrial careers to their current existence as organic farmers near Parma. Vej (macerated 60 days) and its sparkling version Vej Brut are a masterclass in malvasia di candia and its voluptuous aromatics. Vej Bianco Antico Metodo Classico 2014 is possibly unique as a traditional-method sparkler made with 270 days of maceration – it's an extreme but hugely enjoyable wine. I've observed issues in some vintages, due to the lack of SO_2 additions.

Address Via Serravalle 80, 43040 Varano De' Melegari **Tel** +39 0525 552027
Email info@poderepradarolo.com

ITALY / EMILIA-ROMAGNA
Tenuta Croci

Massimiliano Croci is at least the third generation of his family to produce macerated, naturally re-fermented wines in the traditional Emilia-Romagna style. Campedello and Lubigo are deliciously frizzante yet grippy expressions of local varieties such as malvasia di candia and ortrugo. Valtolla is a still version, made with 100% malvasia di candia. Maceration times range from 10 to 30 days.

Address 43040 Varano De' Melegari **Tel** +39 0523 803321
Email croci@vinicroci.com

ITALY / EMILIA-ROMAGNA
Vino del Poggio

Inspired to start bottling wine by La Stoppa's winemaker Giulio Armani, Andrea Cervini pushes the maceration time of his bianco (made from a malvasia di candia-heavy blend) even further than most other producers locally, sometimes reaching a whole 12 months. The Vino del Poggio Bianco is dense, complex and packed with flavour. Bianco, it defiantly is not! The estate also offers an agriturismo with outstanding food.

Address Località Poggio Superiore, 29020 Statto, Travo **Tel** +39.328.3019720
Email info@poggioagriturismo.com

ITALY / UMBRIA
Paolo Bea

Paolo Bea originally made a name for his standout sagrantino, but his son Giampiero (who is now in charge of the winemaking) also makes two macerated whites, including the formidable Arboretus from 100% trebbiano spoletino. These are herbal, aromatic wines with freshness and elegance, but also complexity and profundity. Originally an architect, Giampiero also designed the stunning winery, built in 2006. My only gripe with this winery is the very patchy availability of its wines! Bea also makes two wines for a nearby Cistercian monastery (see Monastero Suore Cistercensi).

Address Località Cerrete, 8, 06036 Cerrete **Tel** +39 742 378128
Email info@paolobea.com

ITALY / MARCHE
La Distesa

Corrado Dottori grew up in Spain and Canada, before working as a stocks trader in Milan. In 1999 he and his wife Valeria decided to downsize to his roots in Marche, farming vineyards bought by his grandfather. Nur is Dottori's rebel cry, a skin macerated blend made in a region devoted to varietal purity. It was born out of the discovery that verdicchio isn't suited to extended maceration. For Gli Eremi, a portion of the grapes are macerated for a few days to kickstart the fermentation, a practice as ancient as the Marche hills. The family runs a peaceful agriturismo.

Address Via Romita 28, Cupramonatana 60034 **Tel** +39 0731-781230
Email distesa@libero.it

ITALY / LAZIO
Le Coste

A collaboration between the winemaking couple Gianmarco and Clementine Antonuzzi, Le Coste was created in 2004 with the purchase of three hectares of abandoned land. White grapes major on procanico (a local clone of trebbiano), plus some malvasia and moscato. Most white wines receive a week of skin contact. The style is rustic, overridingly fresh, light and lively – these are real vins de soif. The viticulture is based on biodynamic principles, but uncertified.

Address Via Piave 9, Gradoli **Tel** +39 328 7926950
Email lecostedigradoli@hotmail.com

ITALY / LAZIO
Monastero Suore Cistercensi

The nuns at this Cistercian monastery near Rome farm their vines entirely manually (organically, but uncertified) and harvest the grapes for their two white blends (made from trebbiano, malvasia, verdicchio and grechetto). The vineyards were planted in 1963, and the resulting wine is an important source of income for the 80 nuns who live on the property. Giampiero Bea is the wine-making consultant who has now presided over more than a decade of these delightful wines. Only Coenobium Ruscum (or Rusticum as it used to be called) has prolonged skin maceration (two weeks).

Address Monastero Trappiste, Nostra Signora di S. Giuseppe, via della Stazione 23, 01030 - Vitorchiano **Tel** +39 761 370017 **Email** info@trappistevitorchiano.org

Cantina Giardino

Antonio and Daniela de Gruttola work with precious plots of very old vines, which they carefully revitalise and then vinify in an ultra-hands-off fashion. All white grapes are macerated for between four and 10 days. These are exciting, wild wines which can be unpredictable, but also wonderful if caught at the right moment. Some require considerable aeration and I would argue they are released too young, a common problem in this genre. The Bianco blend of Coda di Volpe and Greco, helpfully bottled in thirst-quenching magnums, is perhaps the most approachable.

Address Via Petrara 21 B, 83031 Ariano Irpino **Tel** +39 0825 873084
Email cantinagiardino@gmail.com

Podere Veneri Vecchio

Based in the Sannio DOC area, Raffaello Annicchiarico works with several extremely rare local grape varieties (grieco, cerreto and agostinella) all of which are macerated in various blends and varietal cuvées for around 25 days, to produce relatively lean styles with incredible energy and complexity (nothing gets above 12% ABV). The winemaking and the wines are uncompromising, occasionally treading on thin ice for those who don't get along with volatility. My top picks from recent vintages are the Tempo dopo Tempo and Bella Ciao (100% agostinella).

Address Via Veneri Vecchio 1, Castelvenere, 82037, Benevento
Tel +39 335 231827 **Email** libro@venerivecchio.com

Sa Defenza

Pietro, Paolo and Anna Marchi are first generation winemakers, although grape growing runs in the family. Based in the south of the island (Donori), their feisty wines are an absolute joy, but they also present a conundrum. Sullebucce is vermentino with 50 days of skin contact, yet ends up soft and succulent. Maistru takes a local ugly duckling (nuragus) and with a mere 24 hours of maceration transforms it into an intensely tangy, structured beast. Soils are sand and granite. Sulphur is the only additive or processing used.

Address Via Sa Defenza 38, 09040 Donori **Tel** +39 707 332815 **Email** N/A

ITALY / SICILY

Agricola Occhipinti

Arianna Occhipinti is the daughter of COS's Giusto Occhipinti, and created her own estate, also in Vittoria, in 2003. The single white wine SP68 is classic stuff, with around 12 days of skin contact lending it texture and depth. It's a blend of moscato di Alessandria and albanello. Arianna's partner Eduardo Torres Acosta (who arrived from Tenerife to work at the property and gain experience) produces his own Versante Nord line from Etna-grown fruit, and has also released his first skin-fermented bianco.

Address SP68 Vittoria-Pedalino km 3,3 - Vittoria RG Tel +39 0932 1865519
Email info@agricolaocchipinti.it

ITALY / SICILY

Barraco

Since taking on his family's vineyards and creating his winery in 2004, Nino has built a cult following for his vibrant, exciting readings of West Sicily's traditional white grapes – grillo, catarratto and zibibbo. All receive some maceration, from three days to two weeks for Zibibbo. Only a small plot of grillo right on the coast is vinified without any skin contact for Vignammare. The wines have a salty, assertive character and a joie de vivre best paired with fresh sea urchins or prawns – ideally those caught by Nino, also a keen fisherman.

Address C/da Bausa snc - 91025 Marsala Tel +39 3897955357
Email vinibarraco@libero.it

ITALY / SICILY

Cantine Barbera

After her father died in 2006, Marilena Barbera decided to change career and work the family's vines in Menfi. Realising she didn't like the industrial way the wines were made, she began experimenting in 2010 with less intervention and skin maceration for white grapes. There are now three orange wines in the range, Coste al Vento (grillo), Arèmi (catarratto) and Ammàno (zibbibo). All are wild-fermented with their skins for around a week. They're fruit-packed, joyful and varietally expressive, and well worth ageing for a year or two.

Address Contrada Torrenova SP 79 - 92013 Menfi (AG) Tel +39 0925 570442
Email info@cantinebarbera.it

ITALY / SICILY

Cornelissen

How does an ex-financial trader, mountaineer and fine wine broker from Belgium end up making natural wine on a volcano in Sicily? Frank Cornelissen's drive to make fine wine with nothing added led him to Georgia and then to Etna, where he set up his now cult operation in 2000. Preferring grecanico over Etna's indigenous carricante ("If I want acidity, I'll suck on a lemon"), he uses a few days of maceration in two white blends. Winemaking is constantly evolving – the Spanish amphorae have been abandoned in favour of fibre-glass tanks, and maceration has decreased from 30 days to about a week.

Address Via Canonico Zumbo, 1, Fraz. Passopisciaro, Castiglione di Sicilia, 95012
Tel +39 0942 986 315 Email info@frankcornelissen.it

ITALY / SICILY

COS

Giambattista Cilia, Giusto Occhipinti and Cirino Strano were still at university when Cilia's father allowed them to make an experimental harvest and vinification of 1,470 bottles in summer 1980. COS, the acronym of the three friends, has since become a benchmark for Cerasuolo di Vittoria, Sicily's only DOCG. They're also pioneers of amphora use in modern Italy. Visiting Georgia provided inspiration to abandon oak in favour of terracotta, but in 2000 COS settled on Spanish *tinajas* of 440 litres. Pithos Bianco is one of Italy's greatest orange wines, tight and closed in youth but expressive and complex as it opens.

Address S.P. 3 Acate-Chiaramonte, Km. 14,300 97019 Vittoria
Tel +39 393 8572630 Email locanda@cosvittoria.it

New Zealand

After a few decades when New Zealand seemed as though it was only about sauvignon blanc, consolidation and homogenisation, it's thankfully breeding a new generation of winemakers who take a more rootsy and varied approach to their craft. Ideas brought back from European experiences often provide the inspiration, and skin maceration is emphatically on the menu. Orange wines are still very new here, but the availability of cool climate growing zones and a very well educated winemaking community is starting to show really stunning results.

As with Australia, there is a lot of latitude when it comes to wine classification, and there are no particular problems with the inclusion of wording such as 'skin fermented' on the label.

NEW ZEALAND / HAWKES BAY

Supernatural Wine Co.

Vineyards planted (on a lime-rich clay elevation) at Millar Road lodgings between 2002 and 2004 performed above expectations, so owner Gregory Collinge decided to create a winery on the premises in 2009. Sauvignon blanc and pinot gris have been skin fermented since the 2013 vintage and are making quantum leaps in quality each year. Hayden Penny took over from Gabrielle Simmers as winemaker from 2015. These are recognisably bold, new world wines in style, but with excellent balance and poise. The estate is in conversion to biodynamics, and also moving towards no added sulphites.

Address 83 Millar Road, RD10 Hastings 4180, Hawke's Bay **Tel** +64 875 1977
Email greg.collinge@icloud.com

NEW ZEALAND / MARTINBOROUGH

Cambridge Road

This estate was purchased and converted to biodynamics by Lance Redgewell and family in 2006. They've been playing with skin contact for a number of years, using it in a subtle and delightful way to accentuate and add weight to some of the Papillon wines. Cloudwalker is a very moveable feast, for example pinot gris with three days of skin contact in 2015, but a blend with 26 days of contact in 2016. The wines are delicate, refreshing and charming.

Address 32 Cambridge Road, Martinborough **Tel** +64 306 8959
Email lance@cambridgeroad.co.nz

NEW ZEALAND / CANTERBURY

The Hermit Ram

"Ultimately, these are pre-technology wines", says Theo Coles, who started making wine from an old plot of pinot noir in 2012, following winemaking experience in Tuscany. All of his white grapes, and a white-red field blend are skin macerated for a month or more, using a mix of open top fermenters and concrete eggs. He's keen to point out that maceration is merely a technique, not the raison d'être. These are pure, lively wines offering a unique interpretation of the rugged Canterbury landscape and are made without compromise. The Sauvignon Blanc's aromatic definition and finely hewn structure is noteworthy.

Address N/A Tel +64 27 255 1899 Email theo@thehermitram.com

NEW ZEALAND / CENTRAL OTAGO

Sato Wines

Take two Japanese ex-investment bankers turned winemakers, Yoshiaka and Kyoto Sato, filter them through winemaking experience with some of the natural wine world's finest (such as Pierre Frick and Domaine Bizot), and set them down in the increasingly hot, dry Central Otago region – and out come skin-contact wines of positively Burgundian elegance, with Japanese precision and extraordinary purity. Their Northburn Blanc, a blend of chardonnay, pinot gris and riesling fermented on the skins for 20 days is truly outstanding. Uncertified biodynamic viticulture.

Address N/A Tel N/A Email info@satowines.com

Poland

There's a clutch of producers experimenting with skin contact here, and a growing love for the qvevri. So far, there is wild inconsistency and a fair few wines which just seem plain bizarre. Under-ripeness is, as one would expect this far north, a frequent issue, especially given that chaptalising[87] is not something any minimal interventionist producer wants to do. Hybrid grape varieties are popular and while some work with maceration, some clearly don't. One producer has proven their orange chops across two vintages and deserves a mention here.

POLAND / BARYCZ VALLEY

Winnica de Sas

Anna Zuber and Leszek 'Kaukaz' Budzyński are based in Lower Silesia in the Barycz Valley Landscape Park and focus on natural wines. They have the distinction of having produced the first commercially available Polish qvevri wine. Their Kvevri Milvus, 100% gewürztraminer, fermented for six to eight months in Georgian qvevri, is starting to prove itself as Poland's top effort in this genre. The winery has since scaled up to eight qvevris and it will be well worth keeping an eye on future releases. Uncertified organic viticulture.

Address Czeszyce 9A, 56-320, Krośnice **Tel** +48 71 384 56 90
Email zuberdesas@gmail.com

---

87 Adding additional sugar to the ferment to increase the potential alcohol level.

Portugal

Who knew that the vast plains of Alentejo were hoarding a
2,000-year-old Roman tradition of making wine in amphora?
Not many, until the wine world started to go crazy about clay.
Suddenly, wineries in the area realised that their cellars full of
two-century-old *talhas* (large squat amphorae) were gold dust.
Where previously the *talhas* sat empty or were used to make
wine that was quietly blended into other bottlings, now they
are starting to take centre stage, and of course, producers all
over the country are desperate to get their hands on them.

The Douro valley also boasts a venerable skin contact tradition,
but for port rather than still wine. White ports have always
traditionally been foot trodden and fermented on their skins
for at least a few days, with the aim of achieving more stability
and flavour. Since they are often aged oxidatively in wood for
many years, no-one expects them to be white, and indeed they
are not, usually maturing to a nutty brown colour after a few
decades of age.

Most Portuguese winemakers are still in a somewhat experimental phase with their *curtimentas* or skin-fermented white
wines, but there is an increasing number of jewels to seek out.
Talha winemaking still needs some fine-tuning, but given that
it is now officially sanctioned by the Alentejo DO, this should
become a serious playground for Iberian orange wine fans in
the years to come.

PORTUGAL / VINHO VERDE

Aphros

Vasco Croft looks for all the world like an art-school lecturer, with his
philosophical take on life and slightly hippyish style. He's a powerful advocate
of biodynamics, also active as a Waldorf trainer, and makes his own biodynamic
preparations. The Phaunus wines have been made since 2014 in the cellar of the
beautiful quinta, without electricity. Fermentation occurs in squat Alentejano
talhas (amphorae). Phaunus Loureiro, with six to eight weeks' skin contact, is
beguiling, individual and quite unique for the region. Croft's more mainstream
Aphros range is produced since 2004, in a separate and more modern cellar.

Address Rua de Agrelos, 70, Padreiro (S. Salvador), 4970-500 Arcos de
Valdevez Tel +351 935 418 457 Email info@aphros-wine.com

PORTUGAL / DOURO

Bago de Touriga

This collaboration between João Roseiro (Quinta do Infantado) and winemaker Luis Soares Duarte has so far only produced one vintage (2010) of the Gouvyas Ambar, but it is probably the first modern-day macerated white from the Douro. Extended skin contact has long been utilised for white port, but here it's used to make a still wine. It was foot trodden in lagars, and fermented with the skins for 12 days. This is a big-boned, complex beast, only just beginning to show its best, and playing more to oxidative characters. Further vintages have been made since 2015.

Address Rua do Fundo do Povo, 5050-343 Poiares Vila Seca de Poiares **Tel** N/A
Email bagodetouriga@gmail.com

PORTUGAL / DÃO

João Tavares de Pina Wines

The Dão is better known for its elegant, cool-climate reds, and there has been very little activity on the orange wine front. The irrepressible João Tavares has now made two vintages of his Rufia Orange, from a field blend heavy in jampal (shhh, it's not a permitted variety in the region any more!). It's a shame that commercial realities meant the 2016 is now sold out, as it's only just starting to show at its best. The 2017 has so far not impressed me, but if it is as shy as the 2016 then no wonder.

Address Quinta da Boavista, 3550-057 Castelo De Penalva, Viseu
Tel +351 919 858 340 **Email** jtp@quintadaboavista.eu

PORTUGAL / LISBON

Vale da Capucha

I know few winemakers who are as thorough and without artifice in their craft as Pedro Marques. Everything from what to replant, to which varieties respond best to skin contact has been painstakingly explored and fine tuned since 2009, when he took over the family winery. The solera style Branco Especial, blending skin fermented alvarinho, arinto and gouveio was finally bottled in 2018, after three patient years of blending and waiting. It's a triumph. Vineyards are planted on limestone and Kimmeridgian clay soils, just a few kilometres from Lisbon and the Atlantic coast.

Address Largo Engº António Batalha Reis 2, 2565-781 Turcifal
Tel +351 912 302 289 **Email** pedro.marques@valedacapucha.com

PORTUGAL / TEJO

Humus Wines

Rodrigo Filipe's problem is a lack of white grapes in his nine-hectare parcel of vineyards, which is part of an old family estate called Quinta do Paço. His creative solution for the curtimenta was to use 80% touriga nacional, vinified as a blanc de noir, but fermented with the sauvignon and arinto skins which make up the other 20%. The result is entrancing, with a three-month maceration lending gravitas, depth and structure, yet there are fresh, pretty fruit aromatics too. From 2017 he plans to add more orange wines to the range. One to watch.

Address Encosta da Quinta, Lda, Quinta do Paço, 2500-346 Alvorninha
Tel +351 917 276 053 Email humuswines@gmail.com

PORTUGAL / ALENTEJO

Herdade de São Miguel

Part of the Casa Relvas group, this large winery makes two skin-contact wines in its more boutique Art Terra range. The Amphora Branco is perhaps the most convincing talha branco I've yet tasted from the region. With around 60 days of skin contact, this is the real deal, full of herbal, earthy complexity and lovely structure. The Art Terra curtimenta, with eight days' skin contact, feels a little banal in comparison. One has to love the food matching suggestions given for these wines: "Dried fruits, Iberian tapas and a good conversation".

Address Apartado 60 7170-999 Redondo Tel +351 266 988 034
Email info@herdadesaomiguel.com

PORTUGAL / ALENTEJO

José de Sousa (José Maria da Fonseca)

Founded in 1868, this winery has an extraordinary 114 antique talhas still in daily use. Winemakers were not always enamoured of such vessels, which demand serious effort to maintain. However the realisation has hit home that clay is hip now, so this cellar is gold dust. Talha wines are blended into the regular production, but the new Puro Talha range shows the style unadorned. The Talha Branco has an uncontrolled fermentation and around two months of skin contact. Amphoras are then sealed with a layer of olive oil. The result is oxidative and complex with an almost fino-like freshness.

Address Quinta da Bassaqueira – Estrada Nacional 10, 2925-511 Vila Nogueira de Azeitão, Setúbal Tel +351 266 502 729 Email josedesousa@jmfonseca.pt

PORTUGAL / ALGARVE
Monte da Casteleja

Half French, half Portuguese Guillame Leroux wanted to bring something regional and authentic back to a region which is not known for great wine. Using only traditional grape varieties, his Branco is made with 10 days of maceration, with skins and stems, and is a triumph. Leroux achieves body and a grippy structure, with no loss of freshness or fruit. The Branco has been made in this style since 2013, although the winery was established in 2000. Leroux studied oenology in Montpellier.

Address Cx Postal 3002-I, 8600-317 Lagos **Tel** +351 282 798 408
Email admin@montecasteleja.com

Slovakia

The split from Czechoslovakia badly disrupted the wine industry in the mid 1990s, but it's well on the way to recovery. A severe continental climate means that ripening is hard work, and as with the Czech Republic and Poland, disease resistant hybrids and crossings are popular in addition to the perennial staples of grüner veltliner and welschriesling. There's a clutch of younger producers loosely clustered around the village of Strekov who are pioneering macerated white wines. These can be an acquired taste, with rather extreme herbaceous, aromatic characters, but it is one I am certainly acquiring. The enthusiasm amongst this growing scene of natural winemakers is palpable, and it will be well worth watching developments over the next decade.

SLOVAKIA / LESSER CARPATHIANS
Živé Víno

A new project from first-generation winemakers Dusan and Andrej that shows great promise. The two friends currently own two hectares of vines situated on granite bedrock. Their range includes a Blanc (10 days of maceration) and an Oranž (14 days of maceration) – a curious categorisation! The latter, a blend of welschriesling, traminer and grüner veltliner, is quite superb. Živé Vína is their online shop, which also sells the wines of other local producers.

Address Prostredná 31, 900 21 Svätý Jur **Tel** +421 903 253 929
Email info@zivevino.sk

SLOVAKIA / NITRA

Slobodné Vinárstvo

Agnes Lovecka and her team have resuscitated this long-established family estate (called Majer Zemianske Sady), which fell into disuse after Slovakia's separation from Czechoslovakia in 1992. Since 2010, a large range of natural wines are produced, including many oranges. Oranzista (100% pinot gris) and Deviner (devin, grüner veltliner and traminer) are my favourites, for their joyful, herbaceous fruit. The winery purchased two qvevris for the 2014 vintage (Cutis Pyramid) and has invested in Spanish and Tuscan amphoras, too.

Address Hlavná 56, Zemianske Sady Tel +421 907 100030
Email vinari@slobodnevinarstvo.sk

SLOVAKIA / SOUTH SLOVAK

Strekov 1075

Strekov 1075's Heion is one of the benchmarks of Slovakia's small but enthusiastic and fast-growing orange wine scene. It's made from welschriesling with about two weeks of maceration and has the country's distinctive pungent fruit with excellent structure. Zsolt Sütó has adopted the name of his local village for his estate, and it's appropriate enough as this is the epicentre of Slovakia's wine country.

Address Hlavná ul. č. 1075, 941 37 Strekov Tel +421 905 649 615
Email info@strekov1075.sk

Slovenia

Without doubt the beating heart of orange wine, Slovenia has an ever-growing roster of independent, family-run wineries who have dedicated themselves to making macerated white wines. It's a huge irony that their domestic customers still largely shun the style, but their loss is the rest of the world's gain.

Goriška Brda has the greatest concentration of top winemakers, and the longest tradition of working with rebula (the Slovenian name for ribolla gialla), but Vipava is not far behind. The Karst and Slovenian Istra are beautiful regions that deserve more attention – there are really excellent wines being made in both. Thus far there is less of interest for natural or orange-wine fans in the eastern half of the country, but doubtless this will develop.

Slovenia is starting to realise that its tradition of macerated white wines is marketable. While its wine industry was previously held back by the communist era's unifying mediocrity, there's now a renaissance taking place. Evidence of this can be found at several lively events, including the Orange Wine Festival which takes place in the beautiful seaside town of Izola each April, Border Wine which brings together Italian and Slovenian growers, and an annual Rebula Masterclass organised by the Brda tourist board.

SLOVENIA / BRDA

Atelier Kramar

Matjaž Kramar is the brother of Hiša Franko's sommelier and joint owner Valter Kramar. Part of the attraction of this five-hectare estate, created in 2004, is undoubtedly their classy, minimalist labels. Matjaž and his partner Katja Distelbarth have a background in art, hence the atelier tag. The pair began macerating their white wines in 2014. Their Rebula (with between three and five days' maceration) displays great typicity and structure. Friulano is so far less successful.

Address Barbana 12 5212, Dobrovo Tel +386 313 91575
Email info@atelier-kramar.si

Blažič

Borut and Simona Blažič make delicious, typical macerated wines at this estate, which was parcellated by the post-second world war border. Do not confuse them with the identically named Italian estate in Zegla, Cormons, which makes conventional wines. Labelling is admirably clear at this domaine – wines with a black label are macerated, those with an additional orange stripe top and bottom are the premium vineyard selections. Rebula is excellent, the white-blend Blaž Belo selection can also be outstanding.

Address Plešivo 30, 5212 Dobrovo Tel +386 530 45445
Email vina.blazic@siol.net

SLOVENIA / BRDA

Brandulin

This small estate (five hectares) straddles the Italian border around Gorizia. Boris Brandulin started bottling his wines in 1994 (previously the grapes were sold to the local Brda cooperative cellar) and began using longer macerations for the white grapes from 2000. Rebula is now macerated for three weeks, and the white blend (Belo) is made in a similar fashion. These are really outstanding examples of Brda's orange wines and deserve to be much better known than they currently are.

Address Plešivo 4, 5212 Dobrovo v Brdih Tel +386 5 3042139
Email brandulin@amis.net

SLOVENIA / BRDA

Erzetič

A long-established family winery with a passion for amphorae. The move to a larger winery in 2007 allowed for building a small qvevri cellar, which is used to make a number of different wines. Amber offerings include a Pinot Gris and a white blend (rebula plus a smidgen of pinot blanc) which is recommended. The amphora shaped bottles may have seemed like a good idea once upon a time but should probably be abandoned! More conventional wines are also made, and in more conventional bottles, too.

Address Višnjevik 25a, Dobrovo Tel +386 516 43114
Email martin.erzetic@gmail.com

Kabaj

Parisian Jean Michel Morel married into the Kabaj family in 1989 and has been the driving force behind the estate's winemaking since 1993. Previously he worked at the prestigious Borgo Conventi in Friuli. A classic Rebula undergoes 30 days of maceration, while most other wines are made with a short 24-hour maceration and a year in barrique. Since 2008, Morel also makes the Anfora white blend, fermented and aged in a single large Georgian qvevri. Results vary but can be excellent in some years. The family also runs a restaurant and offers accommodation.

Address Šlovrenc 4, 5212 Dobrovo Tel +386 539 59560
Email kabaj.morel@siol.net

Klinec

This long-established winery and restaurant occupies a stunning location perched high in the Brda hills, in Medana village. Aleks Klinec decided in 2005 to focus only on macerated white wines (plus a few reds). Despite "losing the entire Slovenian market", for him it's "more authentic and transmits the terroir much better". Wines spend three years in either oak, acacia, mulberry or cherry wood, before racking into steel and eventual bottling. Their precision and purity are outstanding. Varietal wines are all excellent, but the Ortodox blend is the sensational crowning glory. Uncertified biodynamic agriculture.

Address Medana 20, 5212 Dobrovo v Brdih Tel +386 539 59409
Email klinec@klinec.si

Kmetija Štekar

Staying at Janko Štekar and Tamara Lukman's bucolic agriturismo in the Brda hills is the best way to understand their holistic attitude to farming and winemaking. Wines are made in a simple. natural way, sometimes with and sometimes without added sulphites. Rebula often excels and is usually macerated for one month. Special mention must be made of RePiko, a superb macerated riesling. Janko remarks, "At some point, you have to decide if you're going to make wine for people who like what you like, or whether just to make what the market wants." He's clearly gone for the former.

Address Snežatno 31a, 5211 Kojsko, Tel +386 530 46210
Email janko@kmetijastekar.si

SLOVENIA / BRDA
Marjan Simčič

Situated just opposite the turning for the Movia winery, Marjan Simčič's 18 hectares of vineyards are similarly split between Italy and Slovenia. Marjan is the fifth generation of winemakers, but the first who started seriously bottling in 1988. The estate produces a huge range of wines, from light, fresh styles to the Selection range (some of which are macerated) and finally the grand cru Opoka wines, which were launched in 2008. The rebulas, with a few days of maceration, are amongst the best.

Address Ceglo 3b, 5212 Dobrovo Tel +386 5 39 59 200 Email info@simcic.si

SLOVENIA / BRDA
Movia

Sometimes one wonders if Aleš Kristančič is a genius or a madman, such is his restless drive and passion. There's no doubt about his mastery when you taste the wines though. Movia is an ancient estate, now totalling 22 border-straddling hectares. Aleš is the eighth generation to make wine. The Lunar range, harvested and bottled according to moon phases and made with no added sulphur are impressive, and best enjoyed at ten years old or more. The fresher styles, made with the unusual combination of prolonged maceration and temperature control to retain youthful aromatics, are also excellent.

Address Ceglo 18, 5212 Dobrovo Tel +386 5 395 95 10 Email movia@siol.net

SLOVENIA / BRDA
Nando

This is another border-straddling estate, with most of the 5.5 hectares of vineyard technically in Italy. Andrej Kristančič works organically but is not certified. All of his wines are made in a non-interventionist manner, with spontaneous fermentations and no filtration. The blue label range are released young, and produced only in stainless steel, while the black label wines undergo long maceration (up to 40 days, for the Rebula) and ageing in 500-litre Slavonian oak barrels. They are excellent, typical examples of Brda orange wines.

Address Plešivo 20, Medana, 5212 Dobrovo Tel +386 40 799 471
Email nando@amis.net

Amber Re
Recommended

SLOVENIA / BRDA

Ščurek

Although this winery is not primarily focused on orange wine, their rebula (which goes into two different blends) is always macerated either on the skins or with whole berries in the barrel. This latter is particularly interesting as the flavours of maceration are present but with far less extraction than is usual for this tannic variety. The winery is also recommended for a visit, not only for its commanding hilltop location but also for its secondary purpose as an ad hoc art gallery for local artists.

Address Plešivo 44, Medana, 5212 Dobrovo **Tel** +386 530 4021
Email scurek.stojan@siol.net

SLOVENIA / BRDA

Štekar

Winemaker Jure is Janko Štekar's nephew. His wines are labelled as Štekar which makes life quite confusing for consumers! Luckily, whichever branch of the family one patronises, the wines are excellent. Jure took over the estate from his father Roman in 2012, and briefly became a minor media celebrity after his appearance on Ljubezen na deželi (Love in the Country), a TV dating show. Love didn't blossom then, but the youthful Štekar is now married. His Friulano, with one week of maceration, is recommended, as is the ambitious Rebula Filip dedicated to his son, with six months' maceration.

Address Snežatno 26a, 5211 Kojsko **Tel** +386 530 46540
Email stekar@siol.net

SLOVENIA / BRDA

UOU

Marinko Pintar owns a fleet of trucks, but now in semi-retirement he pours his passion into keeping Slovenia's macerated wine traditions alive. Operating from a tiny cellar in his elderly mum's Nova Gorizian back garden, Pintar produces around 1,000 bottles a year of excellent, typical macerated wines mainly from rebula and malvazija. UOU is the 'Consortium of abandoned vineyards', which, consisting of Marinko together with friends, finds forgotten plots, tracks down elderly or infirm owners and gains permission to harvest and vinify their grapes. His output is never sold, only given away to friends and family.

Address N/A **Tel** N/A **Email** marinko@pintarsped.si

SLOVENIA / VIPAVA

Batič

Ivan Batič laid the groundwork for this important estate by selling bottles door to door in the 1970s. His charismatic son Miha now presides. Big changes were made in 1989, replanting traditional varieties and reverting to a lower intervention style of winemaking. Ivan's drinking pals Radikon, Gravner and Edi Kante certainly had some influence! Most white wines see some skin contact, ranging up to 35 days for older vintages of Zaria and Angel. Zaria, a blend of seven varieties, is my top recommendation – at its best, it's an electrifying wine which achieves complexity, structure and pure drinkability.

Address Šempas 130, 5261 Šempas **Tel** +386 5 3088 676
Email baticmiha@gmail.com

SLOVENIA / VIPAVA

Burja

Primož Lavrenčič started out in partnership with his brother at the family's Sutor winery but broke away to form Burja in 2001. "I'm stuck in the 19th century", says Lavrenčič, by which he means everything he does is based on ancient methods. Well, almost everything. He's in love with the expanding row of concrete eggs in his newly built winery. The Burja blend (seven days' maceration) is consistently good year to year, but his new Stranice single-vineyard cuvée (aged only in concrete, 12 days' maceration) raises the bar still higher with its spicy yet elegant character.

Address Podgrič 12, 5272 Podnanos **Tel** +386 41 363 272 **Email** burja@amis.net

SLOVENIA / VIPAVA

Guerila

Quality estate focused on native grape varieties including pinela and zelen, both made with only one day of skin contact. They're beautiful wines, but to stay on topic, let's turn to the Rebula. Macerated for 14 days, this is a great example of the grape's tannic, honeyed beauty, with elegance to boot. The Retro blend of rebula, zelen, pinela and malvasia is also made traditionally, with four days of maceration. Zmago Petrič created the Guerila brand name in 2005, although winemaking in the family has a much longer history. The labelling is bold and unusual.

Address Zmagoslav Petrič, Planina 111, 5270 Ajdovščina **Tel** +386 516 60265
Email martin.gruzovin@petric.si

SLOVENIA / VIPAVA
JNK

The talented Kristina Mervic has taken over from her father Ivan at this micro-scopic estate (production is 8,000–10,000 bottles a year) situated a stone's throw away from Batič. She's reverted to the traditional style of macerated wines, as made by her grandfather and great-grandfather (the estate made conventional white wines for a short period in the late 1990s). Rebula (two weeks' maceration) and Chardonnay (four days) are outstanding, complex and elegant. Kristina releases the wines at between five and 10 years old, "when they are at their best and showing their natural attributes," as she explains.

Address Šempas 57/c, 5261 Šempas Tel +386 530 8693 Email info@jnk.si

SLOVENIA / VIPAVA
Mlečnik

Valter Mlečnik's winemaking is an exercise in stripping back to the bare mini-mum required. Mentored closely by Joško Gravner in the late 1980s and early 1990s, he rediscovered traditional winemaking and skin contact for white wines. However, Mlečnik and his son Klemen have been careful to follow the Vipava region's traditions closely, so the amount of skin contact is fairly low (three to six days). Since 2015, a simple basket press is the only machinery employed in the winery. The Ana Cuvée is a masterpiece of elegance, understatement and beauty in maceration.

Address Bukovica 31, 5293 Volčja Draga Tel +386 5 395 53 23
Email v.mlecnik@gmail.com

SLOVENIA / VIPAVA
Slavček

This 10-hectare estate is a bit of an insider tip, being highly rated by Dario Prinčič, among others. Franc Vodopivec doesn't have the same international profile as his namesake in the Italian Karst, but his Rebula (which is macerated for five days) has a fresh, creamy charm which is quite distinct from most of its Brda cousins. Certified by the Triple A scheme for natural winemakers.

Address Potok pri Dornberku 29, 5294 Dornberk Tel +386 5 30 18 745
Email kmetija@slavcek.si

SLOVENIA / VIPAVA

Svetlik

Edvard Svetlik has a crystal-clear explanation for his focus on just one grape variety. "We planted our first vineyard in 2000 and in 2005 we first made macerated wine," he says. "We decided on rebula, because the more we know her, the more we believe she is the queen of vines for maceration." Svetlik's project was originally called Grace, after one of his vineyards. His wines stay with their skins for the entire fermentation, usually about two weeks. The Rebula Selection, which undergoes longer ageing in 500-litre barrels, can be excellent, however oak dominates in some vintages.

Address Posestvo Svetlik, Kamnje 42b, 5263 Dobravlje Tel +386 5 37 25 100
Email edvard@svetlik-wine.com

SLOVENIA / KARST

Čotar

The enigmatic Branko and his son Vasja Čotar claim an unbroken history of making macerated white wines with Branko's winemaking experience dating back to 1974. Wine was originally made as an adjunct to the family restaurant but became the main business in 1997. Čotar's almost austere, flinty Vitovska is one of the greatest expressions of this local variety. Malvazija is typically fatter, but ages gracefully for 10 to 15 years. Wines are made without any sulphur additions, and typically receive around seven days of skin contact.

Address Gorjansko 4a, Si-6223 Komen Tel +386 41 870 274
Email vasjacot@amis.net

SLOVENIA / KARST

Klabjan

It is beyond me why the genial Uroš Klabjan has such a low profile worldwide. His pure, defined malvazijas from the stony slopes of the Slovenian Karst are world class, demonstrating that long skin maceration in the right hands creates not only concentration but also elegance, structure and staying power. White-label wines are younger, fresher styles with less maceration, while the black-label range are also aged in large oak barrels. Malvazija Black Label is macerated for around a week.

Address Klabjanosp 80a, 6000 Koper Tel +386 41 735 348
Email uros.klabjan@siol.net

Renčel

Joško Renčel is a man of few words but a wicked, dry humour. White wines have always been made with maceration, varying from a few days to a few weeks. Renčel commercialised the winery in 1991 and more recently has been joined by his son-in-law Žiga Ferlež. Cuvée Vincent is often outstanding, capable of ageing for well over a decade in good vintages. Two wines made from dried grapes are playfully named 'orange' and 'super orange'. Joško says "Gravner printed 'anfora' in orange on his labels and this is my version!" Experiments with a 400-litre qvevri taste delicious so far.

Address Dutovlje 24, 6221 Dutovlje **Tel** +386 31 370 561
Email rencelwine@gmail.com

SLOVENIA / KARST

Štemberger

Long-established producer making good skin-macerated rebula, welschriesling, sauvignon blanc and chardonnay. The wines have a nice subtlety and lightness of touch quite typical of this stony terroir. Macerations are relatively extended for Karst, ranging from six to 12 days. It may not be typical for the region, but their Chardonnay is the top pick.

Address Na žago 1, 8310 Šentjernej **Tel** +386 41 824 116
Email gregor.stemberger@gmail.com

SLOVENIA / KARST

Tauzher

Emil Tavčar uses his family's old German name to differentiate the winery from the many other Tavčars in his village. Short macerations of around three days are used for Malvazija and the region's indigenous Vitovska, as is traditional for the area. The results are surprisingly rich and full bodied for Karst. Production is no more than a minuscule 10,000 bottles a year.

Address Kreplje 3, 6221 Dutovlje **Tel** +386 5 764 04 84
Email emil.tavcar@siol.net

SLOVENIA / ISTRA

Gordia

After 20 years working as a chef, the affable, straight-talking Andrej Cep decided to refocus on wine production in 2012. His restaurant and cellar are situated on an idyllic hilltop with views over the Adriatic. His wines are expertly made, with very long macerations for Malvazija and the white blend, and great care taken in the vineyards, certified organic since the start. Everything at this estate is superbly drinkable, from defiantly cloudy pét-nats to reds. Andrej's latest passion is a small qvevri cellar which he built in 2016. The results taste very promising.

Address Kolomban 13, 6280 Ankaran Tel +386 41 806 645
Email vino@gordia.si

SLOVENIA / ISTRA

Korenika & Moškon

This 22-hectare estate, now Demeter certified, is based close to the pretty coastal village of Izola. Macerated wines, from malvazija, chardonnay and pinot gris, are aged for around six years in the barrel before release onto the market. Maceration times are quite long, varying from 14 to 30 days. The Sulne cuvée (with all three of the above varieties) has been outstanding in some years (2003 and 2005, for example). More recent vintages have failed to excite me as much. A line of fresh, young white wines is also produced.

Address Korte 115B, 6310 Izola Tel +386 41 607 819
Email infokorenikamoskon@siol.net

SLOVENIA / ISTRA

Rojac

Uroš Rojac claims he is primarily a red wine producer, but his three macerated white wines are also well worth getting to know. Typically made with extremely long skin contact (up to 60 days for the Malvazija, which has been part fermented in qvevri since 2010), these are full-bodied and complex wines but with Istra's typical freshness and salinity into the bargain.

Address Gažon 63a, SI-6274 Šmarje Tel +386 820 59 326 Email wine@rojac.eu

SLOVENIA / ŠTAJERSKA

Aci Urbajs

Aci is an iconic figure within Slovenian orange-wine circles. He's also a long-standing proponent and pioneer of biodynamics in the region, and Demeter certified since 1999. The Organic Anarchy cuvée (a blend of chardonnay, welschriesling and kerner) pushes natural winemaking to its limits, and is made without any SO$_2$ additions. The Organic Anarchy Pinot Grigio is a spicy favourite of mine. Both are skin fermented for around two weeks. These can be unpredictable wines but catch them at the right point in their evolution and they are outstanding. The winery is situated in the remote, archaeologically rich area of Rifnik.

Address Rifnik 44b, Šentjur **Tel** +386 3 749 23 73 **Email** aci.urbajs@amis.net

SLOVENIA / ŠTAJERSKA

Bartol

Rastko Tement works as an oenologist making mainstream wines, and this is his pastime! The estate specialises in aromatic varieties such as muscat and traminer, and since 2006 in incredibly long maceration times. The estate's Rumeni Muskat 2009 and Sauvignon 2011 were left with their skins for four years. Tement says he likes the character this brings. I cannot honestly detect a difference between this and macerations of a few months, but the wines are impressively fresh and full of depth and energy.

Address Bresnica 85, 2273 Podgorci **Tel** N/A **Email** vino@bartol.si

SLOVENIA / ŠTAJERSKA

Ducal

Idyllically situated estate in the Trenta valley (on the eastern edge of the Triglav National Park), making very good lightly macerated wines. Welschriesling and Rhine riesling are both macerated for three days. The latter is particularly recommended as one of very few macerated examples which shows an easily recognisable riesling character. Mitja and Joži la Duca also run an agriturismo. A recent development is the installation of some amphorae in the winery. I have not yet tasted the results.

Address Kekčeva domačija, Trenta 76, 5232 Soča **Tel** +386 41 413 087
Email info@ducal.co

SLOVENIA / ŠTAJERSKA
Zorjan

Božidar and Marija inherited their family estate in 1980, pioneering organic and then biodynamic agriculture. Following experiments with small Croatian amphorae in 1995, Božidar now uses Georgian qvevri which are buried under the stars. As he explains, "Cosmic forces turn grapes into wine and give us a unique live wine, where man with his ego is just an observer." Wines are sometimes aged substantially before release. Top picks include the scented, amphora-fermented Muscat Ottonel and the wood-fermented Renski Rizling. The lovable label has the addition 'Dolium' for wines made in amphora.

Address Tinjska Gora 90, 2316 Zgornja Ložnica **Tel** N/A
Email bozidar.zorjan@siol.net

SLOVENIA / JUŽNA ŠTAJERSKA
Keltis

Situated close to the Croatian border, this estate is historically still part of Lower Styria. Marijan and his son Miha Kelhar have been making macerated wines since 2009, inspired by Miha's experience of tasting "amazing wines" made in this style. Their Cuvée Extreme, with two months of skin contact, is noteworthy and complex. A Chardonnay and a Pinot Gris are also made with several weeks of maceration. The estate has worked organically for the past five years and is about to receive its certification at the time of writing.

Address Vrhovnica 5, 8259 Bizeljsko **Tel** +386 31 553 353
Email keltis@siol.net

South Africa

In large part thanks to Craig Hawkins, there's a small but growing trend for producers to use long skin contact in the Cape. Swartland is the main hunting ground for these and other innovations, but Stellenbosch is also increasingly asserting its individuality.

Hawkins' initial experiments with orange wine fell foul of South Africa's Wine & Spirits Board (which oversees wine classification and labelling) and were deemed unfit for export, mainly due to their cloudiness. After petitioning by a small cohort of alternative producers including Hawkins, what was probably the world's first official recognition for skin-fermented white wine became a reality in 2015.

This new breed of Cape winemakers has revolutionised the world's ideas of South African wine by showing that with dry farming (no irrigation), sustainable viticulture and earlier harvesting, there's no reason why it can't produce fresh, lively wines with real tension.

SOUTH AFRICA / SWARTLAND

Intellego

Jurgen Gouws, erstwhile colleague and protégé of Craig Hawkins, owns neither vineyards nor winery, but has built a cult following for his delicate, subtle cuvées. He's a staunch advocate of organic and dry farming (serious business in the drought-ravaged Cape), and personally works his rented plots of chenin blanc and red Rhone varieties. His 13-day macerated Elementis chenin is always a highlight, with its fresh gingery kick. Jurgen's barrels are chalked with favourite tunes or companions, rather than technical detail, and he adds, "Wines are all bottled without filtering and after bottling we go drink gin and tonics!"

Address c/o Annexkloof winery, Malmesbury **Tel** N/A
Email jurgen@intellegowines.co.za

SOUTH AFRICA / SWARTLAND

Testalonga

Craig Hawkins has been a key part of Swartland's new independent producer movement since his time as winemaker for Lammershoek, a partnership that ended rather suddenly in 2015. Hawkins now owns land in the far north of Swartland where he continues his decade-long love affair with skin contact and unusual grape varieties (for the Cape). Hawkins prefers a lean, high-acid profile in his wines, which may not suit everyone but the wines have incredible energy, and age gloriously as a result. El Bandito (macerated chenin) and Mangaliza part II (hárslevelű, 19 days' maceration) are amongst my favourites.

Address PO Box 571, Piketberg, Swartland **Tel** +27 726 016475
Email elbandito@testalonga.com

SOUTH AFRICA / STELLENBOSCH
Craven Wines

Mick and Jeanine Craven hail from Australia and Stellenbosch respectively, and settled back in the region in 2011 after working vintages in Sonoma and elsewhere. Taking inspiration from Craig Hawkins (who is a friend), they macerated 50% of some precious old vine clairette to beef up the texture. The result was a tangy, thirst-quenching triumph that shows a unique side of this maligned variety. A further experiment with pinot gris fermented on the skins was not intended to be commercial, but has since become a bestseller in their range. And no wonder – it's divine.

Address N/A Tel +27 727 012 723 Email mick@cravenwines.com

Spain

There are tantalising glimpses of orange wine heritage all over Spain. There's the *brisat* tradition in Catalonia (an old Catalan word for white wines fermented with the skins), and the widespread use of amphorae across the country, but so far there's no single go-to region or visionary producer to name-check. As with the entire Mediterranean, there's no doubt that white grapes have been skin fermented since time immemorial, if indeed they were separated from red grapes at all, yet this style probably never made it into a bottle until the 21st century. There are plenty of tasty macerated gems being made all over the country, but it's difficult to place them into the same kind of continuum as found in Italy, Slovenia or Georgia.

Spain has however cornered the market for amphora production, with its smaller (and no doubt easier to import) *tinajas* being the vessels of choice for countless European producers, notably COS, Elisabetta Foradori and Frank Cornelissen. Juan Padilla, who works with COS and Foradori, has the reputation of being one of the country's top craftsmen.

SPAIN / GALICIA
Daterra

Tall and dreadlocked, Laura Lorenzo cuts quite an unconventional figure in the rural backwaters of Galicia. After honing her winemaking and viticulture at Dominio do Bibei, she created her own estate in 2013 with a few precious old vineyards purchased from old timers. Two white wines are macerated, the Gavela de Vila (100% palomino, painstakingly extracted from old co-planted vineyards) and Erea da Vila (a field blend of everything else from the same vineyard). For anyone who doubts that the humble palomino can make a great non-fortified wine, the proof is right here.

Address Travesa do Medio, 32781 Manzaneda, Galicia Tel +34 661 28 18 23
Email laura@daterra.org

Loxarel

Josep Mitjans created the Loxarel estate from his first vintage (1985) of just 1,000 litres of xarel-lo. A Pèl Blanco is an amphora-fermented (and thus macerated) version of the variety, showing terrific energy and some pleasing funk. After a five to six week fermentation with the skins, the wine is racked into the same 720-litre *tinajas*, and stays with some of the skins for a further five months. There is no clarification, filtration or addition of any kind.

Address Masia Can Mayol, 08735 Vilobí del Penedès **Tel** +34 93 897 80 01
Email loxarel@loxarel.com

Terroir al Límit

A project created by German Dominic Huber and the now iconic South African winemaker Eben Sadie (who is no longer involved) in 2001. Huber dry farms old vineyards using mostly biodynamic practices. His ambitious aim is to create The Domaine Romanée-Conti of Priorat, his point being that Priorat's terroir demands the same care and attention as top Burgundy. Terra de Cuques and Terroir Històric Blanc are both vinified with a couple of weeks' skin contact. Pedra da Guix, in contrast, is made oxidatively without maceration. Terra de Cuques has very pretty aromas from the small proportion of muscat.

Address c. Baixa Font 10, 43737 Torroja del Priorat **Tel** +34 699 732 707
Email dominik@terroir-al-limit.com

Costador Mediterrani Terroirs

Working with 60 to 110-year-old vines at high altitude (400–800m), Joan Franquet coaxes impressive freshness and fruit focus from a number of amphora cuvées. All are bottled in terracotta under the Metamorphika label. In recent years the Macabeu Brisat has been my hands-down favourite, incredibly expressive, aromatic and fruit forward, with pleasing structure and freshness – everything one wants from an orange wine. Brisat is an old Catalonian term for white wines made with skin contact. Viticulture is organic, but not all plots are certified.

Address Av. Rovira i Virgili 46 Esc. A 5° 2ª Cp.: 43002 Tarragona
Tel +34 607 276 695 **Email** jf@costador.net

Vinos Ambiz

Born and raised in Scotland from Italian parents, Fabio Bartolomei relocated to Spain, "not being able to stand the climate or the prospect of life in the world of accountancy and finance". He started making wine in 2003, securing a permanent winery in 2013. He espouses the Sierra de Gredos area east of Madrid, lamenting the only thing it lacks is other winemakers. White grapes include old varieties such as dolé, albillo and malvar, macerated for between two and 14 days in *tinajas*, steel and wood. They are defiantly cloudy, sometimes divisive but never less than fascinating. Uncertified organic viticulture.

Address 05270 El Tiemblo (Avila), Sierra de Gredos Tel +34 687 050 010
Email enestoslugares@gmail.com

Esencia Rural

Julián Ruiz Villanueva farms 50 hectares of very old and partly ungrafted vineyards in Spain's vast La Mancha region. White grapes are vinified with extremely extended skin contact – up to 14 months in the case of the Sol a Sol Airen, a magnificent wine which plays with residual sweetness and oxidative components. Most wines are made without added sulphites. Results can be variable, but there is plenty of fun to be had here.

Address Ctra. de la Estación, s.n., Quero, 45790, Toledo Tel +34 606 991 915
Email info@esenciarural.es

Joan de la Casa

Although he's been making traditional style wines for over a decade, Joan Pastor only decided they were worthy of selling commercially in 2013. He uses between 15 to 30 days of skin maceration with all three moscatel-based white wines, Nimi, Nimi Tossal and Nimi Naturalment Dolç. The results are superbly aromatic, big and bold, showing the character of this hot, dry part of Spain. That said, the nearby coastline and the llebeig wind help to moderate temperatures and preserve some freshness in the wines.

Address Partida Benimarraig, 27A, 03720 Benissa Tel +34 670 209 371
Email info@joandelacasa.com

Envinaté

Four winemaking friends – Roberto Santana, Alfonso Torrente, Laura Ramos, and José Martínez – came together after university to create this project in 2005, which now occupies four different locations across Spain. Their only white varieties are grown on Tenerife, with grapes sourced from centenarian vineyards on volcanic soils. Taganan and Benje Blanco both have a proportion of their blends traditionally skin fermented, adding texture and intensity to the smoky, mineral character from the soil. Vidueño de Santiago del Teide is a 100% skin fermented red/white blend of ungrafted listan bianco and listan prieto.

Address N/A Tel +34 682 207 160 Email asesoria@envinate.es

Switzerland

The Swiss love their wine so much that they drink nearly all of it themselves. Quality is incredibly high, but there is certainly a slight conservatism when it comes to styles. A few producers are starting to experiment with skin ferments, but as yet there is nothing that qualifies as a movement. There is mention of a "vieille méthode valaisanne" in Viala & Vermorel's *Ampélographie, Tome 6* published in 1905, where white grapes were fermented with their skins, however in the modern age the Germanic style of white winemaking (fermenting without the skins) has prevailed.

Switzerland has a treasure trove of native white grape varieties that could all be interesting if skin fermented. Who knows what lies latent in the skins of neutral chassselas, the aromatic, pin-sharp petite arvine or big-boned completer?

Albert Mathier et Fils

Based in the German speaking part of the Valais, Amédée Mathier's fascination with Georgian qvevri began in 2008. Since then he has consistently produced a compelling qvevri-fermented amber wine, the Amphore Assemblage Blanc, in the traditional Georgian non-interventionist manner. The blend of rèze and ermitage (aka marsanne) stays on its skins for between 10 and 12 months. For me, it outshines almost everything else produced at the property. Mathier has now scaled up to 20 qvevris buried in a smart new cellar and will start experimenting with some lafnetscha in the blend from 2018.

Address Bahnhofstrasse 3, Postfach 16, 3970 Salgesch Tel +41 27 455 14 19
Email info@mathier.ch

United States of America

Wine is now being made in every one of the USA's 50 states. It probably won't be too long before orange wine can claim the same coverage. American winemakers are an adventurous bunch, and with their philosophy of 'if you can't beat it, import it', there is an extraordinary range of grape varieties being grown and macerated.

America's love for Italian food and wine culture has also helped build knowledge and passion for orange wines, and many winemakers cite the pioneers of Friuli in their memoirs. It didn't take long for the output of Radikon, Gravner et al to find its way to the US, and into the glasses of curious winemakers who were quickly inspired by the style.

California still produces around 85% of all American wine, so it is no surprise that producers from that state dominate this list. However, Deirdre Heekin's success with extended maceration in Vermont's cold climate is a clear sign that greatness is achievable in every corner.

USA / OREGON

A.D. Beckham

Andrew Beckham has a unique relationship with his amphorae – as a skilled potter, he made them himself! The A.D. Beckham amphora-fermented wines were originally a sideline from more mainstream production bottled as Beckham Estates, but are now informing the methodology of the entire operation. The amphora Pinot Gris is a dead-ringer for a light, northern Italian red wine, and quite delicious.

Address 30790 SW Heater Road, Sherwood, OR 97140 **Tel** +1 971 645 3466
Email annedria@beckhamestatevineyard.com

USA / CALIFORNIA

Ambyth

Welshman Philip Hart created this estate in the early 2000s, on a pristine patch of Paso Robles land which had never been treated with any synthetic fertilisers or sprays. As an amateur winemaker, he started from the naive belief that all winemaking was natural – and despite later enlightenment, he's never swayed. All white wines are made with maceration, and increasingly also fermented and aged in amphorae. Grenache Blanc 2013 was one of the most sublime orange wines ever produced in the US. The Priscus blend is also highly recommended. No sulphur additions since 2011.

Address 510 Sequoia Lane, Templeton, CA 93465 **Tel** +1 805 319 6967
Email gelert@ambythestate.com

USA / CALIFORNIA

Dirty & Rowdy

Hardy Wallace's rise as a winemaker is a good yarn. Laid off during the 2008 financial crisis, he won a social media contest to move to Napa and work as a marketeer for the Murphy-Goode winery. In 2009 he established Dirty & Rowdy with partner Matt Richardson. The duo make eclectic wines mainly from mourvedre and semillon but partly dictated by the fruit they are able to buy in Napa. Working only with "consciously farmed vineyards" (ie. organic or better), each vintage usually includes an excellent skin contact offering.

Address PO Box 697, Napa, CA 94559 **Tel** +1 404 323 9426
Email info@dirtyandrowdy.com

USA / CALIFORNIA

Forlorn Hope

Napa-based Matthew Rorick could be the archetypal New World winemaker. Trained at UC Davis, he earned his spurs working across the Americas and New Zealand. He loves to experiment, and skin contact finds its way into quite a few of Forlorn Hope's white wines. Most notably, the pretty, aromatic Faufreluches Gewürztraminer spends a few weeks on the skins while Dragone Ramato Pinot Gris is his take on the old Venetian style of pinot grigio. Oh yes, and he also makes and plays electric guitars.

Address PO Box 11065, Napa, CA 94581 **Tel** +1 707 206 1112
Email post@matthewrorick.com

USA / CALIFORNIA

La Clarine

Caroline Hoel and Hank Beckmeyer began farming and making wine in their extremely high-altitude location in the Sierra Nevada hills in 2001. Beckmeyer has moved "beyond biodynamics" to a point where he's trying to implement the teachings of Masanobu Fukuoka (The One-Straw Revolution) as much as possible. Their albariño Al Basc 2015 is an experiment, but a direction I sincerely hope they'll continue to explore. It's an extreme wine made with seven months' skin contact, with the variety's typically expressive fruit and aromatics supported by grippy tannins that would make a Georgian proud.

Address PO Box 245, Somerset CA 95684 **Tel** +1 530 306 3608
Email info@clarinefarm.com

Ryme Cellars

Ryan and Megan Glaab are perhaps one of only two producers in the US who make a varietal ribolla gialla. They don't mess around with the skin contact either, it gets the full six months and is a dark, savoury creature, made with more than a nod to Radikon and Gravner – although sometimes a little too oxidative for my liking. That said, it's wonderful to have a Napa wine with 12% ABV. Their Carneros-grown Vermentino is made two ways, with and without maceration, as the couple do not agree on the optimum way to vinify it. Obviously with ribolla there was no such indecision!

Address PO Box 80, Healdsburg, CA 95448 Tel +1 707 820 8121
Email ryan@rymecellars.com

USA / CALIFORNIA

Scholium Project

Ex-philosophy professor Abe Schoener decided to switch career in 1998 and started with an internship at Stags Leap. He's now made over 10 vintages of The Prince in his Caves, a skin-fermented sauvignon blanc from fruit grown in Napa. It's become one of the US's most iconic orange wines from its first appearance in 2006. This is a defiantly Californian style, often very ripe but with superb varietal expression. The stems are included in some years. Schoener's project has been somewhat itinerant, although a plan is now (2018) well underway to build a winery on the Los Angeles river.

Address Box 5787 1351 Second St, Scholium Project Napa, CA 94581 Tel N/A
Email scholiabe@gmail.com

USA / UTAH AND CALIFORNIA

Ruth Lewandowski

Evan Lewandowski only makes one skin-fermented wine, but Chilion is such a blinder that it deserves inclusion here. Who would think that cortese from Mendocino county could produce this creamy, structured gem? Fermentation happens in egg-shaped tanks and barrels, with six months of skin contact (earlier vintages had just a few weeks). Harvesting and initial fermentation finishes in California, but the tanks are then trucked to the winery in Salt Lake City for ageing. The Ruth in the winery's name refers to Evan's favourite book in the bible, due to its focus on the all-important cycles of life and death.

Address 3340 S 300 W Suite 4 Salt Lake City Tel +1 801 230 7331
Email evan@ruthlewandowskiwines.com

La Garagista

Vermont's chilly mountains are not vine-friendly. Thanks to hybrids developed at the University of Minnesota, Deirdre Heekin is able to produce her fresh, 'alpine' wines. All white grapes receive 15 to 20 days of maceration and are fermented in open-top fibre-glass vats. Harlots and Ruffians, a blend of la crescent and frontenac gris, has piercing acids offset by its generous texture. The project started as a farm and restaurant in 1999, but from 2017 the restaurant has been closed with winemaking as the major focus. Viticulture is based on permaculture and biodynamics, a subject Heekin has written widely about.

Address Barnard, Vermont **Tel** +1 802 291 1295 **Email** lagaragista@gmail.com

Channing Daughters

Winemaker James Christopher Tracy certainly likes to experiment. And he loves skin contact, making no less than eight different wines with extended maceration. There's also a clear love of Friuli's grape varieties and styles, expressed most clearly in the rich, complex Meditazione blend (made since 2004, with around two weeks' maceration). Ribolla is very convincing, as are Ramato and Research Bianco. Thanks to the cool Long Island climate, these wines never stray beyond 12.5% ABV, both literally and figuratively refreshing. Fermentations are spontaneous and uncontrolled, but wines are lightly filtered.

Address 1927 Scuttlehole Road PO Box 2202, Bridgehampton, NY 11932
Tel +1 631 537 7224 **Email** jct@channingdaughters.com

Photo credits

All photos by Ryan Opaz unless otherwise noted below. Every possible effort has been taken to establish and credit copyright owners and/or photographers.

27, 64, 66, 68 Maurizio Frullani, courtesy Gravner family

29, 70, 75 Mauro Fermariello

100–101 Fabio Rinaldi

40 Flamm (16. Korps), collection of K.u.k. Kriegspressequartier, Lichtbildstelle, Wien

44 Copyright unknown, accessed from the Digital Library of Slovenia

58 Reproduction photo by Primož Brecelj, from the original at Podnanos. With the cooperation of priest Tomaž Kodrič and Artur Lipovz, Ajdovščina library

77, 139, 140, 157, 183 (except bottom left by Ryan Opaz), **205, 216i, 219i & ii, 224ii, 225i, 235i, 245ii & iii, 254i, 256ii, 257i, 261, 262ii, 263i, 264i, 267iii, 268i & iii, 270iii, 273ii & iii, 276ii, 278i, 282** Simon J Woolf

114 (×3) Copyright owner unknown. Retrieved from georgiaphotophiles.wordpress.com/2013/01/26/soviet-georgian-liquor-labels

137 Courtesy John Wurdeman

152 © Keiko & Maika, courtesy Luca Gargano (Triple A)

178 Justin Howard-Sneyd MW

213iii, 215, 216ii & iii, 217i & ii, 218, 219iii, 220 - 223, 224i, 225ii & iii, 226 – 228, 229ii, 231, 235ii, 236iii, 237, 238, 239i, 240i, 241, 243i & ii, 244, 245i, 251 - 253, 254ii, 255i, 256, 257ii, 258 - 260, 262i, 263ii & iii, 264ii, 265, 267i & ii, 270i, 271iii, 272iii, 274ii, 276i & iii, 277, 278ii, 279ii, 280, 281, 283, 284, 285i & iii, 286 Courtesy respective producers

213 Tom Shobbrook courtesy The Oak Barrel, Sydney. Sarah & Iwo Jakimowicz by Hesh Hipp, courtesy Les Caves de Pyrene.

217 Rennersistas by Raidt-Lager, courtesy Renner family.

229 Laurent Bannwarth courtesy Just Add Wine Netherlands

230 Yann Durieux, Jean-Yves Péron courtesy Just Add Wine Netherlands. Emmanual Pageot by Alain Reynaud, courtesy Domaine Turner Pageot

233 Nika Partsvania by Hannah Fuellenkemper, Ramaz Nikoladze by Mariusz Kapczyński

236 Niki Antadze by Olaf Schindler

243 Eugenio Rosi by Mauro Fermariello

254 Nuns at Monastero Suore Cistercensi by Blake Johnson, RWM

255 Raffaello Annicchiarico by Bruno Levi Della Vida. Paolo Marchi by Giovanni Segni

266 Sketch of Kramar & Distelbarth by Miriam Pertegato, courtesy Atelier Kramar

269 Marjan Simčič by Primoz Korošec, courtesy Marjan Simčič

273 Ivi & Edi Svetlik by Marijan Močivnik, courtesy Svetlik

279 Mick & Jeanine Craven by Tasha Seccombe, courtesy Craven Wines

285 Abe Schoener by Bobby Pin

Acknowledgements

There is insufficient space to thank everyone who contributed help and advice to make this four-year project happen. I can at least offer the following incomplete list.

Carla Capalbo, Caroline Henry, Wink Lorch and Suzanne Mustacich all provided moral support and invaluable publishing advice at just the right moments. Mauro Fermariello made the wonderful promotional video for my Kickstarter campaign, ensuring this project got off to a rousing start.

Mariëlla Beukers, Stefano Cosma, Hannah Fuellenkemper, Elisabeth Gstarz, Tomaž Klipšteter, Artur Lipovz (director of Ajdovščina library, Slovenia), Vladimír Magula, Tony Milanowski and Bruno Levi Della Vida all contributed valuable research assistance.

Translation of foreign language texts was handled adeptly by Denis Costa (Italian), Barbara Repovš (Slovene) and Elisabeth Gstarz (German).

My winemaking adventures were enabled with the patient support of Teresa Batista, Oscar Quevedo and Claudia Quevedo in Portugal, Ron Langeveld and Marnix Rombaut in the Netherlands.

In Georgia, the support of Sarah May Grunwald, Irakli Cholobargia, his colleagues at the Georgian National Wine Agency, and Dr. Irakli Glonti was invaluable.

Tatjana Familio and Giulia Cantone at FVG Turismo provided generous assistance with accomodation and other logistics in Friuli.

Very special thanks to Joško, Marija, Mateja and Jana Gravner, Valter, Ines, Klemen and Lea Mlečnik, Saša, Stanko, Suzana, Savina and Ivana Radikon, Janko Štekar and Tamara Lukman.

All of the winemakers who opened their cellars, sent me their best bottles and took the time to tell their stories have helped bring this book to life.

David A. Harvey and Doug Wregg were not only generous with their time, but also with their discourse, which greatly helped me shape my own ideas.

The Slovenian Tourist Board provided additional financial support for this book. I am very lucky to have had Her Excellency Ms. Sanja Štiglic, Ambassador of the Republic of Slovenia in the Netherlands as a mentor throughout the process.

Inspiration for chapter nine's title came of course from The Fall (RIP Mark E. Smith).

Elisabeth Gstarz helped make the impossible possible, on several occasions.

Kickstarter supporters

388 wonderful people pledged financial support on the crowdfunding platform Kickstarter, to help make this book happen. Some have asked to remain anonymous, the remainder are listed here.

Sarah Abbott MW ★ James Ackroyd ★ Jesaja Alberto ★ Nicola Allison ★ Paulo de Almeida ★ Diogo Amado ★ Cornell & Patti Anderson ★ Jane Anson ★ Matt & El Bachle ★ Levon Bagis ★ Adrijana & Filip-Karlo Baraka ★ Ariana Barker ★ Fabio Bartolomei ★ Thomas Baschetti ★ Miha Batič ★ Simone Belotti ★ Egon J. Berger ★ Paolo Bernardi ★ Mariëlla Beukers & Nico Poppelier ★ Salvy BigNose ★ Djordje Bikicki ★ BINA37 ★ Ian Black ★ Thomas Bohl ★ Mark Bolton ★ Fredrik Bonde ★ Wojciech Bońkowski ★ Stuart & Vanessa Brand ★ Tjitske Brouwer ★ Elaine Chukan Brown ★ Martin Brown ★ Sam & Charlie Brown ★ Uri Bruck ★ Marcel van Bruggen ★ De Bruijn Wijnkopers ★ Jim Budd & Carole Macintyre ★ BUNCH Wine Bar ★ Inés Caballero & Diego Beas ★ Nicola Campanile ★ Michael Carlin ★ Felicity Carter ★ Damien Casten ★ Matjaz Četrtič ★ Umay Çeviker ★ Remy Charest ★ Daniel Chia ★ André Cis ★ Davide Cocco ★ Gregory Collinge ★ Beppe Collo ★ Alessandro Comitini ★ Helen J. Conway ★ Frankie Cook ★ Steve Cooper ★ Ian FB Cornholio ★ Jules van Costello ★ Giles Cundy ★ Paul V. Cunningham ★ Geoffroy Van Cutsem ★ Barbara D'Agapiti ★ Arnaud Daphy ★ Iana Dashkovska ★ Andrew Davies ★ Steve De Long ★ Cathinca Dege ★ Daniela Dejnega ★ Eva Dekker ★ Juliana Dever ★ Lily Dimitriou ★ La Distesa ★ Martin Diwald ★ Sašo Dravinec ★ Nicki James Drinkwater ★ Darius Dumri ★ Laura Durnford & Steve Brumwell ★ Gabriel Dvoskin ★ Klaus Dylus ★ Eklektikon Wines ★ Souheil El Khoury ★ Magnus Ericsson ★ Jack Everitt ★ Fair Wines ★ Alice Feiring ★ Tom Fiorina ★ Sabine Flieser-Just Dip Somm ★ Stefano & Gloria Flori ★ Luca Formentini ★ Otto Forsberg ★ Ove Fosså ★ Maurizio Di Franco ★ Robert Frankovic ★ Lucie Fricker ★ Andrew Friedhoff ★ Hannah Fuellenkemper ★ Nyitrai Gábor ★ Aldo Gamberini ★ Robbin Gheesling ★ Filippo Mattia Ginanni ★ Leon C Glover III ★ Maciek Gontarz ★ Adriana González Vicente ★ Marcy Gordon ★ Nick Gorevic ★ Nayan Gowda ★ Mateja Gravner ★ Olivier Grosjean ★ Sarah May Grunwald ★ Anna Gstarz ★ Elisabeth Gstarz ★ Gertrude & Josef Gstarz ★ Paulius Gudinavicius ★ Onneca Guelbenzu ★ Chris Gunning ★ Lianne van Gurp ★ Dr Frédéric Hansen von Bünau ★ Marcel Hansen ★ Ian Hardesty ★ Julia Harding MW ★ Rob Harrell ★ David Harvey ★ Susan Hedblad ★ Caroline Henry ★ Nik Herbert ★ Laszlo Hesley ★ Peter Hildering ★ Richard Hind ★ Alicia Hobbel ★ Mike Hopkins ★ Matthew Horkey ★ Janice Horslen ★ Justin Howard-Sneyd MW ★ Niels Huijbregts ★ Diederik van Iwaarden ★ Frankie Jacklin ★ Heidi Jaksland Kvernmo Dip WSET ★ Ales Jevtic ★ Sakiko Jin ★ Gabi & Dieter Jochinger ★ Rick Joore ★ Asa Joseph ★ Jakub Jurkiewicz ★ Jason Kallsen ★ Edgar Kampers ★ Tomaž Kastelic ★ Dan Keeling ★ Fintan Kerr ★ Daniel Khasidy ★ Chris King ★ Tatiana Klompenhouwer ★ Michaela Koller ★ Arto Koskelo ★ Eero Koski ★ Edward Kourian ★ Sini Kovacs ★ Bradley Kruse ★ Roger Krüsi & Agnes Zeiner-Krüsi ★ Peter Kupers ★ Harry Lamers

★ Stef Landauer ★ Esmee Langereis ★ Primož Lavrenčič (Burja) ★ Hongwoo Lee ★ Stéphane Lefèvre ★ Eileen LeMonda Dip WSET ★ Bruno Levi Della Vida ★ Catherine Liao ★ Susan R Lin ★ Richard Van Der Linden ★ Andrew & Tamar Lindesay ★ Allan & Kris Liska ★ Ella Lister ★ Ben Little ★ Icy Liu ★ Angela Lloyd ★ Wink Lorch ★ Laura Lorenzo ★ Brad & Therese Love ★ Dr Ludvig Blomberg ★ Benjamin Madeska ★ Aaron Mandel ★ Tim Reed Manessy ★ Alan March ★ Pedro Marques ★ Alessandro Marzocchi ★ Jerzy Maslanka ★ Rob McArdle ★ Richard McClellan ★ Robert McIntosh ★ Gert Meeder ★ Regina Meij ★ Ayca Melek ★ Ghislaine Melman ★ Tan Meng How ★ Manuchar Meskhidze ★ Karol Michalski ★ Rolv Midthassel ★ Mitja Miklus ★ Tony Milanowski ★ Valter Mlečnik ★ Ana Monforte ★ Gea & Petra Moretti ★ Paddy Murphy ★ Ewan Murray ★ Bernd & Bettina Murtinger ★ Suzanne Mustacich & Pétrus Desbois ★ naturalorange.nl ★ Dr. Nicholas Reynolds ★ Paul Nicholson ★ Patrik Nilsson ★ Domačija Novak ★ Laurie E. O'Bryon & Mario P. Catena ★ Mick O'Connell MW ★ Tobias Öhgren ★ Mark Onderwater ★ Richard van Oorschot ★ Josje van Oostrom ★ Filippo Ozzola ★ Mateusz & Justyna Papiernik ★ Sharon Parsons ★ Antonio Passalacqua ★ Hudák Péter ★ Antti-Veikko Pihlajamäki ★ Adrian Pike ★ Marco Pilia ★ Marco Piovan ★ Zoli Piroska ★ Tao Platón González ★ Helen & David Prudden ★ Luigi Pucciano ★ Melissa Pulvermacher ★ Noel Pusch ★ Alessandro Ragni ★ Christina Rasmussen ★ Rafael Ravnik ★ Simon Reilly ★ Oscar Reitsma ★ Mitch Renaud ★ Magnus Reuterdahl ★ George Reynolds ★ André Ribeirinho ★ Odette Rigterink ★ Thomas R. Riley ★ Treve Ring ★ Nicolas Rizzi ★ Daniel Rocha e Silva ★ Marnix Rombaut ★ Elena Roppa ★ Pieter Rosenthal ★ Gerald Rouschal ★ José Manuel Santos ★ Kjartan Sarheim Anthun ★ Savor The Experience Tours ★ K Dawn Scarrow ★ Carl Schröder ★ Elisabeth Seifert ★ Job Seuren ★ Lynne Sharrock Dip WSET ★ Lizzie Shell ★ Dr Ola Sigurdson ★ Marijana Siljeg ★ Aleš Simončič ★ Jeroen Simons ★ simplesmente... Vinho ★ Robert Slotover ★ Tony Smith ★ Saša Sokolić ★ Spacedlaw ★ Luciana Squadrilli ★ Peter Stafford-Bow ★ Primož Štajer ★ Sverre Steen ★ Janko Štekar & Tamara Lukman ★ Matthias Stelzig ★ Lee Stenton ★ Peter Stevens ★ Melissa M. Sutherland ★ Johan Svensson ★ Dimitri Swietlik ★ Taka Takeuchi ★ Eugene SH Tan ★ Gianluca Di Taranto ★ Famille Tarlant ★ Daphne Teremetz ★ Lars T. Therkildsen ★ Colin Thorne ★ Paola Tich ★ Sue Tolson ★ Mike Tommasi ★ Aitor Trabado & Richard Sanchoyarto ★ Maria W. B. Tsalapati ★ Effi Tsournava ★ Margarita Tsvirko ★ Andres Tunon ★ Ole Udsen ★ Lauri Vainio ★ Eva Valkhoff ★ Joeri Vanacker ★ Sara Vanucci ★ Elly Veitch ★ Alexey Veremeev ★ VinoRoma ★ Priscilla van der Voort ★ Dr José Vouillamoz ★ Filip de Waard ★ Peter Waisberg ★ Arnold Waldstein ★ Evan Walker ★ Timothy & Camille Waud ★ Daniela & Thomas Weber ★ Liz Wells ★ Simon Wheeler ★ Daniela Wiebogen ★ Stefan Wierda ★ Gerhard Wieser ★ De Wijnwinkel Amsterdam ★ Benjamin Williams ★ C Wills ★ The Wine Spot Amsterdam ★ Winerackd ★ Weingut Winkler-Hermaden ★ Adam Wirdahl ★ Michael Wising ★ Keita Wojciechowski ★ Stephen Wolff ★ Diana Woloszyn ★ Chris & Sara Woolf ★ Inigo & Susan Woolf ★ Jon Woolf ★ Stephen Worgan ★ Phillip Wright ★ John Wurdeman ★ Alder Yarrow ★ Aaron Zanbaka ★ Alessandro Zanini ★ Yvonne Zohar

A note about grape varieties

Capitalisation of grape varieties in this book is determined by these rules:

▶ Where we refer to the grape variety itself, it is not capitalised.
▶ Where we refer to a wine which takes its name from the grape variety, it is capitalised.

So, Joško Gravner's Ribolla Gialla is made from ribolla gialla grapes.

Our formatting style conflicts with the standards set by the International Code of Nomenclature for Cultivated Plants (ninth edition, published in 2016 by the International Society for Horticultural Science). However, as *Amber Revolution* is not an academic text, we feel that this style provides a better experience for the vast majority of readers, for two reasons.

Many of the wines discussed in this book are named after their grape variety. Our formatting allows a subtle distinction, showing when we refer to a specific wine and when we refer to the grape variety generically. Furthermore, it avoids text peppered with capitals which can become tiring to read.

Publications such as the *New York Times* and the *Guardian* adopt similar style rules.

Bibliography

Anson, Jane. *Wine Revolution: The World's Best Organic, Biodynamic and Natural Wines.* London: Jacqui Small, 2017.

Barisashvili, Giorgi. *Making Wine in Kvevri.* Tbilisi: Elkana, 2016.

Brozzoni, Gigi, et al. *Ribolla Gialla Oslavia The Book.* Gorizia: Transmedia, 2011.

Caffari, Stefano. *G.* Milan: self-published by Azienda Agricola Gravner, 2015.

Camuto, Robert V. *Palmento: A Sicilian Wine Odyssey.* Lincoln, NE and London: University of Nebraska Press, 2010.

Capalbo, Carla. *Collio: Fine Wines and Foods from Italy's North-East.* London: Pallas Athene, 2009.

Capalbo, Carla. *Tasting Georgia: A Food and Wine Journey in the Caucasus.* London: Pallas Athene, 2017.

D'Agata, Ian. *Native Wine Grapes of Italy.* Berkeley, Los Angeles, London: University of California Press, 2014.

Feiring, Alice. *The Battle for Wine and Love: Or How I Saved the World from Parkerization.* New York: Harcourt, 2008.

Feiring, Alice. *Naked Wine: Letting Grapes Do What Comes Naturally.* Cambridge, MA: Da Capo Press, 2011.

Feiring, Alice. *For the Love of Wine: My Odyssey through the World's Most Ancient Wine Culture.* Lincoln, NE: Potomac Books, 2016.

Filiputti, Walter. *Il Friuli Venezia Giulia e i suoi Grandi Vini.* Udine: Arti Grafiche Friulane, 1997.

Ginsborg, Paul. *A History of Contemporary Italy: Society and Politics, 1943–1988.* London: Penguin Books, 1990.

Goldstein, Darra. *The Georgian Feast: The Vibrant Culture and Savory Food of the Republic of Georgia.* Second edition. Berkeley, Los Angeles, London: University of California Press, 2013.

Goode, Jamie and Sam Harrop MW. *Authentic Wine: Toward Natural and Sustainable Winemaking.* Berkeley, Los Angeles, London: University of California Press, 2011.

Heintl, Franz Ritter von. *Der Weinbau des Österreichischen Kaiserthums.* Vienna, 1821.

Hemingway, Ernest. *A Farewell to Arms.* London: Arrow Books, 2004.

Hohenbruck, Arthur Freiherrn von. *Die Weinproduction in Oesterreich.* Vienna, 1873.

Kershaw, Ian. *To Hell and Back: Europe 1914–1949.* London: Penguin Books, 2015.

Legeron MW, Isabelle. *Natural Wine: An Introduction to Organic and Biodynamic Wines Made Naturally.* London and New York: CICO Books, 2014.

Phillips, Rod. *A Short History of Wine.* London: Penguin Books, 2000.

Robinson, Jancis and Julia Harding. *The Oxford Companion to Wine.* Fourth edition. Oxford: Oxford University Press, 2015.

Robinson, Jancis, Julia Harding and José Vouillamoz. *Wine Grapes: A Complete Guide to 1,368 Vine Varieties, including their Origins and Flavours.* London: Penguin Books, 2012.

Schindler, John R. *Isonzo: The Forgotten Sacrifice of The Great War.* Westport: Praeger, 2001.

Sgaravatti, Alessandro. *G.* Padua: self-published by Azienda Agricola Gravner, 1997.

Thumm, H.J. *The Road to Yaldara: My Life with Wine and Viticulture.* Lyndoch, S. Aust.: Chateau Yaldara, 1996.

Valvasor, Johann Weikhard von. *Die Ehre deß Herzogthums Crain.* Nuremberg, 1689.

Vertovec, Matija. *Vinoreja za Slovence.* Vipava, 1844. Second edition of modern reprint, Ajdovščina: Občina, 2015.

Sunrise on the Collio/Brda border

Index

Regions are listed under their parent countries, so for Carso see 'Italy, Carso'. Recommended producers are listed under 'Recommended producers', so for JNK see 'Recommended producers, JNK'. Producers mentioned in the main text have a main index entry as well.

Slovenia is becoming one of the hottest culinary hubs

Surrounded by Croatia, Italy and Austria, Slovenia is a tiny but diverse country located at the crossroads of the Alpine world, the Mediterranean, Karst and the Pannonian Plain. It is not only a natural gem, but also one of the hottest culinary destinations. In the capital city of Ljubljana and beyond, young and established chefs like Ana Roš (World's Best Female Chef in 2017), Janez Bratovž, Igor Jagodic, Uroš Štefelin, Bine Volčič, Tomaž Kavčič, Luka Košir and many others are being recognised for their enormous talents. Restaurants using locally sourced ingredients are booming and visitors to local markets and food festivals can sample all the flavourful fresh produce that make Slovenian dishes so good.

Slovenia's culinary ingredients vary from region to region, making the country-wide food scene diverse, original and unique. The cuisine focuses traditionally on locally sourced ingredients, placing it at the cutting-edge of a major international food trend. Restaurants throughout Slovenia create culinary experiences featuring ingredients from local gardens, outdoor markets and organic farms. Many dishes incorporate unique hallmarks of the country's 24 gastronomic areas, such as salt from the Piran salt pans, honey harvested from the beehives that Slovenia keeps at the forefront of their conservation efforts, and Carniolan sausage, which is definitely one of the most original and popular Slovenian meat products.

The same goes for Slovenia's stellar wines. With three major wine regions, Slovenia offers varied soils and climates, which make for a multitude of different grape-growing conditions. The grapevine was brought to the area of today's Slovenia by the ancient Romans. Maribor, the second largest city in the country, is home to the oldest vine in the world, which still produces grapes even after 400 years. As Slovenia's wine scene grows, so the accolades roll in. Listed amongst some of the finest wine-producing countries alongside Italy and Spain, Slovenia is proving not just to be at the top of the European food game but the European wine game, too. Also, the country is taking the lead in the production of orange wines. In recent years, orange wines have gained immense popularity as a delicious and fascinating alternative to the standard three options.

This content was contributed by the Slovenian Tourist Board

I FEEL SLOVENIA

Slovenian Tourist Board
Dimičeva ulica 13
1000 Ljubljana
Slovenia

www.slovenia.info

info@slovenia.info
www.slovenia.info/**facebook**
www.slovenia.info/**youtube**
www.slovenia.info/**instagram**

Aleks Klinec slices one of his home-cured Pršut hams, at the Klinec Inn, Medana

About the author

Simon J Woolf is an award-winning English wine and drinks writer, currently clinging to mainland Europe in Amsterdam. This is his first book.

Originally trained as a musician, Simon worked variously as a sound engineer, IT consultant and alternative currency designer before wine took over his life. His writing career began in 2011 with the founding of The Morning Claret – an online wine magazine which has become one of the world's most respected resources for natural, artisanal, organic and biodynamic wine.

He contributes regularly to *Decanter* magazine, *Meininger's Wine Business International* and many other publications on and offline.

When not obsessing about orange wine, Simon is a keen cook and lover of difficult music.

Sign up for Simon's newsletter to stay in touch:
www.themorningclaret.com/subscribe

About Ryan Opaz

Having been a chef, butcher, art teacher, speaker and wine writer, Ryan Opaz eventually found his niche creating specialist wine and food tours in Portugal. He is co-founder of Catavino, which helps people to discover Portugal and Spain through custom tours and events. For eight years he ran the Digital Wine Communications Conference. He currently lives in Porto with his wife, son and cats, where he likes to travel, take photos, and enjoy handmade beverages.